Lecture Notes in Computer Science 6560

Commenced Publication in 1973
Founding and Former Series Editors:
Gerhard Goos, Juris Hartmanis, and Jan van Leeuwen

W0192941

Ngoc Thanh Nguyen (Ed.)

Transactions on Computational Collective Intelligence III

 Springer

Editor-in-Chief

Ngoc Thanh Nguyen
Wroclaw University of Technology
Institute of Informatics
Str. Wyb. Wyspianskiego 27
50-370 Wroclaw, Poland
E-mail: thanh@pwr.wroc.pl

ISSN 0302-9743 (LNCS)   e-ISSN 1611-3349 (LNCS)
ISSN 2190-9288 (TCCI)
ISBN 978-3-642-19967-7   e-ISBN 978-3-642-19968-4
DOI 10.1007/978-3-642-19968-4

Springer Heidelberg Dordrecht London New York

Library of Congress Control Number: 2011923804

CR Subject Classification (1998): I.2, C.2.4, I.2.11, H.3-5, D.2

Typesetting: Camera-ready by author, data conversion by Scientific Publishing Services, Chennai, India

Printed on acid-free paper

Springer is part of Springer Science+Business Media (www.springer.com)

Preface

Welcome to the third volume of *Transactions on Computational Collective Intelligence* (TCCI). It is the second year of this new Springer journal which is devoted to the research in computer-based methods of computational collective intelligence (CCI) and their applications in a wide range of fields such as semantic web, social networks and multi-agent systems. TCCI strives to cover new methodological, theoretical and practical aspects of CCI understood as the form of intelligence that emerges from the collaboration and competition of many individuals (artificial and/or natural). The application of multiple computational intelligence technologies such as fuzzy systems, evolutionary computation, neural systems, consensus theory, etc., aims to support human and other collective intelligence and to create new forms of CCI in natural and/or artificial systems.

TCCI is a double-blind refereed and authoritative reference dealing with working potential of CCI methodologies and applications, as well as emerging issues of interest to academics and practitioners. This issue contains a collection of 10 articles selected from high-quality submissions addressing advances in the foundations and applications of computational collective intelligence.

The research area of CCI has significantly been growing in recent years and we are very thankful to everyone within the CCI research community who has supported the *Transactions on Computational Collective Intelligence*, and its affiliated events including the *International Conferences on Computational Collective Intelligence: Technologies and Applications* (ICCCI). The first ICCCI was held in Wroclaw, Poland in Oct. 2009. ICCCI 2010 was held in Taiwan in Nov. 2010 and ICCCI 2011 will be hosted in Gdynia, Poland in Sep. 2011. With this strong support and a large number of submissions we are very pleased that TCCI and ICCCI are being cemented as high-quality platforms for presenting and exchanging most important and significant advances in CCI research and development. We would like to thank all the authors for their contributions to TCCI. This issue would also not have been possible without the great efforts of the editorial board and many anonymously acting reviewers. Here, we would like to express our sincere thanks to all of them. Finally, we would also like to express our gratitude to the LNCS editorial staff of Springer, in particular Alfred Hofmann, Ursula Barth, Peter Strasser and their team, who have supported the TCCI journal and the editorship of this issue in a very professional way.

February 2011   Ngoc Thanh Nguyen

Transactions on Computational Collective Intelligence

This new journal focuses on research in applications of the computer-based methods of Computational Collective Intelligence (CCI) and their applications in a wide range of fields such as semantic web, social networks and multi-agent systems. It aims to provide a forum for the presentation of scientific research and technological achievements accomplished by the international community.

The topics addressed by this journal include all solutions of real-life problems, for which it is necessary to use computational collective intelligence technologies to achieve effective results. The emphasis of the papers published is on novel and original research and technological advancements. Special features on specific topics are welcome.

Table of Contents

Cooperation of Agents Based on Methods of DES Supervising and Control

František Čapkovič*

Institute of Informatics, Slovak Academy of Sciences
Dúbravská cesta 9, 845 07 Bratislava, Slovak Republic
Frantisek.Capkovic@savba.sk
http://www.ui.sav.sk/home/capkovic/capkhome.htm

Abstract. The cooperation of autonomous agents is synthesized in order to satisfy demands imposed on a group of agents or on MAS (multi agent systems). Petri nets (PNs), especially place/transition PNs (P/T PNs), are used for modelling the agents. The modular approach is utilized on that way. PN-based methods of discrete event systems (DES) control and supervising are utilized in order to synthesize the cooperation of the agents. The usefulness and applicability of the approach is demonstrated by examples and case studies.

Keywords: Agents, bipartite graphs, control, cooperation, discrete-event systems, Petri nets, supervisor, synthesis.

1 Introduction

Discrete-event systems (DES) are widely used in human practice - e.g. flexible manufacturing systems, communication systems of different kinds, transport systems, etc. They are systems driven by discrete events. Thus, the DES behaviour is discrete in nature. The behaviour of agents cooperating each other can also be understood to be a kind of DES. There are many problems in the cooperation of autonomous agents in order to achieve a prescribed global aim. Main aim of this paper is to point out how the methods of DES control theory can be utilized on that way. The supervisor to be synthesized by means of the methods represents the instrument how to realize the cooperation. The causality in the DES behaviour was described in [1]. DES are frequently modelled and analysed by means of Petri nets (PNs), especially P/T PNs (place/transition PNs). The control synthesis for DES modelled by PNs can be performed also in virtue of P/T PN-based methods. In [1] the method of such a kind was introduced. It is based on ordinary reachability graphs (RGs) and yields the space of feasible state trajectories from a given initial state to a desired terminal one. This paper immediately goes on to solve the DES control synthesis problem in order to automate this process as soon as possible, even to achieve the automated control

---

* Partially supported by the Slovak Grant Agency for Science (VEGA) under grant # 2/0075/09.

N.T. Nguyen and R. Kowalczyk (Eds.): Transactions on CCI III, LNCS 6560, pp. 1–24, 2011.
© Springer-Verlag Berlin Heidelberg 2011

synthesis. The earlier results presented in [2],[3] are also utilized in this paper. The original contribution of this paper on the basis of the up-to-date papers consists in giving the methodology how to automate the process of the supervisor synthesis. Starting from PN models of the autonomous agents a step to a supervisor synthesis is performed. The behaviour of such a supervised agents is analyzed (as to satisfying demands) by the method published before. When the behaviour is not satisfied (e.g. because of some absurdities from practical point of view, deadlocks, etc.) an additional demands are imposed on the supervised agents and an additional supervisor is synthesized. Even, we can speak about the hierarchical approach. Although it can hardly be spoken about a 'self-organization', such an approach is very useful especially in case of 'material' agents, e.g. in manufacturing systems. To illustrate such an approach two case studies are introduced.

In the denotation from system theory, the P/T PN-based model of DES can be formally expressed as the linear discrete system constrained by the inequality as follows

$$\mathbf{x}_{k+1} = \mathbf{x}_k + \mathbf{B}.\mathbf{u}_k \quad , \quad k = 0, \, ..., \, N \tag{1}$$

$$\mathbf{B} = \mathbf{G}^T - \mathbf{F} \tag{2}$$

$$\mathbf{F}.\mathbf{u}_k \le \mathbf{x}_k \tag{3}$$

where k is the discrete step of the dynamics development; $\mathbf{x}_k = (\sigma_{p_1}^k, ..., \sigma_{p_n}^k)^T$ is the n-dimensional state vector; $\sigma_{p_i}^k \in \{0, 1, ..., c_{p_i}\}$, $i = 1, ..., n$ express the states of the elementary subprocesses or operations by 0 (passivity) or by $0 < \sigma_{p_i} \le c_{p_i}$ (activity); c_{p_i} is the capacity of the subprocess p_i as to its activities; $\mathbf{u}_k = (\gamma_{t_1}^k, ..., \gamma_{t_m}^k)^T$ is the m-dimensional control vector; its components $\gamma_{t_j}^k \in \{0, 1\}$, $j = 1, ..., m$ represent occurring of elementary discrete events (e.g. starting or ending the elementary subprocesses or their activities, failures, etc.) by 1 (presence of the corresponding discrete event) or by 0 (absence of the event); $\mathbf{B}$, $\mathbf{F}$, $\mathbf{G}$ are matrices of integers; $\mathbf{F} = \{f_{ij}\}_{n \times m}$, $f_{ij} \in \{0, M_{f_{ij}}\}$, $i = 1, ..., n$, $j = 1, ..., m$ expresses the causal relations among the states (as causes) and the discrete events occurring during the DES operation (as consequences) by 0 (nonexistence of the relation) or by $M_{f_{ij}} > 0$ (existence and multiplicity of the relation); $\mathbf{G} = \{g_{ij}\}_{m \times n}$, $g_{ij} \in \{0, M_{g_{ij}}\}$, $i = 1, ..., m$, $j = 1, ..., n$ expresses very analogically the causal relations among the discrete events (as causes) and the DES states (as consequences); the matrix $\mathbf{B}$ is given by means of the arcs incidence matrices $\mathbf{F}$ and $\mathbf{G}$ according to (2); $(.)^T$ symbolizes the matrix or vector transposition.

2   DES Control Problem

Considering the introduced system (1)-(3) to be the model of DES, the problem of control is the problem of finding a suitable sequence of control vectors $\{\mathbf{u}_0, \mathbf{u}_1, ..., \mathbf{u}_{N-1}\}$ transferring the system form a given initial state $\mathbf{x}_0$ to a prescribed terminal state $\mathbf{x}_t$. In any step k, i.e. in any state $\mathbf{x}_k$ of the system, it is

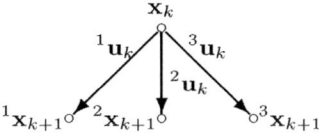

Fig. 1. The example of alternative courses of the DES states development

necessary to find possible alternatives of the further course. In the PN terminology, it is necessary to find PN transitions which are enabled in the step k. In any step k it is possible to proceed on the base of the simple logical consideration: "if we are not able to detect directly which transitions are enabled in the step k, but we are able to detect only which transitions are disabled in this step, we can eliminate the disabled transitions". This can be mathematically described as follows

$$\mathbf{u}_k = \operatorname{neg}\left(\mathbf{F}^T.\operatorname{neg}\left(\mathbf{x}_k\right)\right) \qquad (4)$$

where $\operatorname{neg}(.)$ formally represents the operator of negation. The applying of this operator for a vector $\mathbf{v} = (v_1, v_2, ..., v_n)^T$ of integers yields the vector $\operatorname{neg}(\mathbf{v}) = \mathbf{w} = (w_1, w_2, ..., w_n)^T$. If $v_i = 0$ then $w_i = 1$, otherwise $w_i = 0$. But simultaneously, the condition (3) has to be satisfied. However, because the development of the PN-based model is consecutive (only one transition can be fired in the step k), in case when several transitions are enabled in the step k, only one of them can be chosen to be fired. When the vector $\mathbf{u}_k$ contains more than one non-zero entry, it often does not met (3). But when such $\mathbf{u}_k$ is decomposed into a set of vectors ${}^i\mathbf{u}_k$, $i = 1, ..., r$, each with the different single non-zero entry, any single vector has to satisfy (3) in order to be used as the control vector. It means that there exists only one way how to proceed from the existing state $\mathbf{x}_k$ to another one $\mathbf{x}_{k+1}$ - see illustration in Fig. 1. Every ${}^i\mathbf{u}_k$, $i = 1, 2, 3$ in Fig. 1 has to contain only one non-zero entry. Hence, if $\mathbf{u}_k$ contains in general r non-zero entries (i.e. when r transitions are enabled in the step k), theoretically there are r possibilities of the further development of the system dynamics. Thus, $\mathbf{u}_k$ has to be decomposed into r control vectors ${}^i\mathbf{u}_k$, $i = 1, ..., r$ with single non-zero entry in such a way that $\sum_{i=1}^{r} {}^i\mathbf{u}_k = \mathbf{u}_k$. Thus, the branching makes such a procedure too complicated. Moreover, we do not know which way is a part of trajectory leading to the prescribed terminal state. In general, without additional "backtracking" information we are not able to find solution of the control problem by means of such a "blind" procedure. Therefore, it is better (and simpler in general) to compute the reachability tree (RT) corresponding to P/T PN-based model. The RT yields information about the branching process in the whole. However, even the RT does not give us directly any solution of the control problem. Namely, we have to find the trajectory (or trajectories) between the concrete states from the pair $(\mathbf{x}_0, \mathbf{x}_t)$ and to "extract" the corresponding trajectory (or trajectories) from the global RT. In case of large scale RTs it is not any simple problem. Namely, in general the terminal state can be a multiple leaf of the tree, i.e. there exist many trajectories from $\mathbf{x}_0$ to $\mathbf{x}_t$. Consequently, this paper is motivated by the endeavour to find the automatic procedure yielding control trajectories. Namely, the state trajectories represent only the system responses on the control ones.

3   Forming the Procedure of the Automated Control Synthesis

Starting from results presented in [1]-[3] we are able to compute the functional $(N_{RT} \times N_{RT})$-dimensional adjacency matrix $\mathbf{A}_k$ of the RT as well as the set of feasible state vectors $\{\mathbb{X}_1, ..., \mathbb{X}_{N_{RT}}\}$ reachable from the given initial state $\mathbf{x}_0 \equiv \mathbb{X}_1$ of the PN-based model (including this state too). Such a space of feasible states is represented by the matrix $\mathbf{X}_{reach}$, where the vectors $\mathbb{X}_i$, $i = 1, ..., N_{RT}$ create its columns. The Matlab procedure generating on its output the matrices $\mathbf{A}_k$, $\mathbf{X}_{reach}$ (after entering $\mathbf{F}$, $\mathbf{G}$, $\mathbf{x}_0$ on its input) is introduced in [3]. The method for DES control synthesis based on the intersection of both the straight-lined RT and the backward RT was presented in [1]. Here, the new approach based on bipartite graphs will be presented, because it yields the control trajectories.

3.1   The Procedure for State Machines

A PT/PN is a state machine (SM), if every transition has exactly one input place and one output place. There can not be concurrence in SMs, but conflicts can occur there. Namely, the incidence matrices $\mathbf{F}$, $\mathbf{G}$ have a special structure - any column of $\mathbf{F}$ and any row of $\mathbf{G}$ contains only one non-zero entry. As it is known [12], from the structural point of view PNs are bipartite directed graphs (BDGs) with two kinds of nodes (places and transitions) and two kinds of edges (the arcs directed from places to transitions and the arcs directed contrariwise). Thus, the SM is given as $\langle P, T, F, G \rangle$, where P is the set of PN places, T is the set of PN transitions, F is the set of the edges directed from places to transitions and G is the set of edges directed from transitions to places. The sets F, G can be expressed by the PN incidence matrices matrices $\mathbf{F}$, $\mathbf{G}$. Thus, we can proceed as follows. Let $S = \{P, T\}$ is the set of BDG nodes. Let D is, formally, the set $S \times S$ of BDG edges. Thus, the occurrence of the edges can be expressed by the $((n + m) \times (n + m))$ BDG incidence matrix $\mathbf{A}_{BDG}$ and its transpose $\mathbf{D}$ (as we will see below, it will be very useful)

$$\mathbf{A}_{BDG} = \begin{pmatrix} \emptyset_{n \times n} & \mathbf{F} \\ \mathbf{G} & \emptyset_{m \times m} \end{pmatrix}; \quad \mathbf{D} = \mathbf{A}_{BDG}^T = \begin{pmatrix} \emptyset_{n \times n} & \mathbf{G}^T \\ \mathbf{F}^T & \emptyset_{m \times m} \end{pmatrix} \tag{5}$$

where $\emptyset_{i \times j}$ in general is the $(i \times j)$ zero matrix. The matrices $\mathbf{F}$ and $\mathbf{G}$ are the same as the matrices in the PN-based model (1)-(3). In general, being in a state $\mathbf{x}_k$ the system can develop its dynamic behaviour either in the straight-lined direction or (formally) also in the backward one. The former development is performed by means of the matrix $\mathbf{D}$ given in (5) used in the state equation (6) while the latter one by means of the transpose $\mathbf{D}^T$.

To synthesize the DES control from a given initial state $\mathbf{x}_0$ to a desired terminal state $\mathbf{x}_t = \mathbf{x}_N$ the straight-lined development of the system dynamic can be computed - in analogy with [1] - by means of the following state equation

$$\{\mathbf{s}_{k+1}\} = \mathbf{D}.\{\mathbf{s}_k\}, \; k = 0, 1, \ldots, 2N-1 \tag{6}$$

with $\mathbf{s}_k$ being the augmented $(n+m)$-dimensional vector defined as follows

$$\{\mathbf{s}_k\} = \begin{cases} (\{\mathbf{x}_{k/2}\}^T, \emptyset_m^T)^T & \text{if } k = 0, 2, 4, \ldots, 2N-2 \\ (\emptyset_n^T, \{\mathbf{u}_{(k-1)/2)}\}^T)^T & \text{if } k = 1, 3, 5, \ldots, 2N-1 \end{cases} \tag{7}$$

where $\emptyset_j$ in general is the j-dimensional zero vector; $\mathbf{x}_{k/2} = \mathbf{G}^T.\mathbf{u}_{(k-2)/2}, \; k = 2, 4, \ldots, 2N-2$; $\mathbf{u}_{(k-1)/2} = \mathbf{F}^T.\mathbf{x}_{(k-1)/2}, \; k = 1, 3, 5, \ldots, 2N-1$. To be sure that during the straight-lined development the prescribed terminal state will be met, the backward development of the system dynamic can be computed by means of the following state equation

$$\{\mathbf{s}_{k-1}\} = \mathbf{D}^T.\{\mathbf{s}_k\} = \mathbf{A}_{BDG}.\{\mathbf{s}_k\}, \; k = K, K-1, \ldots, 1 \tag{8}$$

However, because of the special block form of both the matrix $\mathbf{D}$ and the vector $\mathbf{s}_k$ we can alternate step-by-step two procedures - the straight-lined procedure and the backward one. The former procedure is the following

$${}^1\mathbf{X} = (\mathbf{x}_0, \emptyset_{n \times N}); \; {}^1\{\mathbf{u}_0\} = \mathbf{F}^T.\mathbf{x}_0;$$
$${}^1\mathbf{U} = ({}^1\{\mathbf{u}_0\}, \emptyset_{m \times (N-1)}); \; {}^1\{\mathbf{x}_1\} = \mathbf{G}^T.{}^1\{\mathbf{u}_0\}$$
$${}^1\mathbf{X} = (\mathbf{x}_0, {}^1\{\mathbf{x}_1\}, \emptyset_{n \times (N-1)}); \; {}^1\{\mathbf{u}_1\} = \mathbf{F}^T.{}^1\mathbf{x}_1$$
$${}^1\mathbf{U} = ({}^1\{\mathbf{u}_0\}, {}^1\{\mathbf{u}_1\}, \emptyset_{m \times (N-2)})$$
$${}^1\mathbf{X} = (\mathbf{x}_0, {}^1\{\mathbf{x}_1\}, {}^1\{\mathbf{x}_2\}, \emptyset_{n \times (N-2)}); \; \ldots \ldots {}^1\{\mathbf{u}_{N-1}\} = \mathbf{F}^T.{}^1\mathbf{x}_{N-1};$$
$${}^1\mathbf{U} = ({}^1\{\mathbf{u}_0\}, {}^1\{\mathbf{u}_1\}, \ldots, {}^1\{\mathbf{u}_{N-1}\}); \; {}^1\{\mathbf{x}_N\} = \mathbf{G}^T.{}^1\{\mathbf{u}_{N-1}\}$$
$${}^1\mathbf{X} = (\mathbf{x}_0, {}^1\{\mathbf{x}_1\}, {}^1\{\mathbf{x}_2\}, \ldots, {}^1\{\mathbf{x}_N\})$$

where ${}^1\mathbf{U}$ and ${}^1\mathbf{X}$ are, respectively, $(m \times N)$ and $(n \times (N+1))$ matrices. The left upper index ${}^1(.)$ points out performing the straight-lined procedure. The backtracking procedure runs as follows

$${}^2\mathbf{X} = (\emptyset_{n \times N}, \mathbf{x}_N); \; {}^2\{\mathbf{u}_{N-1}\} = \mathbf{G}.\mathbf{x}_N$$
$${}^2\mathbf{U} = (\emptyset_{m \times (N-1)}, {}^2\{\mathbf{u}_{N-1}\}); \; {}^2\{\mathbf{x}_{N-1}\} = \mathbf{F}.{}^2\{\mathbf{u}_{N-1}\}$$
$${}^2\mathbf{X} = (\emptyset_{n \times (N-1)}, {}^2\{\mathbf{x}_{N-1}\}, \mathbf{x}_N); \; {}^2\{\mathbf{u}_{N-2}\} = \mathbf{G}.{}^2\{\mathbf{x}_{N-1}\}$$
$${}^2\mathbf{U} = (\emptyset_{m \times (N-1)}, {}^2\{\mathbf{u}_{N-2}\}, {}^2\{\mathbf{u}_{N-1}\}); \; {}^2\{\mathbf{x}_{N-2}\} = \mathbf{F}.{}^2\{\mathbf{u}_{N-1}\}$$
$${}^2\mathbf{X} = (\emptyset_{n \times (N-2)}, {}^2\{\mathbf{x}_{N-2}\}, {}^2\{\mathbf{x}_{N-1}\}, \mathbf{x}_N); \; \ldots \ldots {}^2\{\mathbf{u}_1\} = \mathbf{G}.{}^2\{\mathbf{x}_2\}$$
$${}^2\mathbf{U} = (\emptyset_{n \times 1}, {}^2\{\mathbf{u}_1\}, \ldots, {}^2\{\mathbf{u}_{N-1}\}); \; {}^2\{\mathbf{x}_1\} = \mathbf{F}.{}^2\{\mathbf{u}_1\}$$
$${}^2\mathbf{X} = (\emptyset_{n \times 1}, {}^2\{\mathbf{x}_1\}, {}^2\{\mathbf{x}_2\}, \ldots, \mathbf{x}_N); \; {}^2\{\mathbf{u}_0\} = \mathbf{G}.{}^2\{\mathbf{x}_1\}$$
$${}^2\mathbf{U} = ({}^2\{\mathbf{u}_0\}, {}^2\{\mathbf{u}_1\}, \ldots, {}^2\{\mathbf{u}_{N-1}\}); \; {}^2\{\mathbf{x}_0\} = \mathbf{F}.{}^2\{\mathbf{x}_0\}$$
$${}^2\mathbf{X} = ({}^2\{\mathbf{x}_0\}, {}^2\{\mathbf{x}_1\}, {}^2\{\mathbf{x}_2\}, \ldots, \mathbf{x}_N)$$

where $^2\mathbf{U}$ is $(m \times N)$ matrix and $^2\mathbf{X}$ is $(n \times (N+1))$ matrix. The left upper index $^2(.)$ points out performing the backtracking procedure. The final phase of the control problem solving consists in the special intersection. Namely, $\{\mathbf{x}_i\} = \max(\{^1\mathbf{x}_i\}, \{^2\mathbf{x}_i\}), i = 0, ..., N; \{\mathbf{u}_j\} = \max(\{^1\mathbf{u}_j\}, \{^2\mathbf{u}_j\}), j = 0, ..., N-1$. Hence, we have at disposal following both kinds of system trajectories - the control trajectories and the corresponding state ones

$$\mathbf{U} = {}^1\mathbf{U} \cap {}^2\mathbf{U}; \quad \mathbf{U} = (\{\mathbf{u}_0\}, \{\mathbf{u}_1\}, \dots, \{\mathbf{u}_{N-1}\}) \tag{9}$$

$$\mathbf{X} = {}^1\mathbf{X} \cap {}^2\mathbf{X}; \quad \mathbf{X} = (\mathbf{x}_0, \{\mathbf{x}_1\}, \dots, \{\mathbf{x}_{N-1}\}, \mathbf{x}_N) \tag{10}$$

Handling the zero blocks is eliminated on this way as well. Although the described approach seems to be very hopeful as to the automated synthesis of the DES control, its usage is limited. In such a form it is suitable only for SMs. In order to utilize such an approach also for P/T PNs that do not fulfill this restriction, we have to work with the RT adjacency matrix appertaining to such PNs.

3.2   The Generalization of the Procedure

Although SMs create the important class of P/T PNs, in comparison with the diversity of P/T PN structure SMs represent only a very small part of P/T PNs in the whole. Consequently, more general methods have to be found in order to deal with general P/T PNs. Here, the generalization of the method introduced above for SMs will be performed in order to be suitable also for P/T PNs with general structure. The main idea emerges from the fact that the P/T PN reachability graph (RG) is state machine in the sense of the SM definition. However, the adjacency matrix of the RG does not contain explicitly the incidence matrices $\mathbf{F}, \mathbf{G}$. Namely, in contrast to SMs, where transitions assigned to edges have only one input place and only one output place (and consequently any ambiguity, as to transitions, cannot occur) in P/T PN with general structure transitions can have more input places and more output ones. Hence, some ambiguities can occur. Therefore, in order to use the previous method here, we have to deal with this problem. Fortunately, the RG adjacency matrix $\mathbf{A}_{RG}$ can be formally decomposed into the fictive incidence matrices $\mathbf{F}_{RG}, \mathbf{G}_{RG}$, provided that the original transitions were renamed before in order to remove any ambiguity. Namely, any column of $\mathbf{F}_{RG}$ and any row of $\mathbf{G}_{RG}$ must not contain more than one non-zero entry. Thus, a fictive SM corresponding to P/T PN arises.

Computing the RG Parameters. The RG adjacency matrix $\mathbf{A}_{RG}$, more precisely the so called k variant adjacency matrix $\mathbf{A}_k = a_{ij}^k, i = 1, ..., N_{RT}; j = 1, ..., N_{RT}$ [1], where N_{RT} is the number of feasible states $\mathbb{X}_k, k = 1, ..., N_{RT}$ reachable from the initial state $\mathbf{x}_0 \equiv \mathbb{X}_1$ (including $\mathbf{x}_0$), can be computed by means the procedure presented in [3]. The $\mathbf{A}_k$ entries a_{ij}^k are the transition functions $\gamma_{t_{\mathbb{X}_i \to \mathbb{X}_j}}^k$. Such an entry concerns the transition fixed to the RG edge connecting two RG nodes $\mathbb{X}_i$, $\mathbb{X}_j$. This matrix is given on the procedure output in the form of *quasi k* variant adjacency matrix $\mathbf{A}_{Qk}$. Its entries are given as integers corresponding to indices of the PN transitions. For example, when $t_{\mathbb{X}_i \to \mathbb{X}_j} = t_q$ - i.e. when it has the index q - the integer q will represent the entry a_{ij}^{Qk}.

Decomposition of the RG Adjacency Matrix. To find the fictive matrices $\mathbf{F}_{RG}$, $\mathbf{G}_{RG}$ we have to disassemble the matrix $\mathbf{A}_{Qk}$. Namely, some of its entries may not be mutually different. They may acquire the same value because the original P/T PN transitions may occur more then once among the entries. Consequently, a confusion could occur during the computational process and decline it. To avoid these difficulties, it is necessary to rename the original P/T PN transitions in order to obtain fictive transitions that occur only once. The number of them is T_r, being the global number of the non-zero elements of $\mathbf{A}_{Qk}$. The renaming is performed raw-by-raw so that the non-zero elements are replaced by integers - ordinal numbers starting from 1 and finishing at T_r. Thus, the auxiliary (fictive) adjacency matrix $\mathbf{A}_{T_r}$ is obtained. The disassembling of the matrix $\mathbf{A}_{T_r}$ into the incidence matrices $\mathbf{F}_{RG}$ and $\mathbf{G}_{RG}$ is accomplished as follows. The elements of these matrices for $i = 1, ..., N_{RT}$, $j = 1, ... N_{RT}$ are

$$\mathbf{T}_{tr}(\mathbf{A}_{Qk}(i,j), \mathbf{A}_{T_r}(i,j)) = \begin{cases} 1 & \text{if } \mathbf{A}_{Qk}(i,j) \neq 0 \,\&\, \mathbf{A}_{T_r}(i,j) \neq 0 \\ 0 & \text{otherwise} \end{cases} \quad (11)$$

$$\mathbf{F}_{RG}(i, \mathbf{A}_{T_r}(i,j)) = \begin{cases} 1 & \text{if } \mathbf{A}_{Qk}(i,j) \neq 0 \,\&\, \mathbf{A}_{T_r}(i,j) \neq 0 \\ 0 & \text{otherwise} \end{cases} \quad (12)$$

$$\mathbf{G}_{RG}(\mathbf{A}_{T_r}(i,j), j) = \begin{cases} 1 & \text{if } \mathbf{A}_{Qk}(i,j) \neq 0 \,\&\, \mathbf{A}_{T_r}(i,j) \neq 0 \\ 0 & \text{otherwise} \end{cases} \quad (13)$$

Here, $\mathbf{T}_{tr}$ is the transformation matrix between the original set of transitions and the fictive ones. Hence, actual $\mathbf{U} = \mathbf{T}_{tr}.\mathbf{U}^*$ where $\mathbf{U}^*$ yields the fictive control strategies given by (9), computed by means of the set of the fictive transitions.

Importance of the Generalized Approach. The generalized approach (i) makes possible the automated control synthesis of the P/T PNs with the general structure - i.e. it extends the applicability of the method originally proposed for SMs; (ii) enables us to analyse the dynamic behaviour of arbitrary structure of agents modelled by P/T PNs. Namely, agents often (even when they are modelled by SMs and supervised by a supervisor) do not represent together any SM but rather P/T PN with a general structure (because of the interconnections between the elementary agents and the supervisor). The supervisor is usually used in order to bring DES subsystems or agents in MAS (e.g. robots, automatically guided vehicles, etc.) to a (better) cooperation or forbid them to be selfish at making use of common sources (like energy, row materials, yard, roads, etc.).

Example 1. Consider an agent modelled by the P/T PN with more general structure (i.e. different from SM) given in Fig. 2 on the left. It represents the

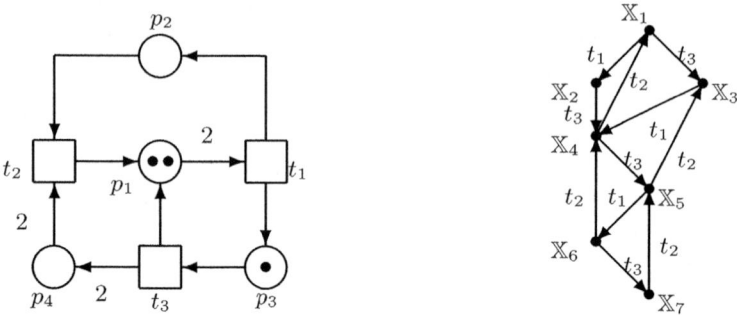

Fig. 2. The PN-based model of the agent (on the left) and the corresponding RG (on the right)

behaviour of the autonomous agent. Let us demonstrate the applicability of the approach introduced in the previous subsections directly on this agent. The corresponding RG is given in Fig. 2 on the right. As we can see $n = 4$, $m = 3$, $\mathbf{x}_0 \equiv \mathbb{X}_1 = (2, 0, 1, 0)^T$, $N_{RT} = 7$. The PN incidence matrices and the RG parameters are the following

$$
\mathbf{F} = \begin{pmatrix} 2 & 0 & 0 \\ 0 & 1 & 0 \\ 0 & 0 & 1 \\ 0 & 2 & 0 \end{pmatrix} \quad
\mathbf{G} = \begin{pmatrix} 0 & 1 & 1 & 0 \\ 1 & 0 & 0 & 0 \\ 1 & 0 & 0 & 2 \end{pmatrix} \quad
\mathbf{A}_{Qk} = \begin{pmatrix} 0 & 1 & 3 & 0 & 0 & 0 & 0 \\ 0 & 0 & 0 & 3 & 0 & 0 & 0 \\ 0 & 0 & 0 & 1 & 0 & 0 & 0 \\ 2 & 0 & 0 & 0 & 3 & 0 & 0 \\ 0 & 0 & 2 & 0 & 0 & 1 & 0 \\ 0 & 0 & 0 & 2 & 0 & 0 & 3 \\ 0 & 0 & 0 & 0 & 2 & 0 & 0 \end{pmatrix} \quad
\mathbf{X}_{reach} = \begin{pmatrix} 2 & 0 & 3 & 1 & 2 & 0 & 1 \\ 0 & 1 & 0 & 1 & 1 & 2 & 2 \\ 1 & 2 & 0 & 1 & 0 & 1 & 0 \\ 0 & 0 & 2 & 2 & 4 & 4 & 6 \end{pmatrix}
$$

After renaming the transitions, decomposing the matrix $\mathbf{A}_{T_r}$ and applying the proposed method we can synthesize the control $\mathbf{U}$ from the initial state $\mathbf{x}_0 \equiv \mathbb{X}_1 = (2, 0, 1, 0)^T$ to a desired terminal state - e.g. to $\mathbf{x}_t = \mathbb{X}_7 = (1, 2, 0, 6)^T$

$$
\mathbf{A}_{T_r} = \begin{pmatrix} 0 & 1 & 2 & 0 & 0 & 0 & 0 \\ 0 & 0 & 0 & 3 & 0 & 0 & 0 \\ 0 & 0 & 0 & 4 & 0 & 0 & 0 \\ 5 & 0 & 0 & 0 & 6 & 0 & 0 \\ 0 & 0 & 7 & 0 & 0 & 8 & 0 \\ 0 & 0 & 0 & 9 & 0 & 0 & 10 \\ 0 & 0 & 0 & 0 & 11 & 0 & 0 \end{pmatrix} \quad
\mathbf{T}_{tr}^T = \begin{pmatrix} 1 & 0 & 0 \\ 0 & 0 & 1 \\ 0 & 0 & 1 \\ 1 & 0 & 0 \\ 0 & 1 & 0 \\ 0 & 0 & 1 \\ 0 & 1 & 0 \\ 1 & 0 & 0 \\ 0 & 1 & 0 \\ 0 & 0 & 1 \\ 0 & 1 & 0 \end{pmatrix} \quad
\mathbf{U}^* = \begin{pmatrix} 1 & 0 & 0 & 0 & 0 \\ 1 & 0 & 0 & 0 & 0 \\ 0 & 1 & 0 & 0 & 0 \\ 0 & 1 & 0 & 0 & 0 \\ 0 & 0 & 0 & 0 & 0 \\ 0 & 0 & 1 & 0 & 0 \\ 0 & 0 & 0 & 0 & 0 \\ 0 & 0 & 0 & 1 & 0 \\ 0 & 0 & 0 & 0 & 0 \\ 0 & 0 & 0 & 0 & 1 \\ 0 & 0 & 0 & 0 & 0 \end{pmatrix}
$$

$$\mathbf{X} = \begin{pmatrix} 1\,0\,0\,0\,0\,0 \\ 0\,1\,0\,0\,0\,0 \\ 0\,1\,0\,0\,0\,0 \\ 0\,0\,1\,0\,0\,0 \\ 0\,0\,0\,1\,0\,0 \\ 0\,0\,0\,0\,1\,0 \\ 0\,0\,0\,0\,0\,1 \end{pmatrix} \quad \mathbf{U} = \mathbf{T}_{tr}.\mathbf{U}^* = \begin{pmatrix} 1\,1\,0\,1\,0 \\ 0\,0\,0\,0\,0 \\ 1\,1\,1\,0\,1 \end{pmatrix}$$

Its graphical expression is on the left in Fig. 3. To obtain the actual matrix $\mathbf{U}$ the fictive matrix $\mathbf{U}^*$ (obtained together with $\mathbf{X}$ at using the proposed procedure) had to be transformed by means of the matrix $\mathbf{T}_{tr}$.

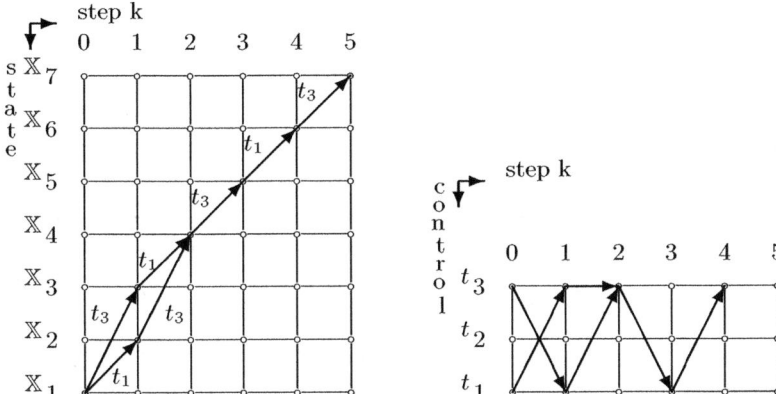

Fig. 3. The state trajectories from $\mathbf{x}_0 \equiv \mathbb{X}_1$ to $\mathbf{x}_t \equiv \mathbb{X}_7$ (on the left) as the responses on the synthesized control trajectories given on the right

4   Synthesis of Agents Cooperation

Using the method presented in [4] we can synthesize the structure of the agent supervisor. The supervisor can be suitable (i) for the avoidance of the egoistic effort of autonomous agents by means of prohibition some states of the global system describing the MAS, e.g. like the so called mutex (<u>mut</u>ual <u>ex</u>clusion) - see examples introduced in [4]; (ii) in order to synthesize the desired cooperation of agents in MAS. The principle of the method is based on the PN place invariants (P-invariants) [12,7,9]. P-invariants are vectors, $\mathbf{v}$, with the property that multiplication of these vectors with any state vector $\mathbf{x}$ reachable from a given initial state vector $\mathbf{x}_0$ yields the same result (the relation of the state conservation)

$$\mathbf{v}^T.\mathbf{x} = \mathbf{v}^T.\mathbf{x}_0, \qquad \text{i.e.} \qquad \mathbf{v}^T.\mathbf{x} = \mathbf{v}^T.\mathbb{X}_1 \tag{14}$$

Hence, taking into account (1) and the consecutiveness of states, for column $col_t(\mathbf{B})$ of $\mathbf{B}$ corresponding to a transition t

$$\mathbf{v}^T.col_t(\mathbf{B}) = 0, \qquad \text{i.e.} \qquad \mathbf{v}^T.\mathbf{B} = \mathbf{\emptyset} \tag{15}$$

where $\mathbf{v}$ is n-dimensional vector (n is the number of PN places) and $\emptyset$ is m-dimensional zero vector. This equation is usually presented as the definition of the P-invariant $\mathbf{v}$ of PN.

The P-invariants can be utilized at the supervisor synthesis [14,13,10,7,9]. In case of several invariants the set of the P-invariants is created by the columns of the $(n \times n_x)$-dimensional matrix $\mathbf{V}$ (n_x expresses the number of invariants) being the solution of the equation

$$\mathbf{V}^T . \mathbf{B} = \emptyset \tag{16}$$

Just this equation represents the base for the supervisor synthesis method. Some additional PN places (slacks) can be added to the PN-model in question. The slacks create the places of the supervisor. Hence, (16) can be rewritten as

$$[\mathbf{L}, \mathbf{I}_s] . \begin{bmatrix} \mathbf{B} \\ \mathbf{B}_s \end{bmatrix} = \emptyset$$

where $\mathbf{I}_s$ is $(n_s \times n_s)$-dimensional identity matrix with $n_s \le n_x$ being the number of slacks, $(n_s \times n)$-dimensional matrix $\mathbf{L}$ of integers represents (in a suitable form) the conditions $\mathbf{L}.\mathbf{x} \le \mathbf{b}$ ($\mathbf{b}$ is the vector of integers), imposed on marking of the original PN and the $(n_s \times m)$-dimensional matrix $\mathbf{B}_s$ yields (after its finding by computing) the structure of the PN-based model of the supervisor. Consequently,

$$\mathbf{L}.\mathbf{B} + \mathbf{B}_s = \emptyset; \quad \mathbf{B}_s = -\mathbf{L}.\mathbf{B}; \quad \mathbf{B}_s = \mathbf{G}_s^T - \mathbf{F}_s \tag{17}$$

where the actual structure of the matrix $\mathbf{L}$ has to be respected. The augmented state vector (i.e. the state vector of the original PN together with the supervisor) and the augmented matrices are as follows

$$\mathbf{x}_a = \begin{bmatrix} \mathbf{x} \\ \mathbf{x}_s \end{bmatrix}; \quad \mathbf{F}_a = \begin{pmatrix} \mathbf{F} \\ \mathbf{F}_s \end{pmatrix}; \quad \mathbf{G}_a^T = \begin{pmatrix} \mathbf{G}^T \\ \mathbf{G}_s^T \end{pmatrix} \tag{18}$$

where the submatrices $\mathbf{F}_s$ and $\mathbf{G}_s^T$ correspond to the interconnections of the incorporated slacks with the actual PN structure. Because of the prescribed conditions we have

$$[\mathbf{L} \mid \mathbf{I}_s] . \begin{bmatrix} \mathbf{x}_0 \\ {}^s\mathbf{x}_0 \end{bmatrix} = \mathbf{b} \quad \text{i.e. the supervisor initial state is:} \quad {}^s\mathbf{x}_0 = \mathbf{b} - \mathbf{L}.\mathbf{x}_0$$

where $\mathbf{b}$ is the vector of the corresponding dimensionality (i.e. n_s) with integer entries representing the limits for number of common tokens - i.e. the maximum numbers of tokens that the corresponding places can possess altogether (i.e. share).

Example 2. Consider two agents with the same structure given in Example 1. Distinguish their models by the left upper index in the vectors and matrices. When the agents are autonomous, their structure can be written as follows

$$\mathbf{F} = \begin{pmatrix} {}^1\mathbf{F} & \emptyset \\ \emptyset & {}^2\mathbf{F} \end{pmatrix}; \quad \mathbf{G} = \begin{pmatrix} {}^1\mathbf{G} & \emptyset \\ \emptyset & {}^2\mathbf{G} \end{pmatrix}; \quad \mathbf{B} = \mathbf{G}^T - \mathbf{F}; \quad \mathbf{x}_0 = \begin{pmatrix} {}^1\mathbf{x}_0 \\ {}^2\mathbf{x}_0 \end{pmatrix}$$

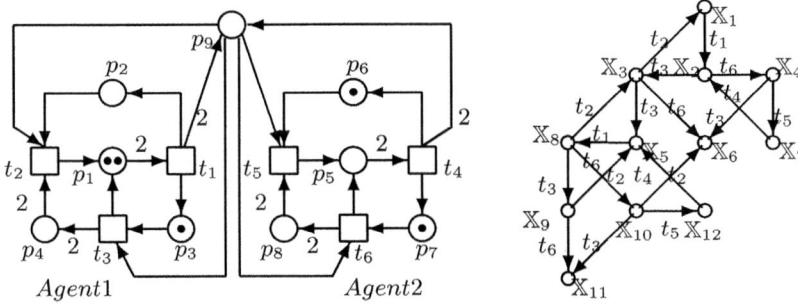

Fig. 4. The PN-based model of the supervised agent cooperation (on the left) and the corresponding RG (on the right)

Consider their initial states $^1\mathbf{x}_0 = (2, 0, 1, 0)^T$, $^2\mathbf{x}_0 = (0, 1, 1, 0)^T$. Let us request that p_1 and p_5 may share (keep together) maximally two tokens, i.e.

$p_1 + p_5 \leq 2$, after introducing the slack p_9: $p_1 + p_5 + p_9 = 2$; $s = 1$; $\mathbf{I}_s = 1$
$\mathbf{L} = (1\,0\,0\,0\,1\,0\,0\,0)$; $\mathbf{b} = 2$; $\mathbf{B}_s = -\mathbf{L}.\mathbf{B} = (2, -1, -1, 2, -1, -1)$
$\mathbf{F}_s = (0\,1\,1\,0\,1\,1)$; $\mathbf{G}_s^T = (2\,0\,0\,2\,0\,0)$; $^s\mathbf{x}_0 = \mathbf{b} - \mathbf{L}.\mathbf{x}_0 = 2 - 2 = 0$

The closed loop structure of the agents together with their supervisor is in Fig.4 on the left. The corresponding RG is given on the right. The supervisor structure (i.e. p_9 together with the interaction edges to and from both agents) and its initial state ensure that the pair of agents will behave in the prescribed fashion (the prescribed condition will never be disturbed). However, in order to know the course of both the the control trajectories and the responses on them (i.e. the state trajectories) we can use the proposed method of the automatic control synthesis. Starting from the initial state $\mathbf{x}_0 \equiv \mathbb{X}_1 = (2, 0, 1, 0\,|\,0, 1, 1, 0\,|\,0)^T$ being the first column of $\mathbf{X}_{reach}$ to the terminal state $\mathbf{x}_t \equiv \mathbb{X}_6 = (1, 1, 1, 2\,|\,1, 1, 0, 2\,|\,0)^T$ being the sixth column of $\mathbf{X}_{reach}$ we have at disposal below the synthesized trajectories in the form of matrices and in the graphical form given in Fig.5.

$$
\mathbf{X}_{reach} = \left(\begin{array}{cccccccccccc}
2 & 0 & 1 & 0 & 2 & 1 & 0 & 0 & 1 & 0 & 1 & 0 \\
0 & 1 & 1 & 1 & 1 & 1 & 1 & 2 & 2 & 2 & 2 & 2 \\
1 & 2 & 1 & 2 & 0 & 1 & 2 & 1 & 0 & 1 & 0 & 1 \\
0 & 0 & 2 & 0 & 4 & 2 & 0 & 4 & 6 & 4 & 6 & 4 \\
\hline
0 & 0 & 0 & 1 & 0 & 1 & 2 & 0 & 0 & 1 & 1 & 2 \\
1 & 1 & 1 & 1 & 1 & 1 & 0 & 1 & 1 & 1 & 1 & 0 \\
1 & 1 & 1 & 0 & 1 & 0 & 0 & 1 & 1 & 0 & 0 & 0 \\
0 & 0 & 0 & 2 & 0 & 2 & 0 & 0 & 0 & 2 & 2 & 0 \\
\hline
0 & 2 & 1 & 1 & 0 & 0 & 0 & 2 & 1 & 1 & 0 & 0
\end{array}\right)
\begin{array}{l}
\left.\rule{0pt}{28pt}\right\}\text{Agent 1} \\[18pt]
\left.\rule{0pt}{28pt}\right\}\text{Agent 2} \\[10pt]
\left.\rule{0pt}{6pt}\right\}\text{Supervisor}
\end{array}
$$

$$\mathbf{X}^T = \begin{pmatrix} 1\,0\,0\,0\,0\,0\,0\,0\,0\,0\,0\,0 \\ 0\,1\,0\,0\,0\,0\,0\,0\,0\,0\,0\,0 \\ 0\,0\,1\,1\,0\,0\,0\,0\,0\,0\,0\,0 \\ 0\,0\,0\,0\,0\,1\,0\,0\,0\,0\,0\,0 \end{pmatrix} ; \mathbf{U} = \begin{pmatrix} 1\,0\,0 \\ 0\,0\,0 \\ 0\,1\,1 \\ 0\,0\,0 \\ 0\,0\,0 \\ 0\,1\,1 \end{pmatrix}$$

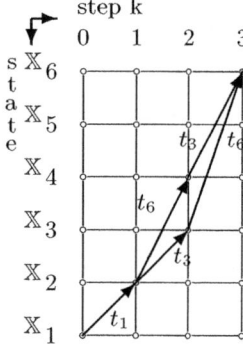 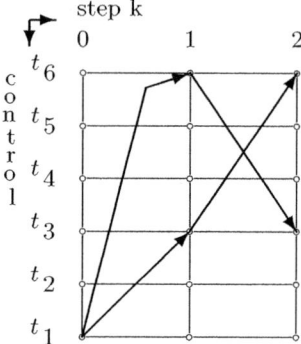

Fig. 5. The state trajectories from $\mathbf{x}_0 \equiv \mathbb{X}_1$ to $\mathbf{x}_t \equiv \mathbb{X}_6$ (on the left) as the responses on the synthesized control trajectories (on the right)

5   Generalized Constraints in the Supervisor Synthesis

The previous constraints utilizing only PN places can be extended as it was already premised above. Namely, the vector $\mathbf{x}_k$ expressing the state of the system is the PN marking vector. However, the vector $\mathbf{u}_k$, named in this paper as the control vector, is the driving vector of the system dynamics development. It represents the cause of the change $\mathbf{u}_k \rightarrow \mathbf{x}_{k+1}$ while $\mathbf{x}_k$ represents a consequence of the change $\mathbf{u}_{k-1} \rightarrow \mathbf{x}_{k1}$. Therefore, it is very useful to utilize it at the synthesis of supervisor too. On this way also the Parikh's vector is very important and useful.

Hence, the general linear constraints were simply described in [8] as follows

$$\mathbf{L}_p.\mathbf{x} + \mathbf{L}_t.\mathbf{u} + \mathbf{L}_v.\mathbf{v} \leq \mathbf{b} \tag{19}$$

where $\mathbf{L}_p$, $\mathbf{L}_t$, $\mathbf{L}_v$ are, respectively, $(n_s \times n)-$, $(n_s \times m)-$, $(n_s \times m)-$dimensional matrices. When $\mathbf{b} - \mathbf{L}_p.\mathbf{x} \geq \mathbf{0}$ is valid - see e.g. [8] - the supervisor with the following structure and initial state

$$\mathbf{F}_s = \max(\mathbf{0}, \mathbf{L}_p.\mathbf{B} + \mathbf{L}_v, \mathbf{L}_t) \tag{20}$$

$$\mathbf{G}_s^T = \max(\mathbf{0}, \mathbf{L}_t - \max(\mathbf{0}, \mathbf{L}_p.\mathbf{B} + \mathbf{L}_v)) - \min(\mathbf{0}, \mathbf{L}_p.\mathbf{B} + \mathbf{L}_v) \tag{21}$$

$$^s\mathbf{x}_0 = \mathbf{b} - \mathbf{L}_p.\mathbf{x}_0 - \mathbf{L}_v.\mathbf{v}_0 \tag{22}$$

guarrantees that constraints are verified for the states resulting from the initial state. Here, the max(.) is the maximum operator for matrices. However, the maximum is taken element by element. Namely, in general, for the matrices $\mathbf{X}$, $\mathbf{Y}$, $\mathbf{Z}$ of the same dimensionality ($n \times m$, the relation $\mathbf{Z} = \max(\mathbf{X}, \mathbf{Y})$ it holds that $z_{ij} = \max(x_{ij}, y_{ij})$, $i = 1, ..., n$, $j = 1, ..., m$.

5.1   Some Remarks

In general (not only the supervisor synthesis) the control synthesis for DES modelled by P/T PNs can be performed also in virtue of P/T PN-based methods. In [1] the method of such a kind was introduced. It is based on ordinary reachability graphs (RGs) and yields the space of feasible state trajectories from a given initial state to a desired terminal one. The modified approach based on bipartite directed graphs (BDGs) was presented in [5].

The supervision ensures fulfilling prescribed conditions imposed on the agents behaviour. However, from the control theory point of view, it does not mean that a single trajectory from the given initial state of the system to a prescribed terminal one will be at disposal. The supervising only limits possibilities of the agents behaviour. Besides, the agents can behave as freely as possible.

6   The Case Study 1

The above introduced exact approach to the supervisor synthesis is sufficiently general for DES modelled by P/T PNs. Hence, it is applicable on very wide class of DES including agents, especially material agents in industry. To illustrate this let us apply the approach to the seemingly simple case, namely to the internal transport of FMS. Combinations of the both kinds of constraints will be used step-by-step in order to synthesize the supervisor for four agents in FMS.

Many times the agents working in a common space - e.g. the tracks for AGVs (automatically guided vehicles) or mobile robots in a kind of FMS, or tracks for trains in a railway, etc. - have to be supervised in order to avoid a crash. To illustrate this, consider N_t tracks of AGVs in FMS. Denote them as agents A_i, $i = 1, ..., N_t$. The AGVs carry semi-products from a place of FMS to another place and then they (empty or with another load) come round. In any track A_i there exist $n_i \geq 1$ AGVs. Consider the tracks with AGVs to be the autonomous agents. The PN model of the single agent A_1 is given in Fig.6. The parameters of the agents PN-based models are the following

$$^i\mathbf{F} = \begin{pmatrix} 1 & 0 & 0 & 0 \\ 0 & 1 & 0 & 0 \\ 0 & 0 & 1 & 0 \\ 0 & 0 & 0 & 1 \end{pmatrix} ; \quad ^i\mathbf{G}^T = \begin{pmatrix} 0 & 0 & 0 & 1 \\ 1 & 0 & 0 & 0 \\ 0 & 1 & 0 & 0 \\ 0 & 0 & 1 & 0 \end{pmatrix} ; \quad ^i\mathbf{B} = \begin{pmatrix} -1 & 0 & 0 & 1 \\ 1 & -1 & 0 & 0 \\ 0 & 1 & -1 & 0 \\ 0 & 0 & 1 & -1 \end{pmatrix} ; \quad i = 1, N_t$$

$$\mathbf{F} = \begin{pmatrix} ^1\mathbf{F} & \emptyset & \cdots\cdots & \emptyset \\ \emptyset & ^2\mathbf{F} & \cdots\cdots & \emptyset \\ \cdots & \cdots\cdots & \cdots \\ \emptyset & \emptyset & \cdots\cdots & {}^{N_t}\mathbf{F} \end{pmatrix} ; \quad \mathbf{G} = \begin{pmatrix} ^1\mathbf{G} & \emptyset & \cdots\cdots & \emptyset \\ \emptyset & ^2\mathbf{G} & \cdots\cdots & \emptyset \\ \cdots & \cdots\cdots & \cdots \\ \emptyset & \emptyset & \cdots\cdots & {}^{N_t}\mathbf{G} \end{pmatrix} ; \quad \mathbf{x}_0 = \begin{pmatrix} ^1\mathbf{x}_0 \\ ^2\mathbf{x}_0 \\ \cdots \\ {}^{N_t}\mathbf{x}_0 \end{pmatrix}$$

$$\mathbf{B} = \mathbf{G}^T - \mathbf{F}$$

During the agents activities n_1 AGVs (represented by means of tokens situated in corresponding PN places) have to pass this track as well as a restricted area (RA) common for all agents, namely, even two times. RA is a "bottle-neck" of the global system. Namely, in case of the AGVs of e.g. the agent A_1: (i) when they carry some semi-products from a place p_1 of FMS to another place p_3 they have to pass the area (expressed by p_2) first time, and (ii) when they come round to the place p_1 they have to pass the same area (expressed now by p_4) once more. However, because the space of the FMS where the agents operate is limited, there exists the restriction that only limited number of different AGVs, namely, $N < \sum_{i=1}^{N_t} n_i$ or often $N << \sum_{i=1}^{N_t} n_i$, can operate in the RA simultaneously, the agents A_i have to be limited in their autonomous activities by a supervisor. The reason is that the agents themselves are not able to coalesce on a procedure satisfying all of them because the autonomous agents are usually egoistic (selfish). A violent driving of individual agents in RA might tend to wrecks with exterminatory effects, including some mechanical devastations, even standing the whole FMS off. Therefore, the supervisor determines a policy of the agents behaviour from the global point of view (i.e. conducive to the whole FMS) in order to achieve the satisfying results of the cooperative interactions among devices and expected behaviour (function) of the global FMS. Besides, it assures that no agent will be discriminated in its activities. The opposite view on the supervisor synthesis process can evoke an impress that such a process expresses e.g. the agents negotiation (although unwilling) or another kind of cooperation. Such a view is not so fantastic, because the supervisor does not drive its own selfish will or interest but its activity represents only the necessary part of the global strategy of the FMS behaviour, even the correct model of a part of the technological subprocess inside FMS. Another view on the supervisor synthesis process (especially from the control point of view) is that the supervisor realizes the objective function of the FMS subprocess. Namely, the supervisor only realizes the global demands on the behaviour of a part of FMS so as to meet the global aim of the whole FMS. In general, considering N_A agents, we can describe

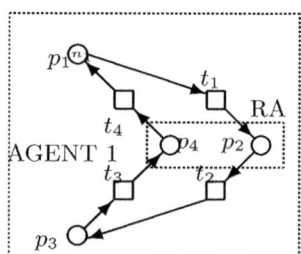

Fig. 6. The PN-based model of the agent. The places p_2, p_4 lie in the RA.

the restrictions in analytical terms as follows

$$\sigma_{p_2} + \sigma_{p_4} \leq n1$$
$$\sigma_{p_6} + \sigma_{p_8} \leq n2$$
$$\cdots \qquad \cdots \qquad \cdots \qquad \cdots$$
$$\sigma_{p_{4N_A-2}} + \sigma_{p_{4N_A}} \leq n_{N_A}$$
$$\sigma_{p_2} + \sigma_{p_4} + \sigma_{p_6} + \sigma_{p_8} + \ldots + \sigma_{p_{4N_A-2}} + \sigma_{p_{4N_A}} \leq N$$

For illustration, consider $N_A = 4$, $N = 2$, $n_1 = n_2 = n_3 = n_4 = 1$. Consequently, we have

$$\sigma_{p_2} + \sigma_{p_4} \leq 1$$
$$\sigma_{p_6} + \sigma_{p_8} \leq 1$$
$$\sigma_{p_{10}} + \sigma_{p_{12}} \leq 1$$
$$\sigma_{p_{14}} + \sigma_{p_{16}} \leq 1$$
$$\sigma_{p_2} + \sigma_{p_4} + \sigma_{p_6} + \sigma_{p_8} + \sigma_{p_{10}} + \sigma_{p_{12}} + \sigma_{p_{14}} + \sigma_{p_{16}} \leq 2$$

Thus, in the sense of [9], the supervisor can be synthesized as follows

$$\mathbf{L} = \begin{pmatrix} 0\,1\,0\,1\,0\,0\,0\,0\,0\,0\,0\,0\,0\,0\,0\,0 \\ 0\,0\,0\,0\,0\,1\,0\,1\,0\,0\,0\,0\,0\,0\,0\,0 \\ 0\,0\,0\,0\,0\,0\,0\,0\,0\,1\,0\,1\,0\,0\,0\,0 \\ 0\,0\,0\,0\,0\,0\,0\,0\,0\,0\,0\,0\,0\,1\,0\,1 \\ 0\,1\,0\,1\,0\,1\,0\,1\,0\,1\,0\,1\,0\,1\,0\,1 \end{pmatrix}$$

$$\mathbf{B}_s = -\mathbf{LB} = \begin{pmatrix} -1\ 1\,-1\ 1\ \ 0\ 0\ \ 0\ 0\ \ 0\ 0\ \ 0\ 0\ \ 0\ 0 \\ 0\ 0\ \ 0\ 0\,-1\ 1\,-1\ 1\ \ 0\ 0\ \ 0\ 0\ \ 0\ 0 \\ 0\ 0\ \ 0\ 0\ \ 0\ 0\ \ 0\ 0\,-1\ 1\,-1\ 1\ \ 0\ 0\ \ 0\ 0 \\ 0\ 0\ \ 0\ 0\ \ 0\ 0\ \ 0\ 0\ \ 0\ 0\,-1\ 1\,-1\ 1 \\ -1\ 1\,-1\ 1\,-1\ 1\,-1\ 1\,-1\ 1\,-1\ 1\,-1\ 1 \end{pmatrix}$$

$$\mathbf{F}_s = \begin{pmatrix} 1\,0\,1\,0\,0\,0\,0\,0\,0\,0\,0\,0\,0\,0\,0\,0 \\ 0\,0\,0\,0\,1\,0\,1\,0\,0\,0\,0\,0\,0\,0\,0\,0 \\ 0\,0\,0\,0\,0\,0\,0\,0\,1\,0\,1\,0\,0\,0\,0\,0 \\ 0\,0\,0\,0\,0\,0\,0\,0\,0\,0\,0\,0\,1\,0\,1\,0 \\ 1\,0\,1\,0\,1\,0\,1\,0\,1\,0\,1\,0\,1\,0\,1\,0 \end{pmatrix} \quad \mathbf{G}_s^T = \begin{pmatrix} 0\,1\,0\,1\,0\,0\,0\,0\,0\,0\,0\,0\,0\,0\,0\,0 \\ 0\,0\,0\,0\,0\,1\,0\,1\,0\,0\,0\,0\,0\,0\,0\,0 \\ 0\,0\,0\,0\,0\,0\,0\,0\,0\,1\,0\,1\,0\,0\,0\,0 \\ 0\,0\,0\,0\,0\,0\,0\,0\,0\,0\,0\,0\,0\,1\,0\,1 \\ 0\,1\,0\,1\,0\,1\,0\,1\,0\,1\,0\,1\,0\,1\,0\,1 \end{pmatrix}$$

When the initial state of the non-supervised agents is

$$\mathbf{x}_0 = \begin{pmatrix} 1\,0\,0\,0\,1\,0\,0\,0\,1\,0\,0\,0\,1\,0\,0\,0 \end{pmatrix}^T$$

$$\mathbf{b} = \begin{pmatrix} 1\,1\,1\,1\,2 \end{pmatrix}^T ; \quad {}^s\mathbf{x}_0 = \mathbf{b} - \mathbf{Lx}_0 = \begin{pmatrix} 1\,1\,1\,1\,2 \end{pmatrix}^T$$

$$\mathbf{F}_a = \begin{pmatrix} \mathbf{F} \\ \mathbf{F}_s \end{pmatrix} ; \quad \mathbf{G}_a^T = \begin{pmatrix} \mathbf{G}^T \\ \mathbf{G}_s^T \end{pmatrix} \quad \mathbf{B}_a = \begin{pmatrix} \mathbf{B} \\ \mathbf{B}_s \end{pmatrix} ; \quad {}^a\mathbf{x}_0 = \begin{pmatrix} \mathbf{x}_0 \\ {}^s\mathbf{x}_0 \end{pmatrix} \qquad (23)$$

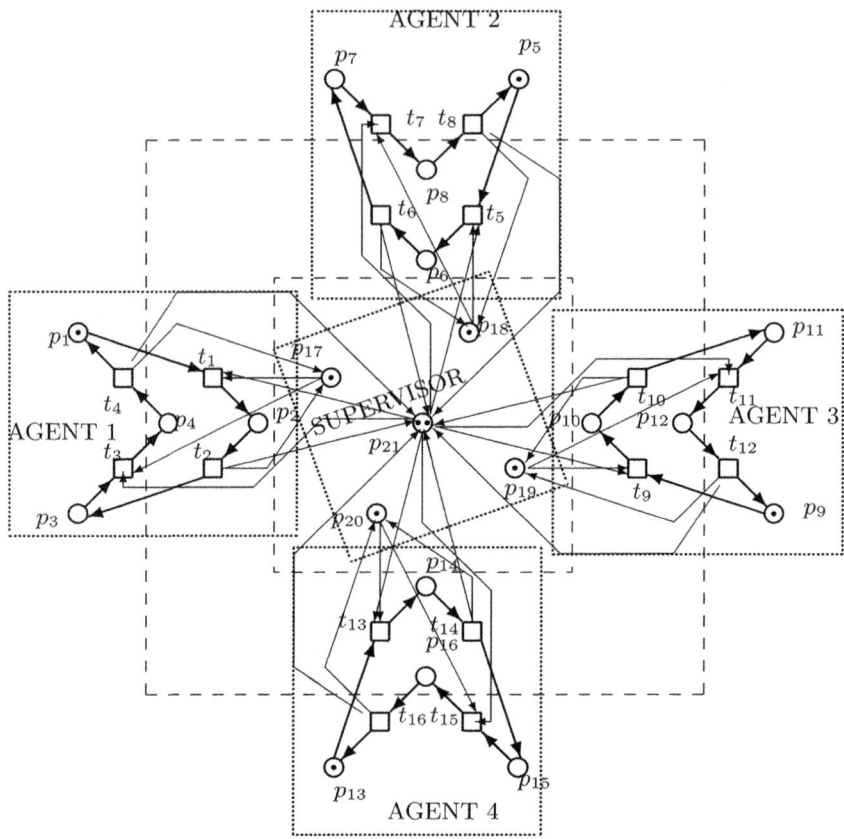

Fig. 7. The PN-based model of supervising 4 agents in order to simultaneously exploit the RA

Having these parameters we can realize the supervisor structure. The structure of the supervised system is displayed in Fig.7. The supervisor guarantees only fulfilling the prescribed restrictions. Therefore, the approach presented in [1],[5], yielding the space of feasible trajectories can help to analyse the supervised plant as to the selection of the most suitable trajectories. In such a supervisor structure only the presence of N AGVs in the RA simultaneously is assured without designation which agents (in our example which $N = 2$ agents from four existing ones) have the priority to enter by their AGV into the area. To resolve this problem it is necessary to ensure priorities Especially, in the given initial state, when all of the agents compete for entering the area, it is necessary to choice N of the N_t agents. During the global FMS dynamics development it is probable that not all of the agents will compete for entering. However, in general, also in such a case more than N agents can compete. However, there is impossible in a real FMS to presume that the agents will negotiate each other to find the global optimum. Usually, there is no time for such a "democratic" negotiation process. However, there exist the way - we can synthesize another supervisor for the system being already supervised by the existing supervisor synthesized above. The advantage of such a multilevel approach consists in a flexibility. Namely, while the first level supervisor assures the stable situation that only two AGVs can occur in the RA, the second level can determine on which track (i.e. to which agent A_i AGVs belong in).

6.1   Another Supervisor

In general, when we want to enter priorities, the new (additional) supervisor can be synthesized. We can consider e.g. that the priorities π_{A_i} of agents A_i descends with the ascending agent number - i.e. $\pi_{A_1} > \pi_{A_2} > \pi_{A_3} > \pi_{A_4}$ (but not only these ones, of course). The Agent 1 has the highest priority as to entering to RA. The priorities of other agents descend with ascending number denoting the agent in question, namely in both directions - i.e. at carrying a part to the corresponding machine as well as on its regress. It means that the constraints imposed on elements of the Parikh's vector are the following

$$v_5 \leq v_1; \ v_9 \leq v_1; \ v_{13} \leq v_1; \ v_6 \leq v_1; \ v_{10} \leq v_1; \ v_{14} \leq v_1$$
$$v_9 \leq v_5; \ v_{13} \leq v_5; \ v_{10} \leq v_5; \ v_{14} \leq v_5$$
$$v_{13} \leq v_9; \ v_{14} \leq v_9$$

Considering the initial condition for the Parikh's vector and the vector $\mathbf{b}$ to be

$$\mathbf{v}_0 = \begin{pmatrix} 0\,0\,0\,0\,0\,0\,0\,0\,0\,0\,0\,0\,0\,0\,0\,0 \end{pmatrix}^T ; \ \mathbf{b} = \begin{pmatrix} 0\,0\,0\,0\,0\,0\,0\,0\,0\,0\,0\,0 \end{pmatrix}^T$$

the process of the supervisor synthesis (respecting the above constraints expressed by the matrix $\mathbf{L}_v$) yields the below introduced structure of the supervisor (the matrices $^{(2)}\mathbf{F}_s$, $^{(2)}\mathbf{G}_s^T$) and its initial state $^{(2)s}\mathbf{x}_0$.

$$\mathbf{L}_v = \begin{pmatrix}
-1 & 0 & 0 & 0 & 1 & 0 & 0 & 0 & 0 & 0 & 0 & 0 & 0 & 0 & 0 & 0 \\
-1 & 0 & 0 & 0 & 0 & 0 & 0 & 0 & 1 & 0 & 0 & 0 & 0 & 0 & 0 & 0 \\
-1 & 0 & 0 & 0 & 0 & 0 & 0 & 0 & 0 & 0 & 0 & 0 & 1 & 0 & 0 & 0 \\
-1 & 0 & 0 & 0 & 0 & 1 & 0 & 0 & 0 & 0 & 0 & 0 & 0 & 0 & 0 & 0 \\
-1 & 0 & 0 & 0 & 0 & 0 & 0 & 0 & 0 & 1 & 0 & 0 & 0 & 0 & 0 & 0 \\
-1 & 0 & 0 & 0 & 0 & 0 & 0 & 0 & 0 & 0 & 0 & 0 & 0 & 1 & 0 & 0 \\
0 & 0 & 0 & 0 & -1 & 0 & 0 & 0 & 1 & 0 & 0 & 0 & 0 & 0 & 0 & 0 \\
0 & 0 & 0 & 0 & -1 & 0 & 0 & 0 & 0 & 0 & 0 & 0 & 1 & 0 & 0 & 0 \\
0 & 0 & 0 & 0 & -1 & 0 & 0 & 0 & 0 & 1 & 0 & 0 & 0 & 0 & 0 & 0 \\
0 & 0 & 0 & 0 & -1 & 0 & 0 & 0 & 0 & 0 & 0 & 0 & 0 & 1 & 0 & 0 \\
0 & 0 & 0 & 0 & 0 & 0 & 0 & 0 & -1 & 0 & 0 & 0 & 1 & 0 & 0 & 0 \\
0 & 0 & 0 & 0 & 0 & 0 & 0 & 0 & -1 & 0 & 0 & 0 & 0 & 1 & 0 & 0
\end{pmatrix}$$

$$^{(2)}\mathbf{F}_s = \begin{pmatrix} 0\,0\,0\,0\,1\,0\,0\,0\,0\,0\,0\,0\,0\,0\,0 \\ 0\,0\,0\,0\,0\,0\,0\,0\,1\,0\,0\,0\,0\,0\,0 \\ 0\,0\,0\,0\,0\,0\,0\,0\,0\,0\,0\,1\,0\,0\,0 \\ 0\,0\,0\,0\,0\,1\,0\,0\,0\,0\,0\,0\,0\,0\,0 \\ 0\,0\,0\,0\,0\,0\,0\,0\,0\,1\,0\,0\,0\,0\,0 \\ 0\,0\,0\,0\,0\,0\,0\,0\,0\,0\,0\,0\,1\,0\,0 \\ 0\,0\,0\,0\,0\,0\,0\,0\,1\,0\,0\,0\,0\,0\,0 \\ 0\,0\,0\,0\,0\,0\,0\,0\,0\,0\,0\,1\,0\,0\,0 \\ 0\,0\,0\,0\,0\,0\,0\,0\,0\,1\,0\,0\,0\,0\,0 \\ 0\,0\,0\,0\,0\,0\,0\,0\,0\,0\,0\,0\,1\,0\,0 \\ 0\,0\,0\,0\,0\,0\,0\,0\,0\,0\,0\,1\,0\,0\,0 \\ 0\,0\,0\,0\,0\,0\,0\,0\,0\,0\,0\,0\,1\,0\,0 \end{pmatrix} \quad {}^{(2)}\mathbf{G}_s^T = \begin{pmatrix} 1\,0\,0\,0\,0\,0\,0\,0\,0\,0\,0\,0\,0\,0\,0 \\ 1\,0\,0\,0\,0\,0\,0\,0\,0\,0\,0\,0\,0\,0\,0 \\ 1\,0\,0\,0\,0\,0\,0\,0\,0\,0\,0\,0\,0\,0\,0 \\ 1\,0\,0\,0\,0\,0\,0\,0\,0\,0\,0\,0\,0\,0\,0 \\ 1\,0\,0\,0\,0\,0\,0\,0\,0\,0\,0\,0\,0\,0\,0 \\ 1\,0\,0\,0\,0\,0\,0\,0\,0\,0\,0\,0\,0\,0\,0 \\ 0\,0\,0\,0\,1\,0\,0\,0\,0\,0\,0\,0\,0\,0\,0 \\ 0\,0\,0\,0\,1\,0\,0\,0\,0\,0\,0\,0\,0\,0\,0 \\ 0\,0\,0\,0\,1\,0\,0\,0\,0\,0\,0\,0\,0\,0\,0 \\ 0\,0\,0\,0\,1\,0\,0\,0\,0\,0\,0\,0\,0\,0\,0 \\ 0\,0\,0\,0\,0\,0\,0\,0\,1\,0\,0\,0\,0\,0\,0 \\ 0\,0\,0\,0\,0\,0\,0\,0\,1\,0\,0\,0\,0\,0\,0 \end{pmatrix}$$

$$^{(2)s}\mathbf{x}_0 = \begin{pmatrix} 0\,0\,0\,0\,0\,0\,0\,0\,0\,0\,0\,0 \end{pmatrix}^T$$

Therefore, the resulting supervised system has the following initial state

$$^{(2)}\mathbf{x}_0 = (\mathbf{x}_{a0}^T,\ {}^{(2)s}\mathbf{x}_0^T)^T$$

with

$$\mathbf{x}_{a0} = \begin{pmatrix} 1\,0\,0\,0\,1\,0\,0\,0\,1\,0\,0\,0\,1\,0\,0\,0\,|\,1\,1\,1\,1\,2 \end{pmatrix}^T$$

Respecting the structure of the system supervised by the first supervisor (see its general form in (18)), the structure of the fully supervised system (i.e. by both supervisors) has the following structure

$$^{(2)}\mathbf{F}_a = \begin{pmatrix} \mathbf{F}_a \\ {}^{(2)}\mathbf{F}_s \end{pmatrix}; \quad {}^{(2)}\mathbf{G}_a^T = \begin{pmatrix} \mathbf{G}_a^T \\ {}^{(2)}\mathbf{G}_s^T \end{pmatrix}$$

Here, $^{(2)}(.)$ expresses that the matrices/vectors belonging to the second supervisor are meant. The second supervisor is synthesized for the augmented system (i.e. the original agents already supervised by the first supervisor). The structure of the second supervisor has to be embedded into the structure presented in Fig. 7. Of course, in case of having the sufficient space also the more detailed constraints could be chosen and analysed.

7 The Case Study 2

Here, the inverted Y form of manufacturing [6] (i.e. one machine and two output transport systems) will be synthesized and controlled. Consider the machine and two AGV. AGV1 transports correct products while AGV2 transports the bad products in case when the machine failures. The PN-models of the devices are displayed in Fig.8. Here, the interpretation of the PN places ($p_{10}-p_{13}$ arise during synthesis) and transitions is as follows: p_1 - part is being carried to completed-parts queue by AGV1; p_2 - AGV1 is free; p_3 - AGV1 is at pick-up position at machine M; p_4 - part is being carried to damaged-parts queue; p_5 - AGV2 is free; p_6 - AGV2 is at pick-up position at machine M; p_7 - M is up and busy (part is

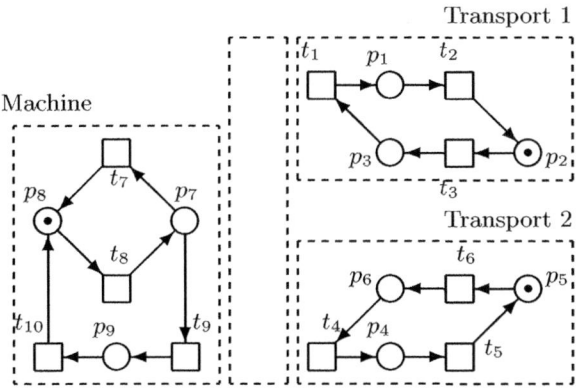

Fig. 8. The PN models of autonomous devices. The empty block will be synthesized.

being processed); p_8 - M is free; p_9 - M is being repaired; p_{10} - completed part is waiting for transfer; p_{11} - damaged part is waiting for transfer; p_{12} - capacity place; p_{13} - machine capacity place; t_1 - part is picked up by AGV1; t_2 - part is deposited in completed-parts queue by AGV1; t_3 - AGV1 moves at pick-up position at machine; t_4 - part is picked up by AGV2; t_5 - part is deposited in damaged-parts queue by AGV2; t_6 - AGV2 moves at pick-up position at machine; t_7 - uncontrollable: part processing is complete; t_8 - part is charged in M; t_9 - uncontrollable: machine fails, part is damaged; t_{10} - M is repaired.

The parameters of the device models are the following (the machine is D_1, the AGV1 realizing the Transport 1 is D_2 and the AGV2 realizing the Transport 2 is D_3)

$$
{}^1\mathbf{F} = {}^2\mathbf{F} = \begin{pmatrix} 0 & 1 & 0 \\ 0 & 0 & 1 \\ 1 & 0 & 0 \end{pmatrix} ; \quad {}^1\mathbf{G} = {}^2\mathbf{G} = \begin{pmatrix} 1 & 0 & 0 \\ 0 & 1 & 0 \\ 0 & 0 & 1 \end{pmatrix}
$$

$$
{}^3\mathbf{F} \begin{pmatrix} 1 & 0 & 1 & 0 \\ 0 & 1 & 0 & 0 \\ 0 & 0 & 0 & 1 \end{pmatrix} ; \quad {}^3\mathbf{G} = \begin{pmatrix} 0 & 1 & 0 \\ 1 & 0 & 0 \\ 0 & 0 & 1 \\ 0 & 1 & 0 \end{pmatrix}
$$

$$
{}^1\mathbf{x}_0 = {}^2\mathbf{x}_0 = (0,\, 1,\, 0)^T,\ {}^3\mathbf{x}_0 = (0,\, 1,\, 0)^T;\ \mathbf{x}_0^T = ({}^1\mathbf{x}_0^T, {}^2\mathbf{x}_0^T, {}^3\mathbf{x}_0^T)^T
$$

7.1   The Step 1

To satisfy the technology - the transport of the good parts produced in D_1 by means of D_2 and the transport of the bad parts produced in D_1 when this device fails by means of D_3 and ensuring the reparation of D_3 - it is necessary to automate this utilizing the "partnership" of t_7 and t_1 as well as that of t_9 and t_4. Consequently, with respect to the conditions $v_1 \leq v_7$ $(v_1 - v_7 \leq 0)$ and $v_4 \leq v_9$ $(v_4 - v_9 \leq 0)$ we have

$$
\mathbf{L}_v = \begin{pmatrix} 1 & 0 & 0 & 0 & 0 & 0 & -1 & 0 & 0 & 0 \\ 0 & 0 & 0 & 1 & 0 & 0 & 0 & 0 & -1 & 0 \end{pmatrix} ; \quad \mathbf{b} = \begin{pmatrix} 0 \\ 0 \end{pmatrix}
$$

Respecting the fact that in this case $\mathbf{L}_p$ and $\mathbf{L}_t$ are zero matrices as well as fulfilling (19)-(22) and considering that $\mathbf{v} = (0, 0, 0, 0, 0, 0, 0, 0, 0, 0)^T$ we obtain

$$\mathbf{F}_{s_1} = \begin{pmatrix} 1\,0\,0\,0\,0\,0\,0\,0\,0\,0 \\ 0\,0\,0\,1\,0\,0\,0\,0\,0\,0 \end{pmatrix}; \mathbf{G}_{s_1}^T = \begin{pmatrix} 0\,0\,0\,0\,0\,0\,1\,0\,0\,0 \\ 0\,0\,0\,0\,0\,0\,0\,0\,1\,0 \end{pmatrix}$$

Because of $\mathbf{b} = (0, 0)^T$ the extension for the initial state of the plant is $^{s_1}\mathbf{x_0} = (0, 0)^T$. Thus the parameters of the plant to be controlled are

$$\mathbf{F}_{P_1} = \begin{pmatrix} \mathbf{F} \\ \mathbf{F}_{s_1} \end{pmatrix}; \mathbf{G}_{P_1}^T = \begin{pmatrix} \mathbf{G}^T \\ \mathbf{G}_{s_1}^T \end{pmatrix}; {}^{P_1}\mathbf{x_0} = \begin{pmatrix} \mathbf{x_0} \\ {}^{s_1}\mathbf{x_0} \end{pmatrix}$$

The synthesized structure is given in Fig.9. Because in such a configuration the number of the reachable states is 267 an the return to the initial state is impossible, this model is insufficient for practical usage. Consequently, the next step of the synthesis is necessary.

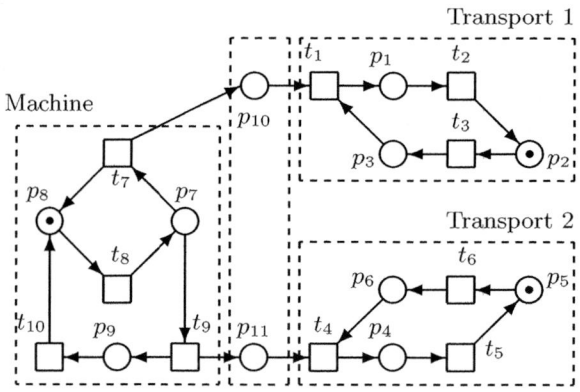

Fig. 9. The structure of the model after the first step of synthesis

7.2   The Step 2

Here, we will use the P-invariant based approach. Now, similarly to the previous example, only matrix $\mathbf{L}_p$ in the general condition (19) will be nonzero. In such a case the simpler approach [11,10,9] will be utilized.

The aim of this step of the synthesis is to ensure the possibility to reach the initial state (to realize the working cycle) and to find the satisfying throughput in order to reduce the number of states and especially the number of possible trajectories. Hence, $p_3 + p_6 \leq 1$ and $p_7 + p_{10} + p_{11} \leq 1$ and consequently

$$\mathbf{L}_p = \begin{pmatrix} 0\,0\,1\,0\,0\,1\,0\,0\,0\,0\,0 \\ 0\,0\,0\,0\,0\,0\,1\,0\,0\,1\,1 \end{pmatrix}; \mathbf{b} = \begin{pmatrix} 1 \\ 1 \end{pmatrix}$$

$$\mathbf{B}_{s_2} = \begin{pmatrix} 1\,0\,-1\,1\,0\,-1\,0\quad0\,0\,1 \\ 1\,0\quad0\,1\,0\quad0\,0\,-1\,0\,0 \end{pmatrix}$$

$$\mathbf{F}_{s_2} = \begin{pmatrix} 0\,0\,1\,0\,0\,1\,0\,0\,0\,0 \\ 0\,0\,0\,0\,0\,0\,0\,1\,0\,0 \end{pmatrix}; \mathbf{G}^T_{s_2} = \begin{pmatrix} 1\,0\,0\,1\,0\,0\,0\,0\,0\,0 \\ 1\,0\,0\,1\,0\,0\,0\,0\,0\,0 \end{pmatrix}$$

for $\mathbf{b} = (1,\,1)^T$ the initial state of the supervisor is $^{s_2}\mathbf{x}_0 = (1,\,1)^T$. Thus, the parameters of the supervised plant are

$$\mathbf{F}_{P_2} = \begin{pmatrix} \mathbf{F}_{P_1} \\ \mathbf{F}_{s_2} \end{pmatrix}; \mathbf{G}^T_{P_2} = \begin{pmatrix} \mathbf{G}^T_{P_1} \\ \mathbf{G}^T_{s_2} \end{pmatrix}; {}^{P_2}\mathbf{x}_0 = \begin{pmatrix} {}^{P_1}\mathbf{x}_0 \\ {}^{s_2}\mathbf{x}_0 \end{pmatrix}$$

The number of states was strongly reduced to 48 and the initial state gone to be reachable, However, there are two deadlocks here - in the states $\mathbb{X}_{11} = (0,\,1,\,0,\,0,\,0,\,1,\,0,\,1,\,0,\,1,\,0,\,0,\,0)^T$ and $\mathbb{X}_{15} = (0,\,0,\,1,\,0,\,1,\,0,\,0,\,1,\,0,\,0,\,1,\,0,\,0)^T$ no transition is enabled. These two states are reachable, respectively, by the sequences $\{t_6,\,t_8,\,t_7\}$ and $\{t_3,\,t_8,\,t_9,\,t_{10}\}$. Consequently, we can use another step of the synthesis as follows. The results are displayed in Fig.10.

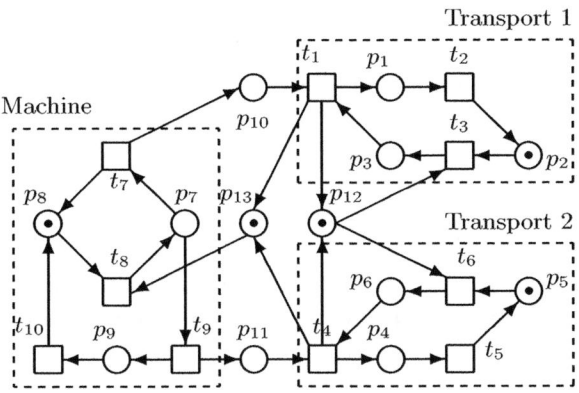

Fig. 10. The structure of the model after the second step of synthesis

7.3 The Steps 3 and 4

Let us remove the deadlocks in this step. Namely, it is necessary to eliminate the collision of the transport systems at the output space of the machine. When the correct part is produced, the Transport 1 has to be there at disposal while the Transport 2 has to be there at disposal when bad part was produced. Thus, $v_3 \le v_7$ ($v_3 - v_7 \le 0$) and $v_6 \le v_9$ ($v_6 - v_9 \le 0$). Consequently,

$$\mathbf{L}_v = \begin{pmatrix} 0\,0\,1\,0\,0\,0\,-1\,0\ \ \,0\,0 \\ 0\,0\,0\,0\,0\,1\ \ \,0\,0\,-1\,0 \end{pmatrix}; \mathbf{b} = \begin{pmatrix} 0 \\ 0 \end{pmatrix}$$

Respecting the fact that in this case $\mathbf{L}_p$ and $\mathbf{L}_t$ are zero matrices as well as fulfilling (19)-(22) and considering that $\mathbf{v} = (0,\,0,\,0,\,0,\,0,\,0,\,0,\,0,\,0,\,0)^T$ we obtain

$$\mathbf{F}_{s_3} = \begin{pmatrix} 0\,0\,1\,0\,0\,0\,0\,0\,0\,0 \\ 0\,0\,0\,0\,0\,1\,0\,0\,0\,0 \end{pmatrix}; \mathbf{G}^T_{s_3} = \begin{pmatrix} 0\,0\,0\,0\,0\,0\,1\,0\,0\,0 \\ 0\,0\,0\,0\,0\,0\,0\,0\,1\,0 \end{pmatrix}$$

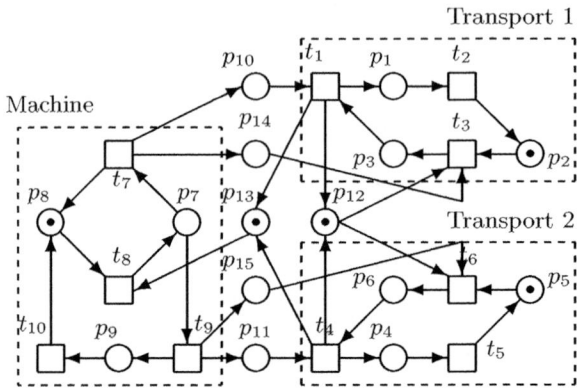

Fig. 11. The structure of the model after the third step of synthesis

For the right side $\mathbf{b} = (0, 0)^T$ of the condition (19) the extension for the initial state of the plant is $^{s_3}\mathbf{x}_0 = (1, 1)^T$. Thus the parameters of the plant to be controlled are

$$\mathbf{F}_{P_3} = \begin{pmatrix} \mathbf{F}_{P_2} \\ \mathbf{F}_{s_3} \end{pmatrix} ; \mathbf{G}_{P_3}^T = \begin{pmatrix} \mathbf{G}_{P_2}^T \\ \mathbf{G}_{s_3}^T \end{pmatrix} ; {}^{P_3}\mathbf{x}_0 = \begin{pmatrix} {}^{P_2}\mathbf{x}_0 \\ {}^{s_3}\mathbf{x}_0 \end{pmatrix}$$

The number of states was reduced to 30 and the deadlocks were removed. The results are displayed in Fig.11. There exists only one 5-steps trajectory $\mathbb{X}_1 \overset{t_8}{\rightarrow} \mathbb{X}_2 \overset{t_7}{\rightarrow} \mathbb{X}_3 \overset{t_3}{\rightarrow} \mathbb{X}_5 \overset{t_1}{\rightarrow} \mathbb{X}_8 \overset{t_2}{\rightarrow} \mathbb{X}_1$ in case of manufacturing good products - on the left in Fig.13. In case of the failure, there exist four 6-steps trajectories - on the right in Fig.13. The same results are achieved when still the fourth step of synthesis is realized by means of the matrix

$$\mathbf{L}_v = \begin{pmatrix} 1 & 0 & -1 & 1 & 0 & 0 & 1 & -1 & 0 & 0 \\ 1 & 0 & 0 & 1 & 0 & -1 & 0 & -1 & 1 & 0 \end{pmatrix}$$

The synthesized structure is displayed in Fig.12. However, when this matrix (which seems to be "chock-full" by exact information) is used in the third step, we have the same results as the results achieved in the step 2 - i.e. 48 states and the 2 deadlocks.

7.4   Concluding Remark

Summarizing experience acquired in the case study in question, it can be said that the successive approach to the synthesis and checking the results in any of its step is rather important in order to avoid problems. The modular approach is favourable for such a kind of synthesis. An excessive endeavour to accelerate the synthesis by a sole step by means of compressing information does not need to bring satisfying results.

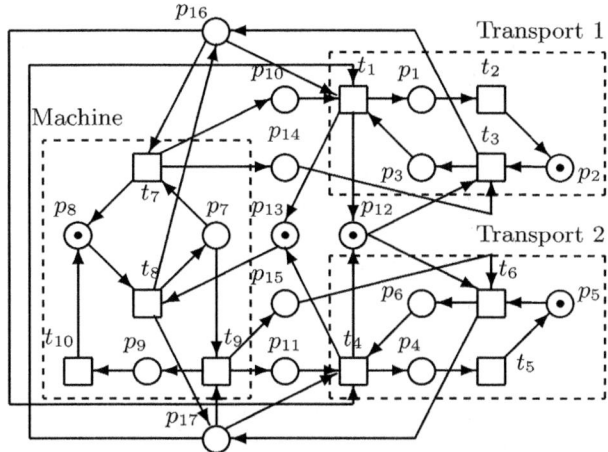

Fig. 12. The structure of the model after the fourth step of synthesis

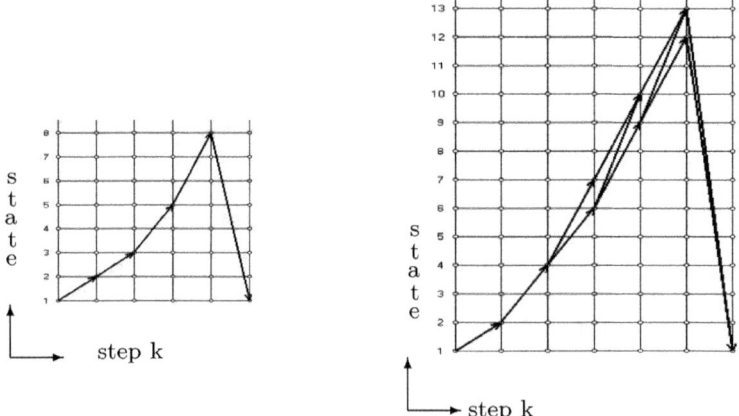

Fig. 13. The trajectories: on the left - the correct working cycle; on the right - four feasible trajectories at failing the machine

8   Conclusion

The approach to synthesis of agents cooperation based on DES control theory methods for control and supervising was introduced in this paper. The individual agents as well as the supervised system were modelled by P/T PNs. Two kinds of constraints were utilized at the supervisor synthesis, namely, the constraints based on P-invariants of PNs and the generalized constraints based not only on PN places but also on PN transitions and/or on the PN Parikh's vector. The examples and case studies were presented in order to document and illustrate the applicability of the approach. In the first case study the synthesis of the cooperation was performed in two steps. First, a constraints based on P-invariants were utilized and the corresponding supervisor was synthesized. Afterwards, the generalized constraints (especially those based on the Parikh's vector) were imposed on this supervised system. The second step was used in order to improve the properties of the global systems. As a matter of fact more than two steps can be used, if it is necessary. Even, different kinds of general conditions can be imposed on that way. Such a situation was illustrated by the second case study where four steps were performed. It appeared that three steps were sufficient.

References

1. Čapkovič, F.: Modelling, Analysing and Control of Interactions among Agents in MAS. Computing and Informatics 26(5), 507–541 (2007)
2. Čapkovič, F.: Control Synthesis of a Class of DEDS. Kybernetes 31(9/10), 1274–1281 (2002)
3. Čapkovič, F.: The Generalised Method for Solving Problems of DEDS Control Synthesis. In: Chung, P.W.H., Hinde, C., Ali, M. (eds.) IEA/AIE 2003. LNCS, vol. 2718, pp. 702–711. Springer, Heidelberg (2003)
4. Čapkovič, F.: Supervisory Control of Agents Cooperation. In: Proceedings of 4th IEEE International Conference on Intelligent Systems, Vol. 1, pp. 6_8–6_13. IEEE Press, Piscataway (2008)
5. Čapkovič, F.: DES Control Synthesis and Cooperation of Agents. In: Nguyen, N.T., Kowalczyk, R., Chen, S.-M. (eds.) ICCCI 2009. LNCS (LNAI), vol. 5796, pp. 596–607. Springer, Heidelberg (2009)
6. Čapkovič, F.: A Modular System Approach to DES Synthesis and Control. In: Proceedings of the 2009 IEEE Conference on Emerging Technologies & Factory Automation - ETFA 2009. CD ROM, 8 pages. IEEE Press, Piscataway (2009)
7. Iordache, M.V., Antsaklis, P.J.: Supervision Based on Place Invariants: A Survey. Discrete Event Dynamic Systems 16(4), 451–492 (2006)
8. Iordache, M.V.: Methods for the supervisory control of concurrent systems based on Petri nets abstraction. Ph.D. dissertation, University of Notre Dame, USA (2003)
9. Iordache, M.V., Antsaklis, P.J.: Supervisory Control of Concurrent Systems: A Petri Net Structural Approach. Birkhauser, Boston (2006)
10. Moody, J.O., Antsaklis, P.J.: Supervisory Control of Discrete Event Systems Using Petri Nets. Kluwer Academic Publishers, Norwell (1998)
11. Moody, J.O.: Petri Net Supervisors for Discrete Event Systems. PhD thesis, University of Notre Dame, Notre Dame, USA (1997)
12. Murata, T.: Petri Nets: Properties, Analysis and Applications. Proceedings of the IEEE 77(4), 541–580 (1989)
13. Ramadge, P., Wonham, W.: Supervisory Control of a Class of Discrete Event Processes. SIAM J. on Control and Optimization 25(1), 206–230 (1989)
14. Yamalidou, E., Moody, J.O., Antsaklis, P.J., Lemmon, M.D.: Feedback Control of Petri Nets Based on Place Invariants. Automatica 32(1), 1–28 (1996)

Role of Thesauri in the Information Management in the Web-Based Services and Systems

Tomasz Kubik

Institute of Computer Engineering, Control and Robotics, Wrocław University of Technology, Wybrzeże Wyspiańskiego 27, Wrocław 50-370, Poland
tomasz.kubik@pwr.wroc.pl

Abstract. Information sharing, exchanging and archiving is the backbone of any organized activity, regardless if it is performed in the sphere of business, home or administration. Semantic Web technologies allow controlling the growth and structure of information, and provide search and inference methods. The article touches one of the main problems in the information-based societies. It refers to the problem of information management and sharing in the heterogonous, complex systems, exposing their functions through the web services.

The main axis of the paper is the implementation of remotely accessible knowledge bases in form of thesauri - dynamic, centrally coordinated dictionaries. Thesauri may contain terms and concepts with an indication of their semantic relationships. They can serve as sources of concept definitions used by various registries, may provide additional information to the search engines, and may support multilingual representation. The article provides some examples of such use cases, targeting special concerns on applications of thesauri in the geospatial domain. The aim of this article was also to show practical aspects of thesauri implementation. The article shows the way of applying officially published standards as guidelines in building interoperable thesauri in form of web service. The implementation of such service, involving the use of SKOS specification as a core information model of the thesauri, and SOAP and REST technologies as a base for communication implementation, is presented. The backend of the service is built on SESAME repository supporting SeRQL and RQL query languages. The examples of implemented clients of the service are: Internet enabled desktop application and web control that can be inserted into any web page.

Keywords: semantic web, web services, thesauri, geospatial information.

1   Introduction

Since many years thesauri are used as tools collecting knowledge from different domains. They were a subject of linguistic studies, which resulted in publication of several books, collecting large number of terms with the use of taxonomies and hierarchies. The interest in the thesauri building has been renewed with

N.T. Nguyen and R. Kowalczyk (Eds.): Transactions on CCI III, LNCS 6560, pp. 25–49, 2011.
© Springer-Verlag Berlin Heidelberg 2011

the development of new technologies. Nowadays thesauri are used not only as printed books, but also as knowledge bases, cataloging and documentation tools, and online search assistants [1]. They are used in the context of structured information management, resource indexing and semantic web.

Semantic web is, roughly speaking, about applying common formats for integration and combination of data drawn from diverse sources. It is also about language for documenting how the data relates to real world objects (a good starting point in discovering this field is a web page of W3C Semantic Web Activity, available at http://www.w3.org/2001/sw/). In consequence, well-defined relations might connect concepts stored in various databases. This idea has been named as *linked data* – the term which is about "using the Web to connect related data that was not previously linked, or using the Web to lower the barriers to linking data currently linked using other methods" (http://linkeddata.org). It is also used "to describe a recommended best practice for exposing, sharing, and connecting pieces of data, information, and knowledge on the Semantic Web using URIs and RDF" (http://en.wikipedia.org/wiki/Linked_Data).

At the bottom of all semantic web solutions are semantic web technologies. These technologies constitute a common framework for data sharing and reusing across application, enterprise, and community boundaries. They allow controlling of, in some senses, growth and structure of information, and provide bases for information discovering. Better decision making requires not only having the broad data, but also knowledge resulting from them at fingertips. Semantic web technologies enable identification of hidden relationships and dependencies and give more than fragmentary information. They provide information in a broader context. They provide knowledge. However, creation of semantic web requires something more. There is a need for formal, standardized methods for information integration, and for services, which would conform to these standards making up really working information infrastructure. This issue was recognized by standardizing bodies, such as: National Information Standards Organization (NISO), British Standards Institution (BSI), International Organization for Standardization (ISO), World Wide Web Consortium (W3C).

NISO provided details on vocabulary terms creation, linking and publishing in its publication [2]. This document covered also the problem of thesauri interoperability and maintenance.

The standardizing efforts undertaken by BSI resulted in publication of set of standards on "Structured Vocabularies for Information Retrieval" under number BS 8723 [3,4,5,6,7]. These documents provide, similar to [2] descriptions of basic principles of thesaurus construction (including facet analysis) and their presentation in electronic and printed media. They also include considerations of the use and management of electronic thesauri, vocabularies and interoperability between vocabularies.

ISO prepared guidelines on construction of monolingual and multilingual thesauri, with the use of descriptors, compound terms and basic relationships [8,9,10]. In these documents some consideration on vocabulary control, indexing terms, display, and management were also presented. The latest standard, [10],

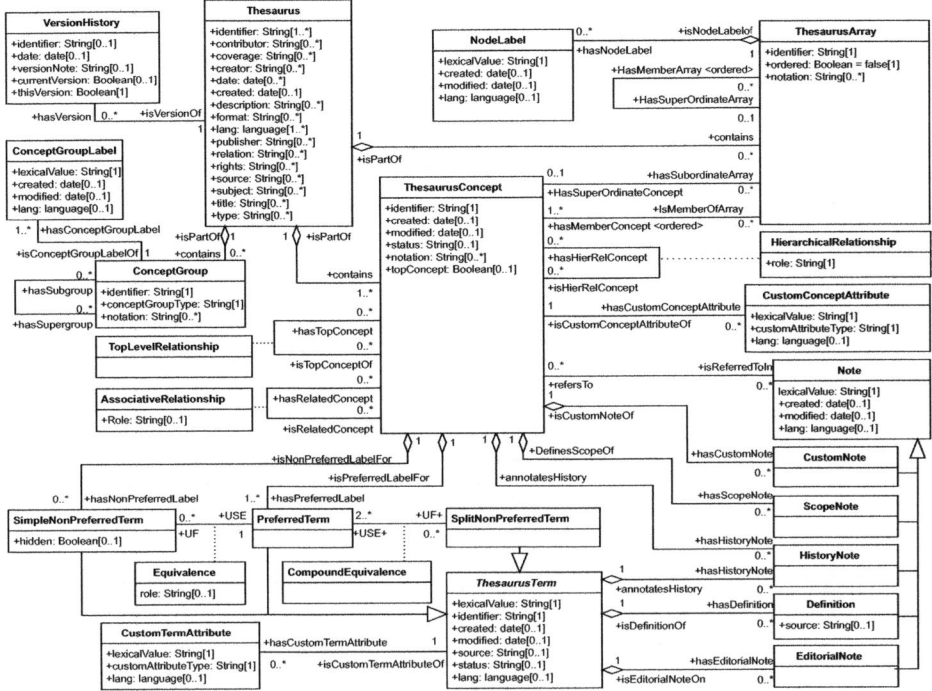

Fig. 1. UML model of thesauri as defined in ISO 25964

derives from the work on BS 8723 standard. The data model that applies to any thesaurus conforming this standard is presented in figure 1. This is UML class diagram, with number of classes and attributes. Such a model can be converted to XML Schema, which can be used then for thesauri data serialization.

The outcome of discussion within W3C Semantic Web Activity on interoperable thesauri took a form of published recommendation. This recommendation contains description of a common data model for sharing and linking knowledge organization systems via the Web named Simple Knowledge Organization System (SKOS) [11]. The recommendation has been supported by informative guide and other documents [12,11]. The SKOS data model is defined as an OWL Full ontology. Although OWL Full as a data modeling language appears intuitively similar in many ways to other modeling approaches, like an UML or an entity-relationship model, there is an important fundamental distinction. This model is based on the open world assumption and can not be simply compared to the UML models. They are simply designed in two different conceptual domains. In figure 2 the hierarchy of SKOS classes, object properties and data properties SKOS core model is shown along with some relationships between SKOS core main classes.

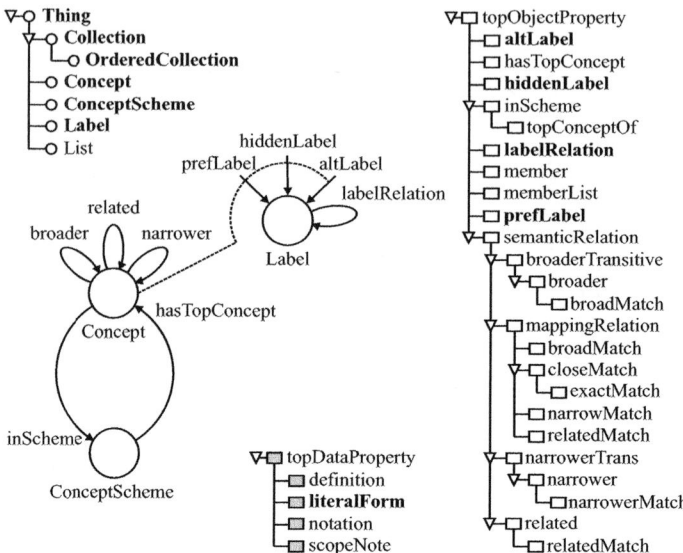

Fig. 2. Hierarchy of classes, object properties and data properties and simplified representation of SKOS core model

The article touches one of the main problems in the information-based societies. It refers to the problem of information management and sharing in the heterogeneous, complex systems, offering their functions through web services. This problem is well known and there are several publications (from beginning of this century) and number of internet accessible resources about it. A good introduction to the concepts of thesauri, subject headings, word lists, classifications and name authority lists, with links to more than 60 vocabulary sources is available at http://www.jiscdigitalmedia.ac.uk/crossmedia/advice/controlling-your-language-links-to-metadata-vocabularies. A collection of printed and electronic publications about the principles of constructing and using thesauri in that context is also accessible at http://www.willpowerinfo.co.uk/thesbibl.htm. Some valuable information on facet analysis, search interfaces, taxonomies, thesauri, ontologies, and topic maps can be found there. M. Middleton collected interesting list of resources on controlled vocabularies at http://www.imresources.fit.qut.edu.au/vocab/. The list includes information on bibliography, classification schemas, thesauri backend, design and use, thesaurus sites and thesaurus software. A.J. Miles compiled another list of thesauri that can be accessed on, or downloaded from the web http://www.w3c.rl.ac.uk/SWAD/thes_links.htm. This compilation includes information on computer encoding formats for thesauri and other concept schemas, plus references to publications, papers and other material.

Thesauri, in general, may contain terms and concepts with an indication of their semantic relationships. Thesauri, implemented as web services, are mainly used for indexing and retrieval of structured data in large datasets (for example NLMs Medical Subject Headings, MeSH, is all about articles collected in a database). Some of them serve as background knowledge for analysis and semantic integration tasks (as for example, lexical database WordNet). Other are just an entry point to internet accessible resources, allowing users to move through large information spaces in a flexible manner without feeling lost, as those build on FLAMENCO (FLexible information Access using MEtadata in Novel Combinations). In most cases these applications offer friendly, graphical user interface that explicitly exposure metadata categories, offer set of possible choices and provide forms with keyword and free text search options. The results of user actions are usually cached to allow further query refinement. The users interactions influence the visual behavior of the interface. An example of domain specific thesaurus with user-friendly interface build on FLAMENCO is shown in figure 3. The application run as web service designed for web browser clients. URL including service address and key-value pairs of parameters identifies the displayed pages.

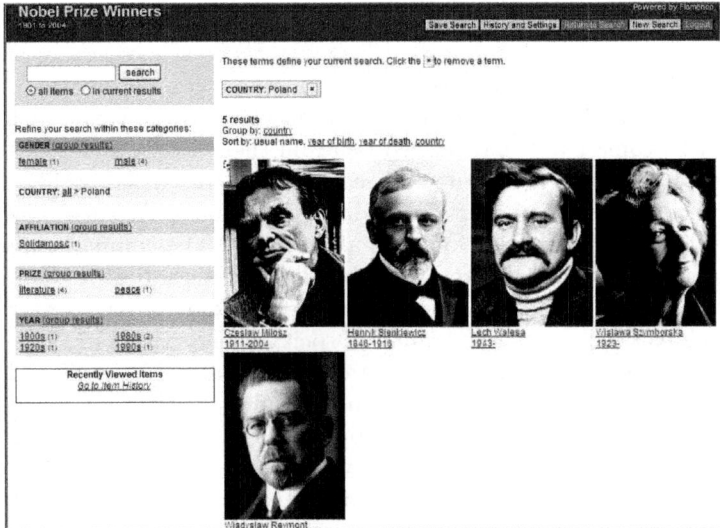

Fig. 3. An example of domain specific thesaurus with user-friendly interface built on FLAMENCO (`http://orange.sims.berkeley.edu/cgi-bin/flamenco.cgi/nobel/Flamenco?q=country:37&group=country`)

The article does not dive deeply into formalism of knowledge modeling nor discuss user interface details. It focuses mainly on an implementation of a thesaurus as a part of information infrastructure – a web service that can be accessed remotely by computers. In general such service's backend can be quite complex solution. It can be distributed, multi-layered, and assure collective work of several search and inference engines, data repositories, security modules etc. More over, it can support variety of models and description languages for data representation. The only requirements are that the service interface is well defined.

Because the standards mentioned above do not provide instructions on implementation, the article shows a proposition of a working solution. The interface of the service implemented was designed to access all elements defined in SKOS. This approach is similar to the approach presented in [13].

The article is organized as follows: after the introduction, some remarks on well-known definition from semantic world are recalled. Then the role of thesauri in geospatial domain is discussed. The remaining part of this article provides the description of implementation of web service offering thesauri functionality via remotely accessible web interface. This solution involves the use of SKOS specification as a core information model of the thesauri, and SOAP and REST technologies as a base for communication implementation. The backend of the service is built on SESAME repository supporting search with SeRQL and RQL query languages. The description of the service is illustrated with examples of two clients: Internet enabled desktop application and web control that can be inserted into any web page.

2   Definitions

The role of thesauri in information management and processing was a subject of several analyses and researches, concerning facet analyses, taxonomy, ontology, fuzzy models, topic maps and related issues in their design and use.

The use of thesaurus to information searching was discussed in [14]. The model presented there focused on user-system interaction and charts the specific stages of searching an indexed collection with a thesaurus. The comparison of thesauri implementations with respect to different criteria was a subject of [15] work. The factor analysis methodology was applied there to the data matrix gathered from users' opinions on a restricted sample of social science thesauri. The thesaurus quality factors uncovered during research were identified as four main components: conceptual framework, performance, format, and external aids (the concept theory was presented in [16]). The process of deciding what terms introduce into thesaurus and how to do it was analyzed in [17]. This process was optimized to maximize performance based on retrospective measurements or estimates of future performance, and decision criteria were developed. A technique based on the notion of similarity, that applies to both thesauri and attribute matching was discussed in [18]. This technique finds a relationship between the terms and a relationship between their attributes. The authors evaluated the precision of the matching and measured the influence of the heuristics through experiments. The authors of [19] worked on converting various thesauri to the RDF/OWL data model used in Semantic Web applications for annotations. The paper presented a case study in which the conversion method was applied to MeSH and Word-Net thesauri. Tindall et al. [20] discussed the problem of creating and using the metadata catalogue and thesaurus for Urban Regeneration and the Environment Research Program (URGENT), enabling its scientific community to discover what data were available. The basic elements of faceted thesauri were described by authors of [21]. They discussed faceted thesaurus use in browsing and searching and compared faceted thesauri and related knowledge organization systems to ontologies. A topic maps-based ontology were a subject of study presented in [22]. The results indicated that a topic maps-based ontology information retrieval system has a significant and positive effect on both recall and search time, compared to a thesaurus-based information retrieval system. Fuzzy relational ontological model applied in information retrieval was a subject of [23] work. The authors recalled, that the fuzzy ontological model uses an ontology comprising words and categories to conceptually represent the content of a documents collection connected by a fuzzy relations with values in [0, 1], where 0 indicates no relationship between word and category and 1 indicates the strongest possible relationship. They also referred to the other fuzzy set-based technique that uses FIS-CRM (Fuzzy Interrelations and Synonymy Concept Representation Model) to represent the indexed documents.

This short overview highlights the main directions of research on thesauri construction and use. In the following sections some common, thesauri-related definitions are provided. These definitions will help in reading the rest of this article.

Categorization – assigns a symbol to a specific group of objects or concepts with specific characteristics, as a "cat" symbol to a group of cats. A set of such symbols becomes an external model of the world as it is understood. This model can be further improved, by introducing a systematic arrangement of objects or concepts, showing the relations between them. The hierarchical arrangement of types in which categories of objects are classified as subtypes of more abstract categories results in taxonomy.

Taxonomy – is a collection of controlled vocabulary terms, organized into hierarchical structure. This structure reflects parent-child relationships between different terms. In general, each term might appear in one or more parent-child relationships. Relationships may have different nature or type, from where the generalization/specialization and "is part of" have special importance. If a taxonomy has a variety of very carefully defined meanings for the hierarchical link, then it bears a stronger resemblance to an ontology.

The process of indexing relies on "assigning preferred terms or headings to describe the concepts and other metadata associated with a content object. Indexing covers any system or procedure in which the selection and organization of terms requires human intellectual decisions at some point in the process. Computer processing may also be a part of the process for storing and manipulating the terms in a controlled vocabulary or to identify content objects to which certain terms or combinations of terms have been assigned or should be assigned. The process of indexing, therefore, involves selecting preferred terms from one or more controlled vocabularies or other sources to describe a content object. The effectiveness of indexing as a means for identifying and retrieving content objects depends upon a well-constructed indexing language." [2].

Controlled vocabulary – is a list of terms that have been enumerated explicitly. This list is controlled by and is available from a controlled vocabulary registration authority. All terms in a controlled vocabulary must have an unambiguous, non-redundant definition. All terms in a controlled vocabulary should have unambiguous, non-redundant definition. This requirement is difficult to maintain. Therefore, registration of new terms should follow some rules: a) in a case of using the same term for different concepts in different contexts, the potential ambiguity should be solved by explicit qualification of this term; b) if multiple terms are used to mean the same thing, one of these terms should play a role of reference, while others should be listed as synonyms or aliases. Controlled vocabulary can contain terms without description of their meanings (as for the generally known terms) or terms with a very detailed description. Taxonomy provides additional meanings for these terms through the definition of their hierarchy.

Controlled vocabularies serve five purposes, [1]: **translation** (provide a means for converting the natural language of authors, indexers, and users into a vocabulary that can be used for indexing and retrieval), **consistency** (promote uniformity in term format and in the assignment of terms), **indication of relationships** (indicate semantic relationships among terms), **label and browse** (provide consistent and clear hierarchies in a navigation system to help users locate desired content objects).

Thesaurus – is "a controlled vocabulary arranged in a known order and structured so that the various relationships among terms are displayed clearly and identified by standardized relationship indicators. Relationship indicators should be employed reciprocally." [2]. The set of relationships can be extends by adding new associations (i.e. new terms definitions). The expressiveness of these relationships may be various, i.e., it can be as simple as "A corresponds to B", or more complex, as "A is like B, but different from C". Thanks to that, it is possible to find "linked" terms, which come from different areas of taxonomy. But usually the number of unions and associations used in the thesauri is limited.

Taxonomies and thesauri can combine terms in a controlled vocabulary through inheritance and associations, but do not provide the grammatical rules, setting out limits on the use of these terms in order to express or model something meaningful within a given domain. If taxonomy has a large selection of carefully defined meanings for hierarchical relationships, then it is very similar to the ontology. On the other hand, the term ontology often serves as a synonym to the glossary and data dictionary, thesaurus and taxonomy, schema and data model, a formalism allowing data typing and inference.

There are several definitions of ontology. Webster's dictionary defines ontology in the computer context as "a systematic arrangement of all of the important categories of objects or concepts which exist in some field of discourse, showing the relations between them. ..." When completed, ontology is a categorization of all of the concepts in some field of knowledge, including the objects and all of the properties, relations, and functions needed to define the objects and specify their actions. Ontology may be visualized as an abstract graph with nodes and labeled arcs representing the objects and relations. In general, ontology considers a part of reality, more or less precisely defined, trying to answer the questions: "How can all be classified?", "What are the classes of entities necessary for describing the processes and reasoning about them?", "What are the bases for reasoning about the truth?", and "What classes of entities allows inference about the future?" In general ontology deals with discovering and describing concepts. Usually it contains taxonomy as one of the important principles of organization.

The creation of ontology models is closely related to modern object-oriented software design. Most of the languages used for ontology modeling represented the model in the same way: with classes, instances and their interrelationships, but with some differences in a power of expression. The number of formal ontology languages is not too large. One can distinguish such languages as: Ontobroker, SHOE (Simple HTML Ontology Extensions), OIL (Ontology Inference Layer or Ontology Interface Layer), DAML (DARPA Agent Markup Language) + OIL (Ontology Inference Layer), OWL (Ontology Web Language). Most of newer languages use RDF (Resource Description Framework) and RDFS (Resource Description Framework Schema) vocabularies. For the older languages, it is possible to translate to/from the KIF (Knowledge Interchange Format), which can be easily translated to/from RDF.

There exists normative specification that provides common data model for sharing and linking knowledge organization systems via the Web. This is SKOS (Simple Knowledge Organization System) specification by W3C. SKOS captures much of similarity of knowledge organization systems, such as thesauri, taxonomies, classification schemas and subject heading systems, enabling data and technology sharing across diverse applications. SKOS also provides a lightweight, intuitive language for developing and sharing new knowledge organization systems. It may be used on its own, or in combination with formal knowledge representation languages such as OWL. The implementation of the thesauri as a web service presented in the section 6 was designed based on SKOS.

All dictionaries, taxonomies, thesauri, and ontology support structuring, classification, modeling and representation of concepts and relationships within a domain of interests (and can be cross domain). They all are targeted at reaching consensus on the use of the same terms in the same way (with the linked data perspective in mind) and use defined vocabulary of terms as a base reference for concepts and relationships (accepted by the community). The meaning of the terms can be specified to some degree of accuracy, thus it might be fuzzy (not precise, as it is in real life). The main differences between concepts mentioned are meaning scope; language, notation and vocabulary; application area (the uses of concepts can be different); and extensibility.

3   Thesauri in the Geospatial Domain

Activities undertaken in the technical and organizational sphere currently play a huge role in the information society building. Information and processes associated with it emerge in wider perspective of infrastructure, going far beyond existing, closed solutions. Exemplification of such actions is an adoption of INSPIRE (The Infrastructure for Spatial Information in Europe) Directive by the European Parliament and European Council [24]. This Directive, oriented on establishing better conditions for the implementation of environmental strategy in the European Union, took over its respective efforts integration of services, spatial data and metadata created by the member countries.

From a technical point of view, the nodes of the information infrastructure proposed are distinguishable, autonomous parts of the complex system build on the SOA (Service Oriented Architecture) paradigm. The nodes may simultaneously play a role of service providers, service consumers or service suppliers and consumers. Once build, they can be potentially a subject of services chaining and orchestration. A particular important part of this model is a services bus - a place of integration of data and services suppliers and consumers. Interestingly, a consumer of a service can be both, human accessing services from using web browser or specific application, and a machine that connects to the service provider automatically while executing its own process. The first step of Directive implementation puts the obligation on member countries of creating and sharing geospatial metadata. Information stored in the metadata record refers to a single products or services (usually it is a description of one thematic layer or geospatial service) and contains the details on how to access them.

The history of the catalogue services implementation correlates with the history of the advances of the information technologies and is closely associated with the development of the Internet. In the initial period, the solutions built made use of library systems. The primary communication protocol was Z39.50 and the common metadata profile was Dublin Core. Current catalogue services should conform metadata model according to the ISO 19115 and ISO 19119 (INSPIRE adapted this model for their own needs), and publish their metadata using XML encoding consistent with the ISO 19139 or profiles thereof (as ISO CSW 2.0.2 profile).

In general, metadata portals allow users to search for data sets based on metadata schemas used by data providers. Current portals use two different approaches for metadata search: (1) searching on distributed catalogues or (2) harvesting catalogues into a central searchable catalogue [25]. Geospatial metadata schemas were subject of standardization performed by two authorities, the U.S. Federal Geospatial Data Committee (FGDC) and the International Organization of Standards (ISO). INSPIRE Drafting Teams derived from their work and published formal INSPIRE Implementing Rules. The metadata elements defined are collections of records about identification, extent, quality, spatial and temporal schema, spatial reference, and distribution of digital geographic data and service description. However, this information does not give a chance to go beyond the area defined by the model of the metadata information. Especially that specific XML Schema defines the way of metadata encoding and because there are some obligatory rules that cannot be checked in XML Schema based validation. Moreover, the interface of discovery services, implemented in form of catalogue services with standardized interface, used for searching within metadata repositories, has its limits. Thus, score relevancy of search results depends on the contents of metadata records. There are no semantic links predefined and before delving into the original resources of data is not possible to get more search details or scope. To gather more information it is necessary to generate further queries, targeted directly to the services providing the data. The use of ontology and semantic web technologies would waive this restriction, opening new opportunities. One option to perform metadata searching using knowledge bases and topic maps as shown in [26]. The other possibility would be enriching metadata with semantic information.

This paper described the use of the thesaurus and topic maps to aid in the retrieval process in SDI metadata catalogs. This works main contributions include: (1) proposal of a method for creating a thesaurus in a SDI; (2) definition of a system to retrieve metadata in SDI supported by thesaurus and topic maps; (3) implementation of an interface based on visual search techniques.

There are some efforts within ISO/TC 211 on finding ways on how the concept of ontology and the Semantic Web can support and facilitate the work of this committee, as well as how ISO/TC 211 may contribute to the Semantic Web in the perspective of improving the interoperability of geographic information. They resulted with another standard proposition: ISO 191150 Geographic information – Ontology. However, as a proposition, this standard does not provide any solution ready to use. Therefore, it seams that the first steps towards porting geospatial information to the semantic web could be realized with the help of thesauri. This is main idea of this article.

Thesauri implementations appears as sets of semantically and hierarchically related terms, facilitating search for derived information or as vocabularies including related terms. Thesauri tend to be specialized to handle the concepts in the selected areas. One example is GEMET (General Multilingual Environmental Thesaurus), developed on behalf of the European Environment Agency, which contains over 6000 concepts developed in 22 languages. The terms from this thesaurus were officially accepted as candidates for keywords in geospatial metadata records. This requirement appeared in the formal regulation, published in the Official Journal of the European Union [27]:

<...>

If a resource is a spatial data set or spatial data set series, at least one keyword shall be provided from the general environmental multilingual thesaurus (GEMET) describing the relevant spatial data theme as defined in Annex I, II or III to Directive 2007/2/EC.

<...>

If the keyword value originates from a controlled vocabulary (thesaurus, ontology), for example GEMET, the citation of the originating controlled vocabulary shall be provided. This citation shall include at least the title and a reference date (date of publication, date of last revision or of creation) of the originating controlled vocabulary.

<...>

(Excerpts from the regulation, part A, section 3. KEYWORD)

Thus, the keywords are the only part of geospatial metadata formally accepted that might have a broader, semantic context. However, the common use of terms from the GEMET is far away from the idea of linked data. The users browse GEMET repository on a web page (see figure 4) or import thesaurus content, as

RDF documents into their own application (from a GEMET web page, `http://www.eionet.europa.eu/gemet/rdf`) for further processing. In general, the geographic information retrieval systems use geographical terms or spatial references as search terms. More complex systems detect locations and spatial references based on geographic entities extraction, semantic analysis, geographical data bases (thesauri, gazetteers), query expansion methods and geographical disambiguation [28].

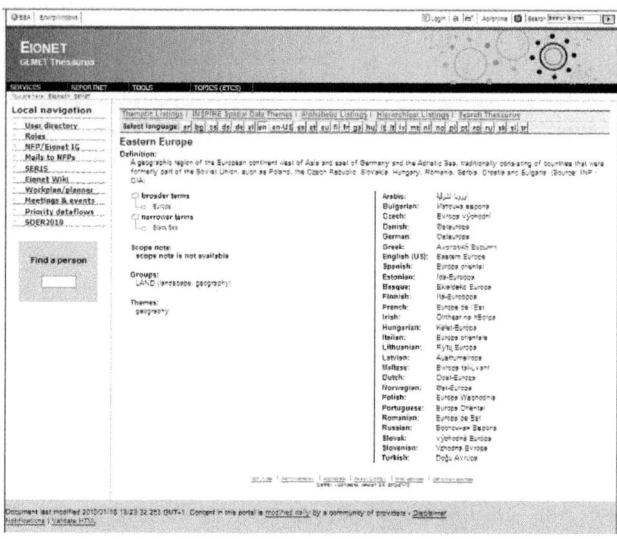

Fig. 4. GEMET user interface (`http://www.eionet.europa.eu/gemet/concept?cp=388&langcode=en&ns=1`)

GEMET's data are exposed through the Web for remote applications using XML (RDF/SKOS), HTTP and XML/RPC. The API (Application Programming Interface) exists for XML/RPC and HTTP, but this API is undergoing a change. This was one of the reasons for a new web service design and implementation. The implementation, presented in the section 6, follows the idea described in the GEMET API proposition. The organization of methods is similar, but the interface binding is different. There are two possible communication options in the implementation presented: SOAP and REST.

Of course, GEMET is not the only knowledge base in the whole geospatial domain. There are some others, as for example: a) the OpenCYC Selected Vocabulary and Upper Ontology - Geography (`http://www.opencyc.org`) providing an example of a classification for geospatial features, using a proprietary ontology language. b) Suggested Upper Merged Ontology (SUMO) [29] that organizes concept definitions into three levels: SUMO Top Level (including high-level abstractions), MILO (including mid-level ontology) and Ontology of Geography (including a number of classes that correspond to geospatial concepts, and instances); c) The Semantic Web for Earth and Environmental Terminology (SWEET) providing an upper-level ontology for the Earth system sciences in which several thousand terms are grouped into facet ontologies, whose classes are connected by properties [30]. There are also ontologies available used in geospatial domain, as for example owl-time (http://www.w3.org/TR/owl-time/). But none of these examples has been widely and practically used in any part of the geospatial information infrastructure. The leading and commonly used solutions are those that offer gazetteer interface (geospatial dictionary, containing lists of geospatial names along with their geospatial locations and other descriptive information, as Geonames available at http://www.geonames.org/) and catalogue service (archives, containing metadata about geospatial data sets and services), accessible from dedicated clients. The clients functionality is similar as web pages of thesauri mentioned before (the example of catalogue service client is shown in figure 5). Clients, behind the scene, allow parameterized querying, provide category-based search option, and display query results in a user friendly form. The functionality of these solutions depends on way of their implementation. It is often the case that clients offer more functions than are originally provided by the catalogue service interface. The clients often extend it with additional functions and features, playing a role of an entry point to the broader information collection. However, such behavior needs additional work on information integration on the clients sides.

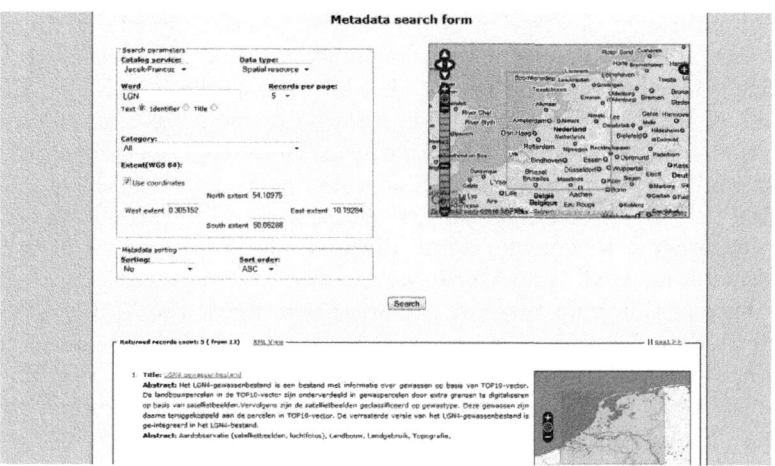

Fig. 5. User interface of the catalog service client

4   Information Integration

Information integration in the context of semantic web technology has holistic nature. This process is built-up from the following steps: a) mapping the various data on an abstract representation of data (it withdraws information from various resources and presents it in a structured form); b) merging the results obtained (it creates a kind of common denominator for all data processed; RDF is a standard for modeling and RDF/XML for encoding); c) processing and querying against the whole information collected (it provides results which are impossible to receive during individual analysis of each data set; it is a place for inference engines application).

It is desirable to perform the information integration in an unmanned way. This should overcome the limits of manual search (which can be spotted in a case of documents retrieving or manual web pages browsing) and shorten the time of getting results. Indeed, the information integration can be automated. What's more, it can rely on using the broad information infrastructure with web services working as data providers. However, this requires digitization of resources and adoption of a methodology for describing their contents in order to convert them into the format understandable by the machines. It is a place for the use of metadata and ontology along with the standards related to them.

Regarding the implementation and organization of information in digital thesauri, many of them are historically based on the ISO 2788 and ANSI/NISO Z39.19 standards. The main structuring concepts are terms and three relations between terms: the Broader Term (BT), Narrower Term (NT) and Related Term (RT) whose names are self explanatory. The main structuring concepts incorporate also terms representing other relations: Use For (UF) and its inverse Use (U) – which relate preferred terms (also known as descriptors) to non-preferred terms, and Definition (DEF) and Scope Note (SN) - used to provide a definition and additional description of a term. In general, the rule of thumb says, that preferred terms should be used for indexing, while non-preferred terms for searching. Only preferred terms are allowed to have the BT, NT and RT relations. Thus, if the thesauri are build on the same model, the mapping between their terms exists. However, their native format, often a proprietary XML, ASCII or relational schema, is not compatible with the Semantic Webs standard format, RDF(S). The problem of converting thesauri to RDF/OWL was addressed in [31], together with guidelines and illustrations of conversions of two known knowledge bases: MeSH and WordNet.

A chance of tiding up thesauri resources is to apply the W3C SKOS proposition for knowledge organization. This standard is easier to use and implement then other standards, and has support from several APIs. The SKOS' use cases were subject of analysis, involving dedicated questionnaire sending to a wide audience. The results were collected in [12] – a document which also features a set of fundamental or secondary requirements derived from the survey, used to guide the design of SKOS.

However, the thesauri implementations sometimes extend core SKOS vocabulary, breaking interoperability. As for GEMET, SKOS core vocabulary has been extended by 4 classes (SuperGroup, Group, Theme, Concept - this class remains unused) and 7 properties (acronymLabel, theme, themeMember, group, groupMember, subGroupOf, subGroup). These additional terms are defined in "GEMET schema" ontology, available at http://www.eionet.europa.eu/gemet/2004/06/gemet-schema.rdf. The classes introduced are used to represent specific taxonomy of the terms collected. The meaning of properties is following: hasConcept – relates theme or group with a concept (equivalent to narrower), theme – relates Concept with Theme (theme is implemented in RDF, but it is unclear whether it is relevant; in general it is equivalent to broader, but a Theme is not a broader concept of a Concept), group – relates Concept with Group (equivalent to broader), subGroupOf – relates Group with one of the four SuperGroups (equivalent to broader), subGroup – inverse of subGroupOf (equivalent to narrower).

One of the possible options when trying to integrate information from various thesauri is to equip them with SPARQL Endpoint. Executing SPARQL queries opens the gate to the whole thesauri structure, regardless its construction and specific features. The experiment with interfacing SKOS Thesauri through such endpoint was already performed [32]. The thesauri proposed in the article uses the same idea. The backend of the implementation is SESAME Framework, which provides SeRQL and RQL query language to its RDF repository.

5   Implementing Thesauri as a Web Service

Implementation of thesauri is not such a difficult task. Several frameworks and software tools can support such implementation. A comprehensive list of such frameworks and tools is available on the W3C web page (http://www.w3.org/2001/sw/wiki/Tools). The description of available semantic APIs (that take unstructured text, including web pages, as input and return the contents) can be found in [33]. The framework discussed there were: Dapper, OpenCalais, SemanticHacker, Semantic Cloud API, Zemanta API, Ontos API. There are also some solutions that are especially designed for the use with thesauri or even are thesauri implementations, as, for example SKOS API (http://www.w3.org/2001/sw/Europe/reports/thes/skosapi.html).

The work presented in [13] is an example of the specification and development of a Web Ontology Service (WOS) according to OGC Web Service Architecture specification. The purpose of this service was to facilitate the management and use of lexical ontologies and to show how to integrate this service with Spatial Data Infrastructure discovery components in order to obtain a better classification of resources and an improvement in information retrieval performance. The architecture of the WOS service consisted of three layers: the repository layer (storing the ontologies managed by the service and the concept core used for the interconnection of ontologies); the application layer (providing an access to ontology concepts and their metadata); the service layer (providing a web service wrapper to enable the access of web clients). Thanks to this architecture user queries could by expanded, making profit of the knowledge behind the lexical ontologies managed by WOS. However, the interface for ontologies management was quite simple. It allowed to get service metadata, to get and set ontology metadata, to import and export an ontology, to make query, to work on: ontologies, concepts, properties, and relations (trough the use of create and delete methods), and to retrieve related concepts.

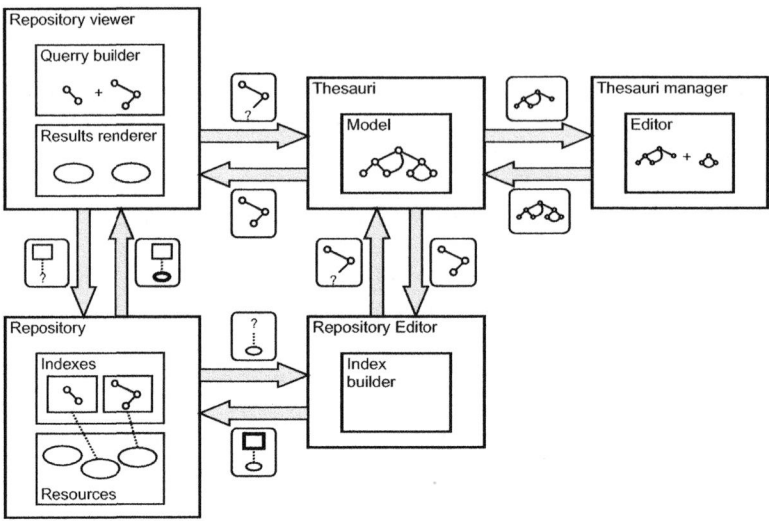

Fig. 6. The use of thesauri for information retrieval and resource indexing

The solution presented in the paper, Tezaurus2010, is another option to be considered by potential users. It is a service that can help in distributed applications creation offering extended searching/indexing capabilities. As a part of information infrastructure this service will offer interface for thesauri management (thesauri edition) and thesauri based search (for building indexes or retrieving indexed resources) what is a common thesauri use case as shown in figure 6.

Tezaurus2010 software consists of two parts: web service implementation and two samples of client implementation (desktop client and browser client, see figure 7). Tezaurus2010 software is open-source solution, distributed along with GPL license. It offers most of the thesauri functions as defined in SKOS. At the current stage the only missing features are: concepts mapping from various thesauri and collections handling.

5.1   Web Service

Web service is a core part of the Thesaurus2010 responsible for running thesauri engine as well as making it available to clients. The main parts of this service are: ThesauriService and SesameFramework (see figure 8). ThesauriService offers two external interfaces for its clients: REST and SOAP. The REST and SOAP interfaces were designed for specific purpose and should be used accordingly. Their implementation is based on JAX-WS library (for clarity, this part was not shown in figure 8).

SesameFramework   serves   as   a   RDF   repository   accessible   trough SesameGraphApi and SesameRepositoryApi - parts of SESAME framework (for more details on SESAME architecture and use please refer to http://www. openrdf.org/doc/sesame/users/userguide.html). ThesauriService contains

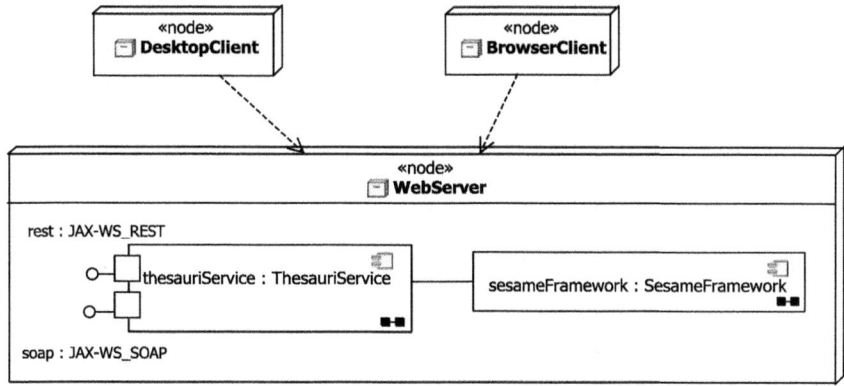

Fig. 7. Sample of Tezaurus2010 deployment diagram

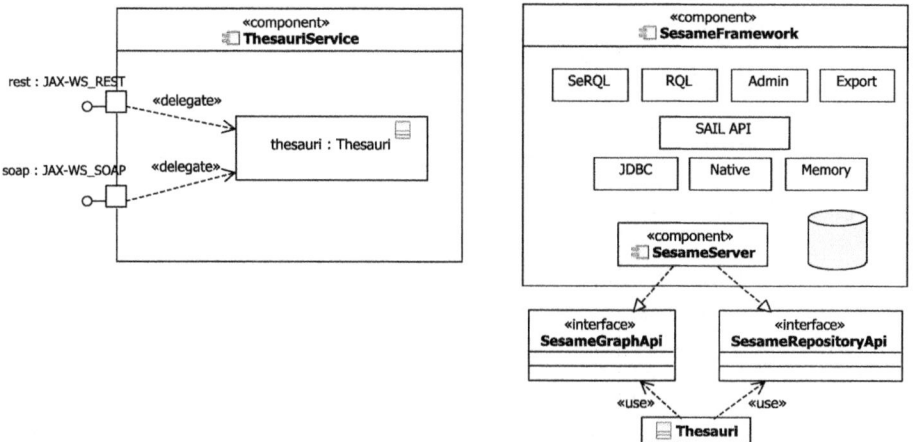

Fig. 8. Main components of Tezaurus2010 web service

an instance of Thesauri class. This instance is responsible for delegation of queries acquired from REST or SOAP interface to SesameFramework. It realizes this task using mentioned parts of SESAME framework (as internal interface). The list of methods offered by the Thesauri class reflects its ability (see figure 9).

The aim of REST interface is to provide an easy way for invoking safe, read only operations. This interface hides most of the Thesaurus2010 functionality. The only available methods are those responsible for finding and getting concepts. The queries are constructed following RESTfull idea. By convention introduced, the REST query should contain a path to the ThesauriService, followed by a method identifier, followed by arguments of this method.

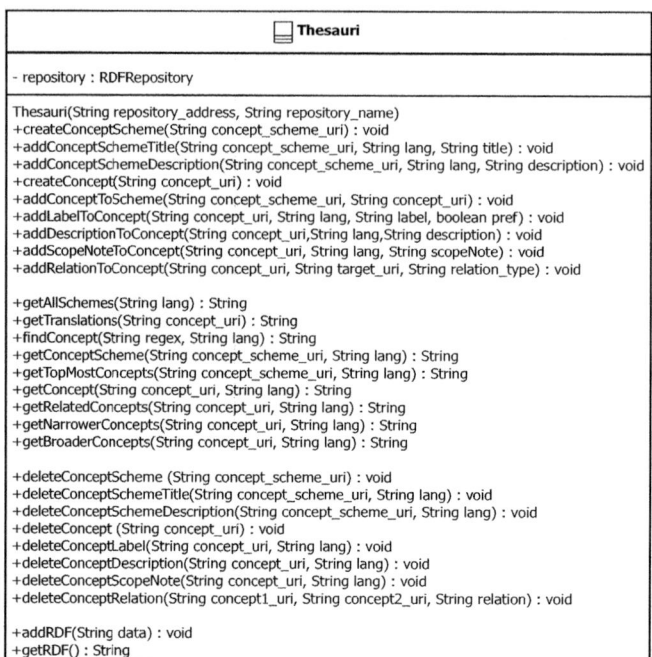

Fig. 9. Thesauri class providing methods for processing queries delegated to it

The methods of Thesauri class can be split into two groups, as it is shown in the table 1: first, taking only one argument (there are 2 such methods), and second, taking two arguments (there are 7 such methods).

The members of each group have ID assigned. This ID is used when constructing REST query. The template of REST query against a method with single argument is following: `@Path("{methodID}/{str1}")` , where `methodID` is a number of the method being invoked, `str1` is a method parameter. In a case of querying methods from the second group, the REST path is defined as follows: `Path("{methodID}/{str1}/{str2}")`, where `str2` , represents the second parameter of the method. Unfortunately, the introduced convention does not work for arguments which are URI containing forward slash / character. The problem was solved by substitution of / by $ character when issuing the queries. Tezaurus2010 server brings the URI back to the normal form before further processing.

Thus, to get all schemas from the repository defined in English language, one could use the following REST path: `Tezaurus2010_server_address/1/en`. To get the concept from the repository, the REST path should be as follows: `Tezaurus2010_server_address/4/http:$$thesaurus.org$concepts$concept1/en`.

REST interface is a perfect candidate for communication with other web applications, plug-ins or light desktop applications. It fits well to the concept of linked data. This interface can be extended to provide also transactional operations, but such functionality was not implemented.

Table 1. Two groups of methods accessible from REST interface, together with methods ID

First group of the methods	ID
getAllSchemes(String lang) : String	1
getTranslations(String concept_uri) : String	2
Second group of the methods	**ID**
findConcept(String regex, String lang) : String	1
getConceptScheme(String concept_scheme_uri, String lang) : String	2
getTopMostConcepts(String concept_scheme_uri,String lang) :String	3
getConcept(String concept_uri, String lang) : String	4
getRelatedConcepts(String concept_uri, String lang) : String	5
getNarrowerConcepts(String concept_uri, String lang) : String	6
getBroaderConcepts(String concept_uri, String lang) : String	7

SOAP interface, on the other hand, was design in order to provide all the functionality of Thesaurus2010 to the end user. Therefore, applications using this interface can communicate with web service in read/write mode allowed. However, implementing Thesaurus2010 in production environment needs some additional efforts. The remarks on safety issues connected with it are presented shortly in the last section of this article.

The implementation of the provided and required SOAP interfaces with JAX-WS is relatively easy. The framework hides all details of message processing thus programmers can use simple, wrapper classes. The SOAP messages conform to SOAP version 1.1 specification. The methods calls and responses are encoded within Body element following RPC convention. Thus, parameters of the method invoked are nested within element with a name corresponding to this method. The response from the thesauri is nested within return element of the element with a name corresponding the name of the method invoked (the responses are encoded as RDF documents using standard XML entities as substitutions of special characters). The example of SOAP request and response messages are shown in figure 10.

5.2 Desktop Client

Tezaurus2010 DesktopClient implementation is fully capable of managing thesaurus through SOAP interface of ThesauriService. It is default web client for Tezaurus2010 web service and it is part of this software. The features list of the client includes:

- connecting to remote web service;
- defining new Thesauri languages;
- support for variety of languages;
- creating new concept schemas (Categories);
- creating new concepts;
- editing existing concepts and schemas;
- deleting data;

SOAP request

```
<?xml version="1.0" ?>
<S:Envelope xmlns:S="http://schemas.xmlsoap.org/soap/envelope/">
<S:Body>
<ns2:getTranslations xmlns:ns2="http://newpackage/">
<concept_uri>http://thesaurus.org/languages</concept_uri>
</ns2:getTranslations>
</S:Body>
</S:Envelope>
```

SOAP response

```
<?xml version='1.0' encoding='UTF-8'?>
<S:Envelope xmlns:S="http://schemas.xmlsoap.org/soap/envelope/">
<S:Body>
<ns2:getTranslationsResponse xmlns:ns2="http://newpackage/">
<return>&lt;rdf:RDF
xmlns:dc=&quot;http://purl.org/dc/elements/1.1/&quot;
xmlns:rdfs=&quot;http://www.w3.org/2000/01/rdf-schema#&quot;
xmlns:ukat=&quot;http://www.ukat.org.uk/downloads/skos-schema-ext/&quot;
xmlns:rdf=&quot;http://www.w3.org/1999/02/22-rdf-syntax-ns#&quot;
xmlns:skos=&quot;http://www.w3.org/2004/02/skos/core#&quot;
&gt;
&lt;skos:Concept rdf:about=&quot;http://thesaurus.org/languages&quot;&gt;
&lt;skos:prefLabel xml:lang=&quot;pl&quot;&gt;Polski&lt;/skos:prefLabel&gt;
&lt;skos:prefLabel xml:lang=&quot;en&quot;&gt;English&lt;/skos:prefLabel&gt;
&lt;skos:prefLabel xml:lang=&quot;de&quot;&gt;Deutsch&lt;/skos:prefLabel&gt;
&lt;skos:prefLabel xml:lang=&quot;fr&quot;&gt;Francoise&lt;/skos:prefLabel&gt;
&lt;/skos:Concept&gt;
&lt;/rdf:RDF&gt;
</return>
</ns2:getTranslationsResponse>
</S:Body>
</S:Envelope>
```

Fig. 10. Example of SOAP request (getTranslation) and response (getTranslationResponce)

- finding concepts in Thesauri;
- exporting Thesauri data to RDF File;
- importing RDF File with new data to Thesauri.

Setting up the client is very easy. It is enough to run the application and provide at start up an URL of Tezaurus2010 web service (i.e. URL of the web service running ThesauriService).

5.3   Browser Client

Thezaurus2010 can be accessed from any web page served with Thesaurus2010 BrowserClient control embedded into its HTML code. From the end user point of view, the use of this control is transparent. It does not differ from opening with a web browser and using any other web page. The control was developed using JavaScript and PHP technologies and jQuery and jsTree libraries. Thezaurus2010 BrowserClient uses REST interface of ThesauriService and is capable to

- connect to the service;
- choose language;
- find concepts in Thesauri;
- browse concepts with tree representation.

Setting up the control requires some work. The control provided cannot live alone by itself. It must be embedded inside the code of web page published on an application server with all supporting libraries installed. More over, it is a web pages administrator responsibility to place this control in the right position (and to prepare adequate stylesheet templates, if required). Only then, users who wish to access this page with their web browsers will have a chance to exploit all functions provided. The control appears in the HTML code placed within div tags. Thus, the installation procedure of Thesaurus2010 BrowserClient control consists of the following steps:

1. copy HTML code (code.html) into BODY section of the index.html page (this is an example of the HTML code with control embedded);
2. copy jquery1.4.2. min.js to the application server (this installs jQuery library used);
3. copy jsTree.v.1.0rc/ folder with default styles to the application server (this installs jsTree library (jQuery plugin) used to display contents of the thesaurus in a three structure);
4. copy communicate.js the application server (this installs JavaScript script which is part of the control implementation);
5. copy webServiceClient.php to the application server (this installs PHP script which implements communication between client side and server side and provides user interface).

The control was tested on lighttpd 1.4 2b (may 2010) application server with PHP 5.2.12pl0 – gentoo interpreter. It worked with Google Chrome, Mozilla Firefox, Opera, and Safari web browsers, but not with Internet Explorer (the web browser should have JavaScript support enabled).

6   Conclusions

In this article the role of thesauri in the information management and processing was considered. Summarizing in a few words, thesauri are mainly used for indexing and retrieval of structured information in large datasets. Thesauri, as all dictionaries, taxonomies, and ontologies, provide support for structuring, classification, modeling and representation of concepts and their relationships within domain of interests (and cross-domain). They are targeted at reaching consensus on the use of the same terms in the same way and use defined vocabulary of terms as a base reference for concepts and relationships.

Thesauri serve as backend of knowledge-based applications, allowing information analysis and semantic integration. There are web services, which use this backend in order to offer friendly, graphical interface to the internet accessible resources, allowing users to move through large information spaces in a flexible manner without feeling lost. Usually this graphical user interface explicitly exposure metadata categories, offers set of possible choices and provides forms with keyword and free text search options. Thesauri implementations appear as sets of semantically and hierarchically related terms, facilitating search for derived information, or as vocabularies of related terms. These implementations tend to be specialized to handle knowledge in the selected areas.

Information integration in the context of semantic web technology has holistic nature and, because of various knowledge models used, – it can be difficult. A chance for solving this issue is to implement standards as W3C SKOS. SKOS is a normative specification that provides common data model for sharing and linking knowledge organization systems via the Web. SKOS captures much of similarity of knowledge organization systems, such as thesauri, taxonomies, classification schemas and subject heading systems. SKOS also provides a lightweight, intuitive language for developing and sharing new knowledge organization systems. SKOS can be used by its own, or in a combination with formal knowledge representation languages such as OWL.

There is a strong need to build thesauri as web services with standardized web interface. Such solutions can play roles of resources of semantic references in the information infrastructure (and semantic networks). This is especially important in the geospatial domain where concepts from the GEMET thesaurus were nominated to be official sources for keywords used in metadata records. This obligation got a legal scope after publishing Commission Regulation of the European Parliament and of the Council [27] – a document providing implementation rules for INSPIRE Directive as regards metadata. The GEMET thesaurus has its own web service API proposed, but this interface is undergoing a change.

The metadata elements are collections of records about identification, extent, quality, spatial and temporal schema, spatial reference, and distribution of digital geographic data and service description. According to INSPIRE Directive, member countries shall establish and operate a network of various services, including discovery services which should make it possible to search for spatial data sets and services on the basis of the content of the corresponding metadata and to display the content of the metadata. Minimal search criteria shall include: keywords; classification of spatial data and services; the quality and validity of spatial data sets; degree of conformity with the implementing rules provided for in Article 7(1); geographical location; conditions applying to the access to and use of spatial data sets and services; the public authorities responsible for the establishment; management, maintenance and distribution of spatial data sets and services. Discovery services are build on catalogue web services specification proposed by OGC. But using catalogue services directly does not give a chance to go beyond limits of the model of the metadata information. Especially that specific XML Schema defines the way of metadata encoding, because there are some obligatory rules that cannot be checked in XML Schema based validation, and because there is no bridge between metadata model and semantic network world defined yet (excluding ISO 19150 standard proposition, which is under going project). This was a motivation for research and implementation described.

The implementation of Thesauri2010 presented is an option which can be considered by potential users and developers who wish to work with information infrastructure in order to build semantic bridges between different nodes. Tezaurus2010 software consists of two parts: web service implementation (offering REST and SOAP communication interfaces) and samples of desktop and browser client applications. Tezaurus2010 software is open-source solution, distributed along with GPL license. REST interface is a perfect candidate for communication with other web applications, plug-ins or light desktop applications. It fits well to the concept of linked data. This interface can be extended to provide also transactional operations, but such functionality was not implemented. SOAP interface, on the other hand, was design in order to provide all the functionality of Thesaurus2010 to the end user. Because of the component based architecture, there are some security issues which have to be considered when using Thesausur2010. First, the backend of the implementation is SESAME repository. Users of the implementation proposed should assure that this repository is well protected against unauthorized use (the only connections allowed are from the ThesauriService instance). Next, the service provided does not include any authentication nor authorization mechanisms. These can be implemented as an additional access layers (for example, by using OpenID – an open, decentralized standard for authenticating users).

References

1. Harpring, P.: Introduction to Controlled Vocabularies: Terminology for Art, Architecture, and Other Cultural Works. Getty Research Institute, Los Angeles (2010)
2. ANSI/NISO Z39.19-2005: Guidelines for the Construction, Format, and Management of Monolingual Controlled Vocabularies (R2010) (2005)
3. Structured Vocabularies for Information Retrieval - Guide - Exchange formats and protocols for interoperability (DD 8723-5:2008). British Standard (2008)
4. Structured Vocabularies for Information Retrieval - Guide - Vocabularies other than thesauri (BS 8723-3:2007). British Standard (2007)
5. Structured Vocabularies for Information Retrieval - Guide - Interoperability between vocabularies (BS 8723-4:2007). British Standard (2007)
6. Structured Vocabularies for Information Retrieval - Guide - Definitions, symbols and abbreviations (BS 8723-1:2005). British Standard (2005)
7. Structured Vocabularies for Information Retrieval - Guide - Thesauri (BS 8723-2:2005). British Standard (2005)
8. Documentation – Guidelines for the establishment and development of monolingual thesauri (ISO 2788:1986). Paperback (August 2007)
9. Documentation - Guidelines for the Establishment and Development of Multilingual Thesauri (ISO 5964:1985=BS 6723:1985). International Standard (1985)

10. Information and documentation – Thesauri and interoperability with other vocabularies – Part 1: Thesauri for information retrieval (ISO/DIS 25964-1). International Standard (2010)
11. SKOS Simple Knowledge Organization System. Reference. W3C Recommendation (August 18, 2009), http://www.w3.org/TR/skos-reference
12. SKOS Use Cases and Requirements, W3C Working Group Note (August 18, 2009), http://www.w3.org/TR/skos-ucr
13. Lacasta, J., Nogueras-Iso, J., Bjar, R., Muro-Medrano, P., Zarazaga-Soria, F.: A web ontology service to facilitate interoperability within a spatial data infrastructure: Applicability to discovery. Data & Knowledge Engineering 63(3), 945–969 (2007)
14. Blocks, D., Cunliffe, D., Tudhope, D.: A reference model for user-system interaction in thesaurus-based searching. Journal of the American Society for Information Science and Technology 57(12), 1655–1665 (2006)
15. Pinto, M.: A user view of the factors affecting quality of thesauri in social science databases. Library and Information Science Research 30(3), 216–221 (2008)
16. Hjrland, B.: Concept theory. Journal of the American Society for Information Science and Technology 60(8), 1519–1536 (2009)
17. Losee, R.M.: Decisions in thesaurus construction and use. Information Processing and Management 43(4), 958–968 (2007)
18. Leme, L.A.P., Brauner, D.F., Breitman, K.K., Casanova, M.A., Gazola, A.: Matching object catalogues. Innovations in Systems and Software Engineering 4(4), 315–328 (2008)
19. van Assem, M., Malaisé, V., Miles, A., Schreiber, G.: A method to convert thesauri to SKOS. In: Sure, Y., Domingue, J. (eds.) ESWC 2006. LNCS, vol. 4011, pp. 95–109. Springer, Heidelberg (2006)
20. Tindall, C.I., Moore, R.V., Bosley, J.D., Swetnam, R.D., Bowie, R., De Rudder, A.: Creating and using the urgent metadata catalogue and thesaurus. Science of the Total Environment, The 360(1-3), 223–232 (2006)
21. Tudhope, D., Binding, C.: Faceted thesauri. Axiomathes 18(2), 211–222 (2008)
22. Yi, M.: Information organization and retrieval using a topic maps-based ontology: Results of a task-based evaluation. Journal of the American Society for Information Science and Technology 59(12), 1898–1911 (2008)
23. Pereira, R., Ricarte, I., Gomide, F.: Fuzzy relational ontological model in information search systems. In: Sanchez, E. (ed.) Fuzzy Logic and the Semantic Web. Capturing Intelligence, ch. 20, vol. 1, pp. 395–412. Elsevier, Amsterdam (2006)
24. DIRECTIVE 2007/2/EC OF THE EUROPEAN PARLIAMENT AND OF THE COUNCIL of 14 March 2007 establishing an Infrastructure for Spatial Information in the European Community (INSPIRE) (2007)
25. Schindler, U., Diepenbroek, M.: Generic xml-based framework for metadata portals. Computers and Geosciences 34(12), 1947–1955 (2008)
26. Silva, O.C., Lisboa-Filho, J., Braga, J.L., Borges, K.A.V.: Searching for metadata using knowledge bases and topic maps in spatial data infrastructures. Earth Science Informatics 2(4), 235–247 (2009)
27. COMMISSION REGULATION (EC) No 1205/2008 of 3 December 2008 implementing Directive 2007/2/EC of the European Parliament and of the Council as regards metadata (2008)
28. García-Cumbreras, M.A., Perea-Ortega, J.M., García-Vega, M., Alfonso Urena-López, L.: Information retrieval with geographical references. Relevant documents filtering vs. query expansion. Information Processing and Management 45(5), 605–614 (2009)

29. Niles, I., Pease, A.: Towards a standard upper ontology. In: Welty, C., Smith, B. (eds.) Proceedings of the 2nd International Conference on Formal Ontology in Information Systems (FOIS 2001), Ogunquit, Maine, October 17-19 (2001)
30. Raskin, R., Pan, M.: Semantic web for earth and environmental terminology (sweet). In: Proceedings of the Workshop on Semantic Web Technologies for Searching and Retrieving Scientific Data (2003)
31. Assem, M.V., Menken, M.R., Schreiber, G., Wielemaker, J., Wielinga, B.: A method for converting thesauri to rdf/owl. In: McIlraith, S.A., Plexousakis, D., van Harmelen, F. (eds.) ISWC 2004. LNCS, vol. 3298, pp. 17–31. Springer, Heidelberg (2004)
32. SKOS/RDF Version of GEMET, SPECIES2000, WWF Ecoregions and EUNIS thesauri, `http://xmlgroup.iit.cnr.it/SPARQL/`
33. Dotsika, F.: Semantic apis: Scaling up towards the semantic web. International Journal of Information Management 30(4), 335–342 (2010)

On Efficiency of Collective Intelligence Phenomena

Tadeusz (Ted) Szuba, Paweł Polański, Paweł Schab, and Paweł Wielicki

Dept. of Control, AGH University, Cracow, Poland
szuba@ia.agh.edu.pl

Abstract. This paper will attempt to formally analyze the problem of individual existence of a being versus its existence in a social structure, through evaluation of Collective Intelligence efficiency. On the basis of two simulation models of two very distant cases of Collective Intelligence, some results to this problem will be given and discussed. Cases are: survival abilities of a bacterial colony, and hunter and dog versus rabbit. This paper also presents the methodology of identification and translation of the mentioned cases of Collective Intelligence phenomena into simulation models. The results show a strong increase of the social structure ability when the Collective Intelligence is functioning. The problem of the Collective Intelligence is so complex, that the results presented here should be considered as a case study. In general, on the basis of presented results, the paper advertises and advocates the theory of Collective Intelligence based on molecular model of computations.

Keywords: Social structure, bacterial colony, cooperation, Collective Intelligence, social structure as inference system, nondeterministic models of computations.

1 Introduction

When observing the surrounding world, we see an almost infinite variety of local environments (probably many more are possible in outer space). We can also see a great complexity of beings starting from viruses up to mammals; living individually or in groups; or united into single organisms at different levels of integration. In this spectrum, even in the same local environment very simple and very complex beings exist in parallel. Interactions between them can also be very different, starting form hostile interactions (e.g. prey vs. predator), through different forms of biological co-operation (e.g. symbiosis), up to interaction based on mental relationships. The inter-action can be very loose; e.g. wolves hunting together only in winter or very close like those beings that cooperate by merging into one organism. Thus from this point of view, three abstract dimensions can be proposed as presented in Fig. 1, creating an abstract space where the problem weather to exist individually or in a group can be analyzed. An additional question emerges here: "Why was there no final unification in the course of evolution?" i.e. (except human) why is there no universal (best) being for all environments and why no universal (best) social structure emerge?

In the paper [11] a hypothesis that the Evolution performs the spiral conversion between individual and group existence is proposed, as presented in Fig. 2.

N.T. Nguyen and R. Kowalczyk (Eds.): Transactions on CCI III, LNCS 6560, pp. 50–73, 2011.
© Springer-Verlag Berlin Heidelberg 2011

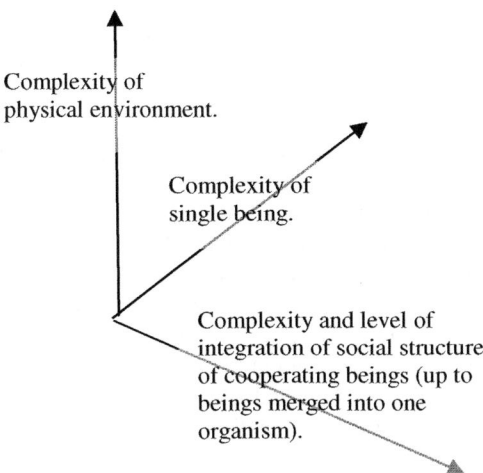

Fig. 1. Abstract dimensions for space where Collective Intelligence can emerge

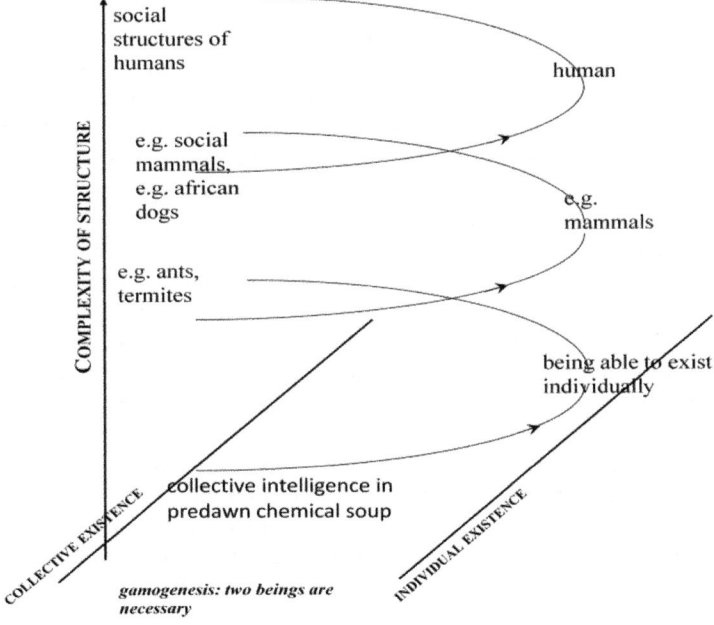

Fig. 2. Spiral relation between complexity of being, individual intelligence and collective existence (Collective Intelligence)

Considering this issue, a fundamental question emerges: *"For a given environment and for a given (assumed) complexity of a single being (organism organization and its intellectual power i.e. ability to process information) – which is better: to exist individually or in a group"*?

The individual decision i.e. the answer to this question strongly implies further requirements on the being's proper education and training, to allow it to exist individually or in a group, and even requires a structural change (adaption) of the whole organism to individual or group existence. This can be for example a development of specific communication abilities, development of proper muscles and so on. In the long term perspective (evolution) it may imply serious genetic changes resulting in the development of a new species even.

The analysis of existing literature, shows a lack of papers dealing with this matter more thoroughly. There is much literature on swarm behavior, e.g. related to Ant Systems e.g. [2], but considerations there focus on the efficiency (advantage) of related algorithms applied to our, i.e. human applications when comparing to traditional computer algorithms (Turing Machine). There is a serious lack of analysis of individual vs. group existence from a biological being's point of view.

The approach applied in this paper tries to shed some light on this problem with the help of formalism of Computational Collective Intelligence. Comparison of individual existence vs. group existence is done through comparison of individual abilities vs. group abilities measured by their Collective Intelligence (*CI*). The question of efficiency of *CI* is a very important strategic question for a single being, as there are no clear terms of trade for the decision: *relying on being's own, individual performance (intelligence) - or to joining a social structure and relying on CI.* This question reaches an almost international level: in some nations, individualism is considered as something valuable, whereas other nations prefer collectivism.

There are high personal costs of participating in social structures, but profit, i.e. the increase of personal incomes of a single being, can be lower than expected. Social structures provide more safety for the individual, but sometimes a social structure is willing to sacrifice single beings relatively easily for group interest.

Beings with low individual intelligence will easily find, that joining a social structure which has a higher *CI*, is personally profitable, even decisive for the survival of an individual for example. Contrary to this, outstandingly intelligent individuals (comparing to other social structure participants) will profit proportionally to their intelligence only if they manage to take a higher position in the social hierarchy and to multiply their incomes this way. Otherwise, as it is widely observed, profits from their individual intelligence are "socially dispersed", nationalized by the rest of the social structure.

Two cases representing two important situations in the real world were found; one where the simulation model can be build for an individual and one for cooperating group existence. On this basis, quantitative results were calculated (simulations) allowing the comparison of individual versus group existence through Collective Intelligence measure.

The structure of the paper is as follows.

At first, difficulties as well as great opportunities related to the research on Collective Intelligence will be presented. Later on, a formal definition of the *CI* will be given, based on the theory presented in the author's book [10]. Next, a computational model of Collective Intelligence will be discussed. This is the theory's key point, because a social structure is considered by the *CI* theory as "a live computer" (inference machine), however using mathematical logic, not binary logic (Boolean algebra). In this computer, beings participate in data processing in an unconscious way; they work both as data processing units (processors) and as data transferring elements. As a whole computational system, such "live computer" is non-Turing; i.e. works in quite different way to what we observe in digital processors[1].

The following parts of the paper will discuss simulation models and simulation results for two above-mentioned social structures. Cases of Collective Intelligence for which quantity analysis is presented in the paper, are almost extremely distant from a biological and mental (individual Intelligence) point of view. This validates the generality of the assumed computational model of Collective Intelligence and forecasts well for the theory of Collective Intelligence presented in this paper. The paper will be concluded with the analysis of results and scientific extrapolations.

2   Difficulties and Opportunities of Research on Collective Intelligence and Basic Formalization Concepts

The question "what Collective Intelligence is" should be considered as part of a more general question "what is Intelligence". At the moment, we can enumerate: individual, collective and artificial Intelligence. Most probably, other types of Intelligence are possible.

Research work of Alan Turing who should be considered as one of founders of today's Computer Science, demonstrates that considerations on the nature of computational processes immediately bring the researcher to a question on the model of computations and in then leads to general considerations on Intelligence. Alan Turing designed his famous test[2] of a machine's ability to demonstrate Intelligence in 1950, whereas AI as a discipline was founded in 1956. Turing' works also provided foundations on how to evaluate complexity of processes related to Intelligence, under the assumption that a computational model of Intelligence is given.

Turing's famous model of computations widely known as the Turing Machine has been designed to formally describe "what can a clerk calculate with help of paper and pencil". Thus it can be said, that Individual Intelligence was a starting point. This model of computations beyond all other progress in computer science has lead researchers today to define and find practical uses of Artificial Intelligence[3].

The authors in this paper follow Allan Turing's research approach, claiming that best way to work with Collective Intelligence is to start at first with a feasible model of computations for Collective Intelligence. To the author's knowledge, no other, alternative model of computations has been proposed as yet for Collective Intelligence processes.

Relations between the complexity of computations, models of computations and Individual Intelligence visible in Alan Turing's works, clearly demonstrate the real difficulty level of research on Collective Intelligence.

---

[1] This should not be surprising, because the so called electronic analog computers also outperform digital computers in the area of differential and integral equations.
  http://www.owlnet.rice.edu/~elec301/Projects99/anlgcomp/
[2] http://en.wikipedia.org/wiki/Turing_test
[3] Newell, A.; Shaw, J.C.; Simon, H.A. (1959). Report on a general problem-solving program. *Proceedings of the International Conference on Information Processing*. pp. 256-264.

In Wikipedia webpage[4] referring to Collective Intelligence we see that the concept of Collective Intelligence is widely investigated in sociology, biology, business, computer science and mass communications. However all research there starts from a specific point of interest (expected application, e.g. market forecast) or observation (Wikipedia as symptom of Collective Intelligence). Researchers try to use alternative terms to name Collective Intelligence symptoms and their perception of the problem is only partially common. Nobody intends to build a general theory of Collective Intelligence.

However, according to the authors, there can be only one common and well defined model of computations for all such research.

Beyond the difficulty in correctly defining a computational model for Collective Intelligence, there is yet another "hard" problem, which authors have faced several times. The problem is how to translate a given characteristic social structure into a corresponding computational model, where Collective Intelligence can be observed. A crucial role will be played by researchers working on Collective Intelligence in other disciplines. Perhaps the best example is Shaw's book [7] "Group Dynamics", where social experiments related to Collective Intelligence are precisely described and enriched with excellent observations and conclusions, i.e. that the construction of a computational model is much easier and becomes well-anchored to real situations.

It is a paradox that the evaluation of the Collective Intelligence of social structures can be easier than the evaluation of the IQ of a single being.

Individual Intelligence can only be evaluated based on the external results of behavior during the problem-solving process. Neuropsychological processes in the brain necessary for problem-solving are still very far from being observable. Consequently, it is necessary to create abstract models of brain activity based on neuropsychological hypotheses, or to create computer-oriented models like Artificial Intelligence.

In contrast, many other elements of collectively intelligent activity can be observed, measured, and evaluated in a social structure e.g. [7]. We can easily observe spatial organization, displacements and actions of beings and their logical results, as well as exchange of information between beings e.g. language or the ant pheromone communication system.

Individual intelligence and behavior is scaled down as a factor – to accidental, local, and probabilistic processes. It can often be observed in the field of economics.

Collective Intelligence can be formalized and evaluated with the help of abstract chaotic[5] models of computations, and statistical evaluation of the behavior of beings in structured environments. Molecular model of computations performing parallel, nondeterministic inference processes seems to be the appropriate tool here.

Some basic observations underlie such model of computations:

1. In a socially cooperating structure, it is difficult to differentiate thinking and non-thinking beings (abstract beings must be introduced).
2. The individuals inside a social structure usually cooperate in chaotic, often non-continuous ways. In a social structure, beings move randomly because needs and opportunities of real life force them to do so.

---

[4] http://en.wikipedia.org/wiki/Collective_intelligence
[5] It is still unclear, whether *CI* processes are random or chaotic.

3. Predicate calculus where facts, rules and goals are used to build inferences; seems to be the most suitable mathematical formalism to describe behavior of beings.

4. Inference processes performed by beings are made randomly, starting when there is a need, when higher level needs are temporarily not disturbing a given being, or when there is a chance to rendezvous and make inference(s). Most inferences are never finished. This makes the similarity to Brownian movements almost striking, and suggests using quasi-Brownian movements[6] for modeling behavior in a social structure.

5. Individual inferences are also accidental and chaotic.

6. Resources for inferences are distributed in space, time, and among beings.

7. The performance of a given social structure is highly dependent on its organization.

8. Facts and rules in inference system can create inconsistent systems. Multiple copies are allowed.

9. Probability over the domain of problems must be used as an IQ measure for a social structure.

It is expected that research on Collective Intelligence should in future result with a variety of direct profits, than profits resulting from research on Individual Intelligence[7].

For example, the efficiency of a company on the market and it's ability to adapt to any changes in the environment (a crisis), can be considered and quantitatively analyzed in terms of it's internal Collective Intelligence.

There are strong evidences that "A. Smith's invisible hand" phenomenon can be analyzed, formalized and most probably explained[8] in terms of Collective Intelligence of the so called Free Market. It is expected that this way, some characteristics of the Free Market can be explained and even forecasted.

Also in medicine, the theory of Collective Intelligence can be used to evaluate "the problem solving power" of a bacterial colony, to find a method of neutralizing a new drug. The example given in the paper addresses this problem. Two factors are important here: 1) whether a bacterial colony of the given size is able to find a method of neutralizing the applied drug (and to acquire constant resistance) 2) how much time is necessary for a bacterial colony to neutralize this drug. If this time is sufficient, the patient's general condition should improve and other immunity components should resume action to fight off the bacterial colony.

3   Computational Model for Collective Intelligence Phenomena

The discrete nature of social structures strongly suggests use of molecular models of computations[9]. The model designed for *CI* phenomena [10] is described below.

---

[6] http://en.wikipedia.org/wiki/Fractional_Brownian_motion

[7] Strong demand on Individual Intelligence testing emerged at the end of 19-century due to requirements from industry and army.

[8] Author and his Ph. D. student are working on it.

[9] One possible realization of this model is the famous DNA-computer:
http://en.wikipedia.org/wiki/DNA_computer

Let's name this model *mCIm* for "*molecular CI model*". The whole model is composed on the basis of only two[10] elementary abstract concepts: information_molecule and membrane.

The 1st level Computational Space *(CS)* with internal quasi-random traveling Information Molecules *(IMs)* of facts, rules, and goals c_i is denoted as the multiset $CS^1 = \{c_1, ..., c_n\}$. Thus, facts, rules, and goals are themselves 0-level *CS* i.e. CS^0. For better readability, CS^0 let's denote as c_i, c_j etc..

For a given *CS*, we define a membrane similar to that of the Chemical Abstract Machine [3] denoted by $|\cdot|$ which encloses inherent facts, rules, and goals. It is obvious that $CS^1 = \{c_1, ..., c_n\} \equiv \{|c_1, ..., c_n|\}$. For a certain kind of membrane $|\cdot|$ its type p_i is given, which will be denoted as $|\cdot|_{p_i}$ to define which *CMs* can pass through it.

Such an act is considered as an Input/Output for the given *CS* with a given $|\cdot|$. It is possible to define degenerated membranes marked with $|\bullet$ or $\bullet|$ in the *mCIm* i.e. a collision-free (with membrane) path can be found going from the exterior to the interior of an area enclosed by such a membrane, for all types of *CMs*.

The simplest possible application of degenerated membranes in the *CS* simulating a given social structure is to make boundaries or streets for example. If the *CS* contains clauses c_i of facts, rules, goals as well as other *CSs*, then it is considered a higher order one, depending on the level of internal *CS*. Such internal *CS* will be also labeled with $\hat{v}_i$ e.g.

$$CS^2 = \{|c_1, ... CS^1_{\hat{v}_j}, ... c_n|\} \qquad iff \qquad CS^1_{\hat{v}_j} \equiv \{|b_1, ..., b_n|\}$$

$$where \quad b_i \quad i = 1...m \quad and \quad c_j \quad j = 1...n \quad are \quad clauses$$

Every c_i can be labeled with $\hat{v}_i$ to denote characteristics of its individual quasi-random displacements. The general practice will be that higher level *CSs* will take fixed positions, i.e. will create structures, and lower level *CSs* will perform displacements.

Specific (even low-level) *CSs* "settling" in specific locations of the main *CS*, after a certain period of quasi-random displacements are also allowed in *mCIm* model of computations. Some inference processes require this because for inference, local unions are necessary which *emerge (evolve)* on the basis of *cooperation* or specific forms of *trade* between *Computational_Spaces*.

For a given *CS* there is a defined position function *pos*:

$$pos : O_i \rightarrow \langle position \ description \rangle \cup undefined \quad where \ O_i \in CS$$

Understanding of the position space is formal, i.e. the metrics depends on a specific case which is analyzed. For example, if information_molecules will be traveling along a network of any abstract neurons, this network will define metrics.

---

[10] It is interesting to note that much like the digital computer where information coding and processing is based on 0/1 system, the computations in *mCIm* are also based on two elements: information molecule and membrane.

If there are any two internal CS objects O_i, O_j in the given CS, then there is a defined distance function $D\left(pos\left(O_i\right), pos\left(O_j\right)\right) \to \Re$ and a rendezvous distance d. We say that during the computational process, at any time t or time period Δt, two objects O_i, O_j come to rendezvous iff $D\left(pos\left(O_i\right), pos\left(O_j\right)\right) \leq d$. The rendezvous act will be denoted by the rendezvous relation ®, e.g. O_i ® O_j which is reflective and symmetric, but not transitive. For another definition of rendezvous as the λ-operator, see Fontana, et al [4]. In the $mCIm$ model, the computational process for a given CS is defined as the sequence of frames F labeled by t or Δt, interpreted as the time (given in standard time units or simulation cycles) with a well-defined *start* and *end,* e.g. $F_{t_0}, ..., F_{t_e}$. For every frame the multiset $F_j \equiv \left(\left|c_1, ..., c_m\right|\right)$ is explicitly given, with all related specifications: $pos(.)$, membrane types p, and movement specifications v if available. The simplest case of $mCIm$ used in author's simulations was the 3-D cube with randomly traveling clauses of facts, rules, and goals inside. The $mCIm$ process is initialized to start the inference process after the set of clauses, facts, rules, and goals (defined by the programmer) is injected into proper CS.

More advanced examples of CS for the $mCIm$ include a single main CS^2 with a set of internal CS^1 which take fixed positions inside CS^2, and a number of CS^0 which are either local for a given CS^1_i (because the membrane is not transparent for them) or global for any subset of $CS^1_j \in CS^2$. When modeling the Collective Intelligence of certain closed social structures, interpretations in the structure will be given for all CS^m_n, i.e. "this CS is a message"; "this is a single human"; "this is a village, a city", etc. The importance of properly defining $\hat{v}_j$ for very CS^i_j should be emphasized. As has been mentioned, the higher level CS^i_j will take a fixed position to model substructures like villages or cities. If we model a single human as CS^1_j, then $\hat{v}_j$ will reflect the displacement of a human being. Characteristics of the given $\hat{v}_j$ can be purely Brownian or can be quasi-random, e.g. in lattice, but it is profitable to subject it to the present form of CS^i_j. When $\hat{v}_j$ has the proper characteristics, there are the following essential tools:

- The goal clause, when it reaches the final form, can migrate toward a defined *Output* location. This can be a membrane of the main CS or even a specific, local CS. Thus the appearance of a solution of a problem in the CS can be observable.
- Temporarily, the density of some *information_moleculecs* can be increased in a given area of CS in such a way that after a given low-level CS^i_j reaches the necessary form, it migrates to a specific area or areas to increase the speed of selected inferences.

The above discussed model of computations $mCIm$ requires defining a new inference pattern due to its nature. In general, the idea of Prolog has been used as an inspiration however, clauses are carried out not by strings of characters, but molecular structures, which they are carried by. This requires major changes, but the concept of Prolog is still visible here.

3.1 The Inference Model in the *mCIm*

The pattern of inference in *mCIm* generalized for any CS has the form:

DEFINITION 1. GENERALIZED INFERENCE IN CS^N

Assuming that $CS = \left\{ ...CS^i_j...CS^k_l... \right\}$, on this basis we can define

$$CS^i_j \circledR CS^k_l \text{ and } U(CS^i_j , CS^k_l) \text{ and } C(\text{one or more } CS^m_n \text{ of conclusions}) \quad \vdash$$

one or more CS^m_n of conclusions, $R(CS^i_j \text{ or } CS^k_l)$ ∎

The above description should be interpreted as follows:

$CS^i_j \circledR CS^k_l$ denotes a rendezvous relation;

$U(CS^i_j , CS^k_l)$ denotes that unification of the necessary type can be successfully applied;

$C(\textit{one or more } CS^m_n \textit{ of conclusions})$ denotes that CS^m_n are satisfiable.

Note that the reaction $\rightarrow$ in chemical abstract machine [3] semantics is equivalent to inference $\vdash$.

$R(CS^i_j \text{ or } CS^k_l)$ denotes that any parent *CMs* are retracted if necessary.

The standard PROLOG inferences are simple cases of the above definition. Later, when discussing the N-element inference, we will only be interested in "constructive" inferences, i.e. when a full chain of inferences exists. Thus the above diagram will be abbreviated as

$$CS^i_j ; CS^k_l \xrightarrow{\quad RPP \quad} \sum_n CS^m_n$$

without mentioning the retracted *CMs* given by $R(CS^i_j \text{ or } CS^k_l)$. In general, a successful rendezvous can result in the "birth" of one or more child *CMs*. All of them must then fulfill a $C(...)$ condition; otherwise, they are aborted.

Since our proposed *mCIm* is designed to evaluate the inference power of closed social structures, simplifying assumptions based on real life observation can be made. It is difficult to find cases of direct rendezvous and inference between two CS^m_i and CS^n_j if $m,n \geq 1$ without an intermediary involved CS^0_k $k = 1,2...$ (messages, pheromones, observation of behavior, e.g. the bee's dance, etc.). Even in Genetic Algorithms, the crossover of genes can be considered as the inference of two genomes, $CS^0_i \text{ and } CS^0_j$. Only if we consider CS^n at the level of whole nations, where mutual exchange (migration) of humans takes place, can such a case be considered as an approximation to higher level rendezvous and inferences. This is, however, just an approximation because eventually this exchange is implemented at humans' personal contact level, which are just rendezvous and inferences of two CS_i^0 and CS_j^0 with the help of CS_k^0 $k = 1,2...$. Thus, rendezvous and direct inference between two CS_j^i if $i \geq 1$ will be left for further research. In this paper, we only make use of a single CS_{main}^n for $n > 1$ as the main CS. Single beings like humans or ants can be represented as $CS_{individual}^1$. Such beings perform internal inferences (in their brains), independently of higher level, cooperative inferences inside CS_{main} and exchange of messages of the type CS^0. Internal CS^k inside the main CS will be allowed, but only as static ones (taking fixed positions) to define sub-structures such as streets, companies, villages, cities, etc.

For simplicity, however, we will try to approximate beings as CS^0; otherwise, even statistical analysis would be too complicated. It is also important to assume that the results of inference are not allowed to infer between themselves after they are created. Products of inference must immediately disperse; however, later inferences between them are allowed (Giarratano and Riley call this *refraction* [5]).

4   Formal Definition of Collective Intelligence

The entry assumption is that *CI* itself is a property of a group of beings and is expressed/observable and measurable. Surprisingly, it is <u>not necessary to assume</u> that beings are cooperating or are conscious or not; nothing must be assumed about the communication; we don't even assume that these beings are alive. Thus because nothing specific must be assumed about beings, the definition given later on, works for software agents, bacterial colonies, ants, small social animals, humans, and nations as well. To better understand the above issues, let's look at some examples. Suppose that we observe a group of ants which have discovered a heavy prey that must be transported, and we also observe a group of humans who gather to transport some heavy cargo. Ant intelligence is very low, and a simple perception/communication system is used – however, it is clear that ants display *CI*. On the other hand, humans, after a lot of time, thought, and discussion will also move the cargo; this is also *CI*. Because of such situations, the definition of *CI* must be abstracted from possible methods of thinking and communication between individuals. The definition must be based on the results of group behavior. Let's look into another case. In medieval cities there were streets with shoemaker shops only. They gravitated there because the benefits gained exceeded the disadvantages, e.g. when some customers decided to buy shoes from a neighbor. Some shoemakers were sometimes in fact, even enemies. In this example, *CI* emerges without any doubt; this is obvious just looking at the high amount and quality of shoes produced on such streets. Thus we cannot assume willful cooperation for *CI*, or the definition of cooperation would have to be very vague.

Bacteria and viruses cooperate through exchange of (genetic) information; we know the power of Genetic Algorithms, which creates their *CI* against antibiotics, but it is questionable whether they are alive. Thus, the assumption about the existence of live agents must also be dropped. The definition we give now is based on these assumptions, and will formally cover any type of being, any communication system, and any form of synergy, virtual or real.

Let there be given a set S of individuals $indiv_1,\ldots, indiv_n$ existing in any environment Env. No specific nature is assumed for the individuals nor for their environment. It is necessary only to assume the existence of a method to distinguish $indiv_i$ $i=1,\ldots,n$ from the Env. Let there be also given a testing period $t_{start} - t_{end}$ to judge/evaluate the property of CI of $S\{\ldots\}$ in Env. Let there now be given any universe U of possible problems $Probl_i$ proper for the environment Env, and be given the complexity evaluation for every problem $Probl_i$ denoted by $f_o^{Probl_i}(n)$.

CI deals with both *formal* and *physical* problems; thus we should write the following:

$$f_0^{Probl_i}(n) \overset{def}{=} \begin{cases} \textit{if } Probl_i \textit{ is a computational problem, apply the standard} \\ \textit{definition of computational complexity, where n gives} \\ \textit{the size of the problem;} \\ \textit{if } Probl_i \textit{ is any problem of a "physical" nature, use} \\ \textit{physical measure units, e.g. mass, size, etc. for expressing n.} \end{cases}$$

Let's also denote in the formula the ability to solve the problems of our set of individuals S over U when working/thinking without any mutual interaction (absolutely alone, far from each other, without exchange of information):

$$Abl_U^{all\,indiv} \overset{def}{=} \bigcup_{Probl_i \in U} \max_{S} \left(\max_{n} f_0^{Probl_i}(n) \right)$$

This set defines the maximum possibilities of S when individuals are asked, e.g. one by one, to display their abilities through all the problems. Observe that if any problem is beyond the abilities of any individual from S, this problem is not included in the set.

DEFINITION 2. COLLECTIVE INTELLIGENCE AS A PROPERTY
Now assume that individuals coexist together and interact in some way. We say that CI emerges because of cooperation or coexistence in S, iff at least one problem $Probl'$ can be pointed to, such that it can be solved by a lone individual but supported by the group, or by some individuals working together:

$$f_o^{Probl_i}(n') \overset{significantly}{>} f_o^{Probl_i}(n) \in Abl_U^{all\,indiv}$$
or
$$\exists Probl' \text{ such that } \left(\forall n\, Probl' \notin Abl_U^{all\,indiv}\right) \wedge \left(Probl' \in U\right) \qquad \blacksquare$$

The basic concept of the definition is that the property CI emerges for a set of individuals S in an environment U iff a new problem $\in U$ emerges which can be solved from that point, or similar but even more complex problems can be solved. Even a small modification in the structure of a social group, its communication system, or even in the education of some individuals, can result in *CI* emergence or increase. An example is shoemakers moving their shops from remote villages to the City. This could be the result of a king's order or creation of a "free trade zone". The important thing is that the distance between them has been reduced so much that it triggers new communication channels of some nature (e.g. spying). Defining *CI* seems simple but measuring it is quite a different problem. The difficulty with measuring *CI* lies in the necessity of using a specific model of computations, which is not based on the DTM Turing Machine.

5 Collective Intelligence Quotient IQS

The two basic definitions for *CI* and its measure IQS (IQ Social) have the following forms:

DEFINITION 3. N-ELEMENT INFERENCE IN CS^N

There is a given *CS* at any level $CS^n = \left\{ CS_1^{a_1}, ... CS_m^{a_m} \right\}$, and an allowed Set of Inferences *SI* of the form

$$\{ set\ of\ premises\ CS \} \xrightarrow{I_j} \{ set\ of\ conclusions\ CS \},$$

and one or more CS_{goal} of a goal. We say that $\left\{ I_{a_0}, ..., I_{a_{N-1}} \right\} \subseteq SI$ is an N-element inference in CS^n, if for all $I \in \left\{ I_{a_0}, ..., I_{a_{N-1}} \right\}$ the premises $\in$ the present state of CS^n at the moment of firing this inference, all $\left\{ I_{a_0}, ..., I_{a_{N-1}} \right\}$ can be connected into one tree by common conclusions and premises, and $CS_{goal} \in \left\{ set\ of\ conclusions\ for\ I_{a_{N-1}} \right\}$.   ∎

DEFINITION 4. COLLECTIVE INTELLIGENCE QUOTIENT (IQS)
IQS is measured by the probability *P* that after time *t*, the conclusion CM_{goal} will be reached from the starting *state of CS^n*, as a result of the assumed N-element inference. This is denoted as $IQS = P(t, N)$.   ∎

For evaluating *CI* the last two definitions fulfill these requirements:

- N-element inferences can be allowed to be interpreted as any problem-solving process in a social structure or inside a single being, where N inferences are necessary to get a result; or any production process, where N-technologies/elements have to be found and unified into one final technology or product. Therefore, in the same uniform way we model inferring processes or production processes within a social structure. This is very important because some inference processes can be observed only through resultant production processes or specific logical behavior (of ants, bees, bacteria).
- Simulating N-element inferences in the *mCIm* computational model allows us to model the distribution of inference resources between individuals, dissipation in space or time, or movements (or temporary concentration) in the *CS*. This reflects

well the dissipated, moving, or concentrated resources in a social structure of any type.

- Cases can be simulated where some elements of the inference chain are temporarily unavailable, but at a certain time t, another inference running in the background or in parallel will produce the missing components. This is well known in human social structures, when for example a given research or technological discovery is blocked until missing theorems or sub-technology is discovered.

- Humans infer in all directions: forward - improvements of existing technology, backward - searching how to manufacture a given product going back from the known formula, and also through generalization - two or more technologies can be combined into one more general and powerful technology or algorithm. The N-element inference when simulated reflects all these cases clearly.

EXAMPLE: A HUMAN SOCIAL STRUCTURE FACING A SIMPLE PROBLEM
This example seems simple, but on the basis of simulation experiments turns out to be less trivial. Let us consider a human social structure suffering from cold weather. Assume that:

a) There are some humans with matches only, moving somewhere inside the social structure (let's name them: owners);
b) Others have matchboxes only (let's also name them: owners);
c) There is a small group with an idea of how to use the matches and matchbox together to make fire (let's name them: engineers);
d) Some humans are conscious that fire gives heat (let's name them: physicists);
e) There are humans (perhaps there is only one?) conscious of the fact that heat is necessary (let's name them: politicians, managers).

Other humans are logically void (from CI point of view). Nobody has total knowledge of all the necessary elements and their present position; everybody can infer, but only locally. For this social structure the CS^1 in $mCIm$ can be defined as a set of CS^0:

```
CS¹ ={matches. matchbox. matches∧matchbox→fire.
fire→heat. ?heat.}
```

Please remember, that clauses will have multiple occurrences in CS^1 depending on how many humans have copies of given logical object in the social structure.

Now it is necessary to make assignments:

- The displacement abilities v stand for above defined CS^0. We can use pure or quasi-Brownian movements, e.g. humans run chaotically around on foot looking for the necessary components. Public transportation can change the characteristics of displacement. Virtual travel by telephone or Internet search can also be defined. Traveling may be on a daily/weekly/yearly scale.

- The internal structure of CS^1 which affect rendezvous probability should be defined (internal membranes reflecting boundaries, e.g. streets).

- Artificial restrictions can be imposed on unification, e.g. different languages, casts, racial conflicts, etc. This system is an example of the 4-element inference.

The IQS can be computed here for this social structure on the basis of simulations as a curve showing how probability changes in the given time period, or as the general analytical function $P(4, t)$, if we can manage to derive it.

6   Collective Intelligence of Simple Beings: A Cooperating Bacterial Colony

The bacterial world is so diverse, that is no chance to define any common bacterial representative for simulation purposes. Thus our choice was to design at biochemistry textbook level e.g. [6]. We discussed a well-balanced and simple model of a bacterial colony which will be representative and easily acceptable for any microbiologist. Two aspects of bacterial existence were emphasized in the model because of Collective Intelligence research: survival of bacterial colony (not single bacterial being) when the environment rapidly changes, and the information exchange between bacteria.

An antibiotic attack against a bacterial colony can indirectly be considered as a kind of rapid change of the environment. It has been assumed, that the bacteria respond to this through the change of its internal structure and structure of successors, which implies better adoption to the new state of their environment.

The simulation model has been based on some selected, abstract parameters which are derived from the analysis of the life of a bacterial colony. These basic parameters were:

- A parameter describing the abstract health and vital ability of the bacteria. This parameter was named HVA. It has been assumed that when this parameter will reach maximum value, specific bacteria will reproduce, but when it reaches zero – the bacteria will die. The increase (or decrease) of vital ability depends on the speed of feeding, which is implied by the level of adoption of the given bacteria to the present environment. This implication is rather obvious: "unhealthy" bacteria will not feed.
- Abstract DNA of the bacteria is considered as a parameter. DNA coding is usually based on the long string(s) of symbols; giving myriads of possibilities. Here the DNA concept has been simplified to just R,G,B color – which gives 255^3 possibilities. There is an important bit of intuition behind this: the color of an animal (e.g. human face) is a very important, simple, but useful health indicator. Coding DNA with color is very important for presented simulation model, because it implies further useful simplifications.
- Alarm indicator. This parameter shows how the health and vital ability parameter HVA changes and how severe the situation is for the bacteria at the given moment.

As mentioned before, bacterial life cycle is based on feeding, however in order to feed, the bacteria must be adapted to the present environment in a sufficient way. In our model an adaptation measure is defined: better adaptation implies faster feeding, which implies faster growth of vital abilities. The threshold below which feeding is not possible, is also defined.

Adaptation level is simply calculated on the basis of comparison of the colors (codes as RGB values) describing the present state of the environment and the color of given bacteria. Here, intuition also works: we frequently evaluate the environment or its elements on the basis of color; e.g. food, sky, etc. In our model, the given bacterium can not directly observe the color of the environment to compare with its own color, and in this way to infer how well it is adapted to the environment – the bacteria can only observe its own feeding efficiency.

Every bacterium can observe (in certain predefined radius) the prosperity tendency of neighbors through the alarm indicator, and the amount of neighbors in wider a radius. The observation process is not cost-free: bacteria are foraging a bit slower.

When the health and vital abilities parameter HVA reaches maximum, bacteria reproduce in such way that the parent bacterium will continue its existence with 1/3 of the previous HVA parameter. Similarly, child bacteria will inherit 1/3, while the other 1/3 is considered as lost for reproduction purpose.

The bacteria in our model, is able to displace and the displacement target is to have sufficient number of neighbors around. This will increase its survival ability, since bacteria can observe who is best adapted to the environment. On this basis bacteria can become similar.

To preserve the genetic diversity of the bacterial colony, single bacteria will display interest with the neighbors only if the alarm indicator will force it to act. When bacteria reach any acceptable level of adaption to the environment, it will stop changing DNA. Thus, in our model, bacteria do not optimize – genetic diversity is more important.

In our simulation model the DNA parameter can change in several ways:

- Intentionally: given bacteria (let's say A) notices that its HVA goes down due to insufficient adaption to the environment. Consequently, neighbors in a certain perimeter are observed, the most prosperous one is found (let's say B) and DNA of A is slightly changed, with variation, in the area of color component where the difference between A and B is biggest. In the next cycle the process is repeated if necessary.
- In an alarm situation where no neighbors are found, single bacteria will try macro-mutations of its DNA, desperately trying to adapt to the environment which has changed. In most cases it leads to the death of bacteria. Macro-mutations are also allowed for bacteria with neighbors around – however probability of this is very low.
- DNA of single bacteria may also randomly change, even if there is no need for this (HVA is OK). In such cases, the changes to DNA are slight and random.

A simulation program has been written in C++ with OpenGL to implement the visualization interface. The program was 822 lines of code long and the .exe form was approx. 276 kB. It was necessary to write for four consecutive versions of simulation model to reach its satisfactory behavior. The bacterial world was 2D, like a Petri dish is. Experiments were performed is following way. At first, an environment was initialized with bacteria, settled in quasi random way (e.g. to avoid overlapping). The DNA of bacteria (its color) also was initialized randomly. At first, the environment is set to a grey color. For all experiments this starting color was the same. Later on, the environment will vary (fluctuate) in a random way, with given parameter T defining the mean fluctuation period. Simulation steps are used as time units. Some bacteria will not survive fluctuation of the environment, but others with the help of reproduction, mutation and cooperation, are able to survive. For the given experiment settings, because of multiple random generators built-in in many points of the simulation model, every experiment has been repeated 50 times, and the (average) values were presented in form of charts. It is estimated, that the simulation model has been run 1500 – 2000 times. The key point of our research is the Collective Intelligence efficiency; thus the reference point for every performed experiment was the behavior of the same bacterial colony, but with mutual communication stopped.

Fig. 3 presents general view of bacterial world.

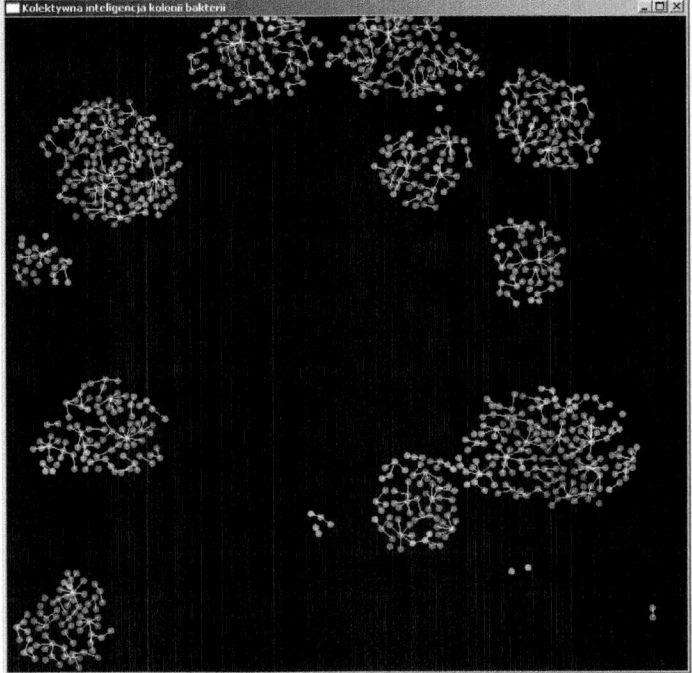

Fig. 3. Simulation snapshot. Fine line segments show communication acts between two bacteria. Colors define state of the bacteria: green marks bacteria with low HVA, red with high HVA, violet color marks bacteria which is reproducing. It is clearly visible that local sub-colonies do better than single, lone bacteria.

Fig. 4 and Fig. 5. shows results of first experiment where the probability that a bacterial colony will increase its population after 1000 simulation cycles, while the environment fluctuates with different speeds is checked. To increase the reader's interest in the given images, conclusions and remarks are given in advance.

Comments and remarks to Fig. 3, 4, 5:

- It is clearly visible, that calm, quiet environment which changes slowly, allows the existence of bacteria without cooperation (information exchange). In such an environment, the bacteria manage to produce enough successors, that mutations will always provide a variant of bacteria able to survive the unfavorable change of environment. Many animals follow this strategy. They produce a great number of successors, very fast in terms of speed of changing environment. Sporadic appearance of a predator as a change of environment will not create a thread for such species. Such animals do not display cooperation, but simply try to survive on their own.

- If the environment changes faster, the Collective Intelligence provides a solution. However, if the environment changes too fast, even this is not sufficient.
- As mentioned in [10], the phenomenon of Collective Intelligence is a temporary one: it can emerge in certain social structures in certain situations and after a certain time can vanish. Collective Intelligence also strongly depends on (is very sensitive to) different environmental and social parameters. This is well visible in this experiment: Collective Intelligence is very profitable for bacterial colony in a rather narrow range of environmental parameter T.

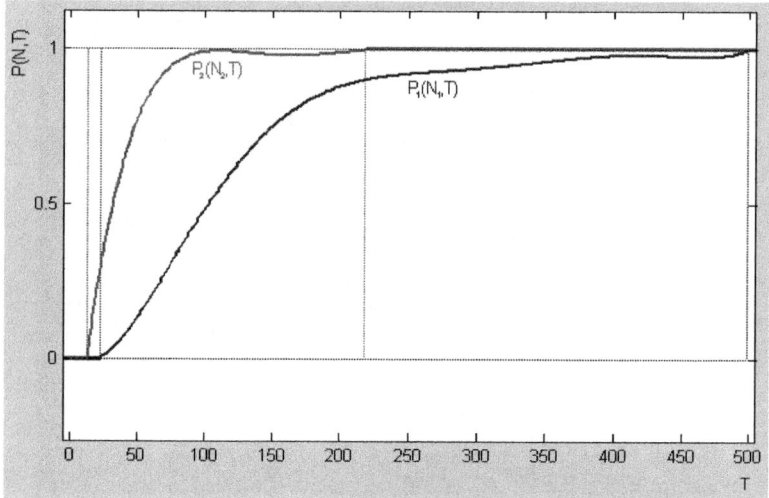

Fig. 4. Results. Red (upper) line show bacterial colony with mutual communication switched on; whereas blue means that communication is "off". Diagrams are refined with help of polynomial approximation. Y axis code probability of the success, X axis gives mean fluctuation period in terms of number of simulation cycles.

The zero-Collective Intelligence (zero-IQS) denoted in [10] as $\emptyset_{IQS}^{S}$ is defined here as a case where bacteria do not communicate, i.e. a case described by blue line in Fig. 4. The increase of IQS referred to $\emptyset_{IQS}^{S}$ is given by the formula bellow.

$$\Delta IQS = \frac{\int (IQS - \emptyset_{IQS}^{S})}{\int \emptyset_{IQS}^{S}} \approx 0.345$$

The second experiment presented here provides some hints to the question on how the Collective Intelligence phenomena depend on number of beings participating in the process. In other words, how efficient Collective Intelligence is in terms of required resources, i.e. how many "live computational elements" are required to get it to function. For beings to engage in something and to make it function, means "to make it profit".

The goal of the experiment was to check how the number of neighbor information-exchanging bacteria affects the speed of solving the basic problem - how to adapt to the environment.

It was assumed in the experiment, that the problem was successfully solved, when after a certain number of simulation steps, at least 50% of bacteria manage to adapt to the environment in such way, that their further growth was possible.

In this experiment, bacteria were not moving nor dying. As mentioned before, 50 experiments were used to estimate the average value of every K for given value of N.

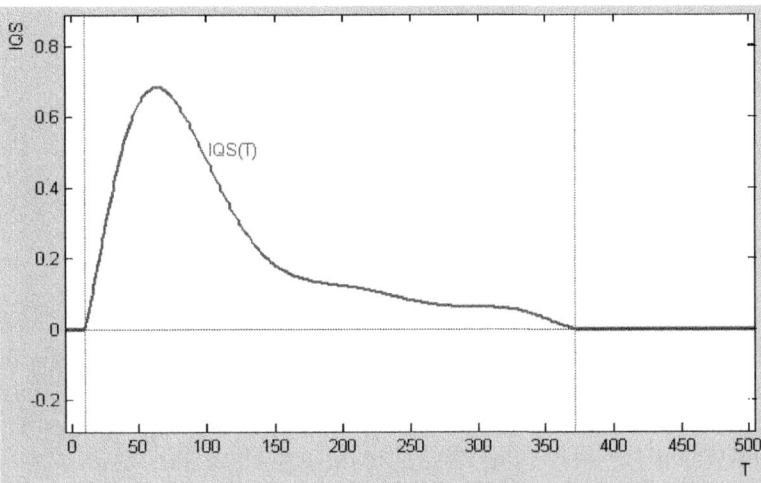

Fig. 5. Results. This chart shows the difference in terms of probability, between cooperating bacteria and bacteria trying to survive alone. It is well visible that a fast changing environment requires Collective Intelligence, whereas a slow changing environment allows individual existence. Environment changing too quickly give no chances for survival.

Comments and remarks.
The experiment demonstrated that if the number of communicating bacteria was greater than 5, the speed of ability to solve this specific problem increased rapidly.

This experiment models specific situation and specific social structure. However, it is immediately visible, that this method can be used to estimate the optimal size of a social structure from the Collective Intelligence point of view. The structure would also be able to survive in the given environment generating the set of problems and imposing the required speed of response. Here, the number of 20 bacteria is optimal. However, this "optimality" can be questioned, because a bigger population does not increase the speed of problem solving, but works as a "bigger static memory" of possible solutions, coded in genetic diversity. This problem is left for future research.

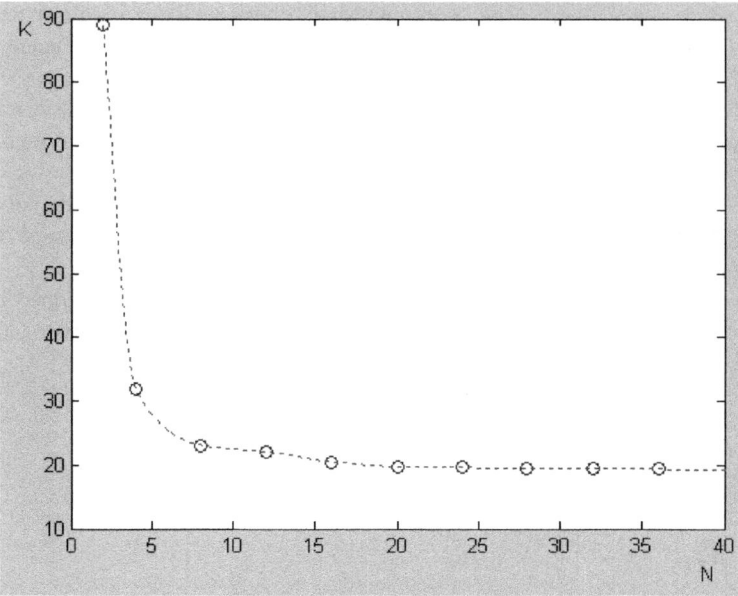

Fig. 6. Results. K denotes the average number of cycles necessary to solve the problem. N denotes the number of bacteria exchanging information.

Real, individual beings need "life space" - thus density of beings (in these case bacteria) cannot be arbitrarily increased, to increase the exchange of information. Perhaps this explains why some biological individual beings decide to merge into one, multi-cell organism able to collectively displace and forage.

There are three basic social structure parameters here: density of beings, communicating distance and communication speed.

When humans were organized into ancient, small villages, with primitive agriculture, the communication abilities were very low. Then, the distance and safety of travel was low, thus in practice, in case of any need (problem to be solved), only some tenth of other humans were within the distance of efficient communication. Collective Intelligence of such a village was low. Communication between villages considered as objects, was low.

An increase in communication abilities occurred when ancient cities started to emerge, which immediately resulted in higher Collective Intelligence and fast technological and cultural progress. In such a city surrounded by a city wall (membrane), a single human in case of a need, was able to safely communicate with hundreds of other humans in the period of hours.

However, the emerging and intensifying exchange of information between cities, based on merchants and caravans was still low in terms of speed and amount of exchanged information.

Even today, long distance traveling is expensive - thus is restricted to low percentage of human population.

Therefore the next major step in Collective Intelligence development should be considered - the Internet. It provides mass, cheap, bidirectional communication, for all classes of information.

Human beings at any given time do not face one but many problems characteristic of the environment they live in. Other humans and beings do not have the same knowledge, abilities and resources. Thus the second dimension of the problem emerges: "who has the solution to the given problem and where". In a medieval city it was possible to remember "who and where" owned certain knowledge and resources - and this human was in walking distance, inside the city wall. The real breakthrough fundamental for Collective Intelligence has happened when people started to widely use the Internet, because it is equipped with browsing capabilities, reducing this dimension.

7 Inter-species Collective Intelligence of Complex Beings: Hunter and Dog versus Rabbit

In the previous experiment, the efficiency of Collective Intelligence was analyzed for almost extremely simple beings, i.e. for a bacterial colony. Possible internal data processing for bacteria is also relatively simple; they do not have a brain. For the same reason their perception of the environment and possible methods of information exchange with other bacteria are not based on any complex data processing.

The second simulation model of Collective Intelligence presented in this paper analyses mammals with a higher level brain and a sophisticated system of senses. The social structure of a hunter and dog, versus a rabbit is very intuitive for us and seemingly simple. However, this structure is very interesting for several reasons. The hunter and dog communicate on the basis of guesses – the interpretation of partner's mental state and will. All this is based on the education (training) and experience of previous joint huntings. All three intelligent beings: human, dog and rabbit are different species - thus represent most probably different ways of thinking[11] (and strategies) when solving problems implied by the hunting process.

For the above reasons, the simulation model has been written in a different way: not as a simulation of physical-style process which was suitable for bacteria without a brain, but as a simulation system using inference engines. Here, Jess[12] software has been used. In such systems, the behavior of beings and their way of thinking is coded with the help of inference rules. Later on such rules are processed by the inference engine.

The simulation experiment has been designed in the following way:

The hunter, the dog and the rabbit exist in a common 2D scene, which is closed and defined as a hunting ground.

---

[11] They are all mammals. It can be assumed, to some extent, that their brains work in a similar way. This is important, because the same inference engine has been used for simulating their intelligence.

[12] Official Website: http://herzberg.ca.sandia.gov/. We would like to thank to Mr. Craig A. Smith from Sandia National Lab for an academic license of Jess, which allowed for the above mentioned simulations and M. Sc. dissertation.

At the beginning of the simulation, the hunter and dog are located (initialized) at the entry to the hunting ground, and the rabbit's initial position is generated randomly. At the beginning, the rabbit is quietly foraging and slowly moves around in a random way.

The complex nature of real hunting ground i.e. bush, trees, hills and ravines, is not directly modeled here, but instead the displacements of actors (when not affected by the inference process) are defined by Brownian movement. This reflects terrain randomness quite well, affecting the rabbit's displacements when foraging and the hunter's and dog's displacements, while looking for the rabbit. Brownian displacements of actors are later on modified (become deterministic) on the basis of logical decisions of the hunter, the dog and the rabbit, resulting from integration between the actors.

Neither the dog nor the hunter, are able to catch the rabbit alone – they are too slow. However, the hunter is equipped with a rifle and if the rabbit is spotted and is sufficiently near, the rabbit will be hunted, which effectively finishes the simulation. Alternatively, the time limit finishes the simulation.

The simulation model was built in an evolutionary way, which finally concluded in the following structure of the simulation model:

Rules for the hunter, the dog and the rabbit were defined using Fuzzy Logic approach with CF (Certainty Factor). Simulations have demonstrated that the necessary number of rules is:

- o   Hunter: 11 rules,
- o   Dog: 18 rules,
- o   Rabbit: 15 rules.

Rules are not complex and the example rule for dog has form:

```
rete.executeCommand("(defrule rabbitClose " +
"(rabbit_close)"
    + " => " + "(assert (track 1))" + "(assert (signal
6)) )");
```

Testing IQS was based on calculating at first the zero-Collective Intelligence (zero-IQS) denoted in [10] as $\emptyset^{S}_{IQS}$. It has been assumed that this case happens when the hunter and dog for some reason do not cooperate, e.g. the dog is young and ignores the hunter resulting in the dog running around for its own pleasure or interest. In this simulation model, such behavior of the dog affects the position and behavior of the rabbit i.e. frightening him. The second possibility is that the hunter is inexperienced, and after a certain time, cooperation between the two vanishes, resulting in the dog once again running around for pleasure, leaving the hunter to hunt the rabbit alone.

Fig 7. Shows how cooperation increases hunting efficiency. Results are based on repeating every simulation 100 times.

The increase of efficiency resulting from Collective Intelligence is relative very high.

Similarly as in case of a bacterial colony, Collective Intelligence rapidly increases hunting efficiency when time given for hunting is short.

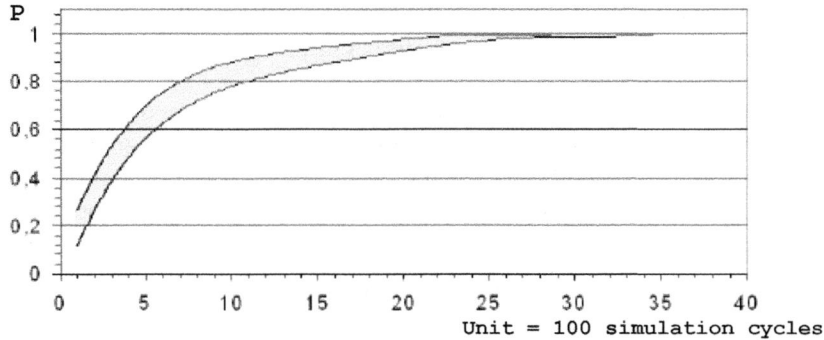

Fig. 7. Increase of hunting efficiency as the result of Collective Intelligence. Vertical axis gives probability of hunting.

In this case, the increase of IQS referred to $\varnothing_{IQS}^{S}$ given by the formula (as used before), is:

$$\Delta IQS = \frac{\int (IQS - \varnothing_{IQS}^{S})}{\int \varnothing_{IQS}^{S}}$$

$$\Delta IQS = \frac{(45.7 - 27.1)}{27.1} \approx 0.68$$

It is a very high increase, almost double to what bacteria gain when using *CI*. Assuming that according[13] to Terman's classification IQ range 80-90 means "dullness", the increase of IQ in this case by 68% shifts it to range 134-151. In Terman's classification range 140 and over means genius or near genius.

8 Conclusions

The paper presents an analysis of Collective Intelligence (*CI*) efficiency based on two simulation models representing two social structures of beings, taken from very distant areas of the real, biological world. Most important conclusions on *CI* efficiency can be summarized in the form of following statements:

- In both cases the increase of problem solving abilities of social structure, when using the *CI* is spectacular. It is interesting that beings with higher individual intelligence profit almost double with Collective Intelligence, even if the population of the social structure is just composed of two beings. Most probably the reason for this is that the higher individual intelligence allows more sophisticated communication and data processing. This in turn points to the suggestion that an evolutionary pressure toward higher intelligence exists. In [11] there is a strong

---

[13] IQ Basics: http://www.iqcomparisonsite.com/IQBasics.aspx

suggestion that the relation between Individual and Collective Intelligence is based on the spiral growth, where one form of intelligence transforms into another in a cyclic (spiral) way.

- The increase of problem solving abilities resulting from Collective Intelligence is:
  o Highest if the speed of problem solving is required. When time-pressure is not high, Collective intelligence is not so profitable for the social structure;
  o One, very strong maximum is observed. Fig. 5 is representative for both experiments.

There are also several concerns regarding results and conclusions presented above:

❖ Only two cases of Collective Intelligence were modeled and analyzed, whereas many more are required to complete this study.

❖ In the Collective Intelligence theory [10], the intelligence quotient IQS for a social structure is defined not as a scalar value (or array of scalars) as human's IQ defined is, but as a function of probability over the domain of time and complexity of problems to be solved. In the above mentioned experiments, both social structures were tested against a specific problem, thus only a single intersection of general IQS function has been received. It is an important issue, because the social structure, during its life, faces a complex mix of simple daily life problems as well as some very complex ones. The presented models were too simple to be able to test social structure against a well-composed benchmark of problems, and to calculate a credible IQS function. We should also keep in mind that a real social structure solves a mix of problems at the same time (in parallel) and not just one problem.

❖ The simulation models were tested in a basic way i.e. how the problem solving ability of a social structure is sensible to internal social and external environmental parameters. However, this objection can be questioned. The real world is so rich with local, sometimes very strange 'ecological niches' that organisms are able to create specific individual and social structures, filling this niche and thus creating specific, high problem oriented Collective Intelligence – *CI* can be really unbeatable there. Specific parameter settings in such cases are irreversibly connected with Collective Intelligence. This observation is also a hint on why some species immediately vanish if some environmental change takes place.

References

1. Ben-Jacob, E., Cohen, I., Gutnick, D.L.: Cooperative organization of bacterial colonies - from genotype to morphotype. Annu. Rev. Microbiol. 52 (1998)
2. Bonabeau, E., Dorigo, M., Theraulaz, G.: Swarm Intelligence: From Natural to Artificial Systems. Oxford University Press, Oxford (1999)
3. Berry, G., Boudol, G.: The chemical abstract machine. Theoretical Computer Science, 217–248 (1992)
4. Fontana, W., Buss, L.W.: The arrival of the fittest. Bull. Math. Biol. 56 (1994)
5. Giarratano, J., Riley, G.: Expert systems, 2nd edn. PWS Pub. (1994)
6. Kunicki-Goldfinger, W.: Life of bacteria (student's textbook), 7th edn., 616 pages. PWN Press, Warsaw (2006) (in Polish)

7. Shaw, M.E.: Group Dynamics, 4th edn. McGraw-Hill, New York (1971)
8. Szuba, T.: A Molecular Quasi-random Model of Computations Applied to Evaluate Collective Intelligence. Future Generation Computing Journal 14(5-6) (1998)
9. Szuba, T.: A formal definition of the phenomenon of collective intelligence and its IQ measure. Future Generation Computing Journal 17 (2001)
10. Szuba, T.: Computational Collective Intelligence. Wiley Series on Parallel and Distributed Computing. Wiley & Sons, Chichester (February 2001)
11. Szuba, T.: Was there Collective Intelligence Before Life on Earth? (Considerations on the Formal Foundations of Intelligence, Life and Evolution). World Futures - The Journal of General Evolution 58(1) (2002)

Enhancing the Computational Collective Intelligence within Communities of Practice Using Trust and Reputation Models

Iulia Maries and Emil Scarlat

University of Economics, Economic Cybernetics Department, 15-17 Dorobanti Avenue,
Sector 1, Bucharest, Romania
iulia.maries@hotmail.com, emil_scarlat@yahoo.com

Abstract. Knowledge assets are a critical resource that can generate a competitive advantage for organizations. Generally, knowledge can be divided in explicit knowledge and tacit knowledge. Organizations focus on managing the explicit knowledge, but also on capturing the tacit knowledge embedded in the individuals' experiences. Through the interactions in social networks, community-based knowledge development has become a very effective tool. In this context, more and more organizations are developing communities of practice as a strategic tool for knowledge development and sharing within the organization and across organizational boundaries. In the last years numerous contributions and approaches pointed out the importance of communities of practice in the knowledge economy. The most relevant argument is that communities of practice are the core of collective learning and collective intelligence, relaying on a permanent exchange of knowledge and information related to the practice. Communities of practice enhance particular knowledge that exist in the organizations and contribute to its coherence. Communities of practice can provide a social reservoir for practitioners, knowledge producers and policy makers to analyze, address and explore new solutions to their problems. These communities are emerging in knowledge-based organizations. They can enhance the efficiency of production and can improve the innovative processes. The paper addresses the new trends and challenges of knowledge dynamics within communities of practice and examines the emergence of this type of communities. We show how computational techniques enhance collective intelligence within communities of practice and suggest a way to model communities' dynamics. The main objective of the paper is to simulate computational collective intelligence using agent-based models.

Keywords: Computational Collective Intelligence, Community of Practice, Trust and Reputation Models, Multi-Agent Systems.

1 Introduction

Knowledge represents a critic asset, the main source of power and competitive advantage in modern organizations. In a global perspective, knowledge represents a dynamic entity that is processed and analyzed through intelligent networks to serve the knowledge society. Knowledge sharing in communities has attracted attention in

N.T. Nguyen and R. Kowalczyk (Eds.): Transactions on CCI III, LNCS 6560, pp. 74–95, 2011.
© Springer-Verlag Berlin Heidelberg 2011

fields like knowledge management or sociology, in both research and practice. Inter-organizational forms of network organizations are more and more accentuated.

A new organizational form has emerged that complements existing structures and emphasizes knowledge sharing and learning, called the community of practice. The concept has received much attention from researchers and practitioners in the management area, especially in knowledge management. Communities of practice are considered important components of the strategies regarding knowledge exchange and innovation processes.

Communities of practice represent social structures suitable for creating, developing and sharing knowledge in organizations and provide an efficient organizational framework for achieving the creative and learning functions of organizations. The organization of the future is that organization which learns to adapt and to benefit from the creative power of project communities, knowledge networks, and open source teams based on free associations of persons passionate about what they do together.

In the context of knowledge-based society, individual intelligence cannot face all the problems. To successfully deal with problems we need to develop collective intelligence as a global civilization. Collective intelligence improves competitiveness within organizations on a global market and leads to collective performance, a critical factor in the organization's development. Thus developing and sustaining collaboration among members within teams is the core that leads to performance.

Collective intelligence include collective perception and discernment, collective memory, collective imagination and intuition, collaborative learning. And self-organizing learning communities like communities of practice are communities which share knowledge.

The remainder of this paper is organized as follows: the concept of community of practice, the emergence and dynamics of such communities are presented in Section 2. Then collective intelligence is defined in the context of communities of practice in Section 3 and Section 4 proposes a selection of computational trust and reputation models is reviewed, on the basis of the concepts of trust and reputation. In Section 5 we present an adapted trust and reputation model. Then agent-based simulations and experiments are introduced in our framework in Section 6. Finally, Section 7 comes up with conclusions, relevant implications and directions for future work.

2 The Emergence and Dynamics of Communities of Practice

Communities of practice are free associations of persons who choose to improve their skills together. Furthermore, they develop new productive collective capabilities, which are sources of value creation in knowledge-based economies. Communities of practice are groups of self-governing people who are challenged to create value by generating knowledge and increasing capabilities.

2.1 About Communities of Practice

The concept "community of practice" was outlined by Lave and Wenger in early 90's, to describe "a group of people who share a concern, a set of problems or a passion about a topic, and who deepen their knowledge and expertise by interacting on an ongoing basis" [33].

Table 1. Key characteristics of communities of practice

• Sustained mutual relationships, both harmonious and conflictual
• Shared ways of engaging in working together
• Knowing what others know and what they can do
• Common background, shared stories
• Certain styles and habits recognized as displaying membership
• Mutually defining identities
• Specific tools, representations and artifacts
• Rapid propagation of innovation
• Absence of introductions, if is not the first interaction
• Quick setup of a problem to be discuss
• Shared repertoire reflecting a certain perspective on the world

Source: Compiled from [33].

Communities of practice can be defined as "groups of people informally bound together by shared expertise and passion for a joint enterprise" [32]. Within communities of practice the individual knowledge and experiences are shared, new knowledge is developed and problems are solved through interactions between members of the communities.

In respect to the above definition, a community of practice is delimited by three dimensions:

• What it is about: the "joint enterprise", as understood and continually renegotiated by its members;
• How it functions: the relationships of "mutual engagement" that bring members together into a social entity;
• What capability it has produced: the "shared repertoire" of communal resources (routines, habits, artifacts, vocabulary, styles) that members have developed over time.

Communities of practice represent "self-organizing and self-governing groups of persons who share a passion for the common domain of what they do and strive to become better practitioners. They create value for their members and stakeholders through developing and spreading new knowledge, productive capabilities and fostering innovation." [24]

2.2 The Emergence Process

The emergence of centralized structures in communities of practice is the result of a self-organizing process. A starting point of the emergence of communities is related to the existence of problems with current solutions or a shared need. The evaluation of relevant knowledge and information, and also of "best practices" related to the practice represents the most important activities in communities of practice. Through these activities, members are able to engage and participate in collective learning process. Therefore, many communities of practice emerge naturally from existing relationships and trustfulness.

In general, individuals do not consider themselves to be part of a community, knowledge sharing taking place in non-hierarchical groups, beyond the formal work description. This phenomenon has been identified as the "emergent communities of practice" [13]. The emergent communities of practice are created by the complexity, diversity and fluidity of the individuals.

"Communities of practice do not usually require heavy institutional infrastructures, but their members do need time and space to collaborate. They do not require much management, but they can use leadership. They self-organize, but they flourish when their learning fits with their organizational environment. The art is to help such communities find resources and connections without overwhelming them with organizational meddling. This need for balance reflects the following paradox: no community can fully design the learning of another; but conversely no community can fully design its own learning." [33]

A community of practice represents "an intrinsic condition for the existence of knowledge" [13]. Learning in communities of practice is not only replicating instances of practice, but also "learning as legitimate peripheral participation". Legitimate peripheral participation means learning as an integral part of practice, learning as "generative social practice in the lived world". Participation represents the key of understanding communities of practice, because they imply participation in an activity about which all participants have a common understanding. Therefore, both the community and the degree of participation in it are inseparable from the practice.

Communities of practice are characterized by the absence of any contractual scheme, agents being able to set the nature of their commitment to the community. The individual expertise underlies the existence of communities of practice, while members are endowed with different experiences. The heterogeneity determines specialization in different fields implied by the personal background of the individuals. The specialization effect shows that each member develops specific knowledge related to his field of enquiry and ignoring other parts. Furthermore, communities often develop specific structures of organization. This implies a differentiation in the roles played by specific members. As a result, each member is endowed with different objectives and motivations. The individuals are also characterized by the deepness of their experience in the community representing the time spent in the community and conditioning the level of knowledge of the practice. The core participants of the community develop common cognitive frames and knowledge. This facilitates coordination among community members, but also restricts the capacity to find solutions to new problems. Original solutions to problems are given by the peripheral members. The process of learning at the boundary is the base of the legitimacy of peripheral members [33].

Communities of practice represent the core of the collective learning and collective invention processes which relies on a constant exchange of knowledge and information. Temporary organizations are motivated to perform specific actions in order to achieve immediate goals. The emergence of such temporary and network-based organizations has determined the creation of communities of practice, which become active temporary in network-based organizations.

2.3   The Dynamics of Communities of Practice

The success of a community depends on the ways of interaction between community members, depends on communication, cooperation, coordination and knowledge exchange, but also depends on certain characteristics of the setting, characteristics of the individuals, characteristics of the community and even characteristics of the environment (Fig. 1). These characteristics are not static; they can change continually, especially in the early phases of a community. In such a dynamic perspective, these characteristics represent conditions for the input and output of the community process. Therefore, a successful community depends on the degree to which the processes mutually match each other.

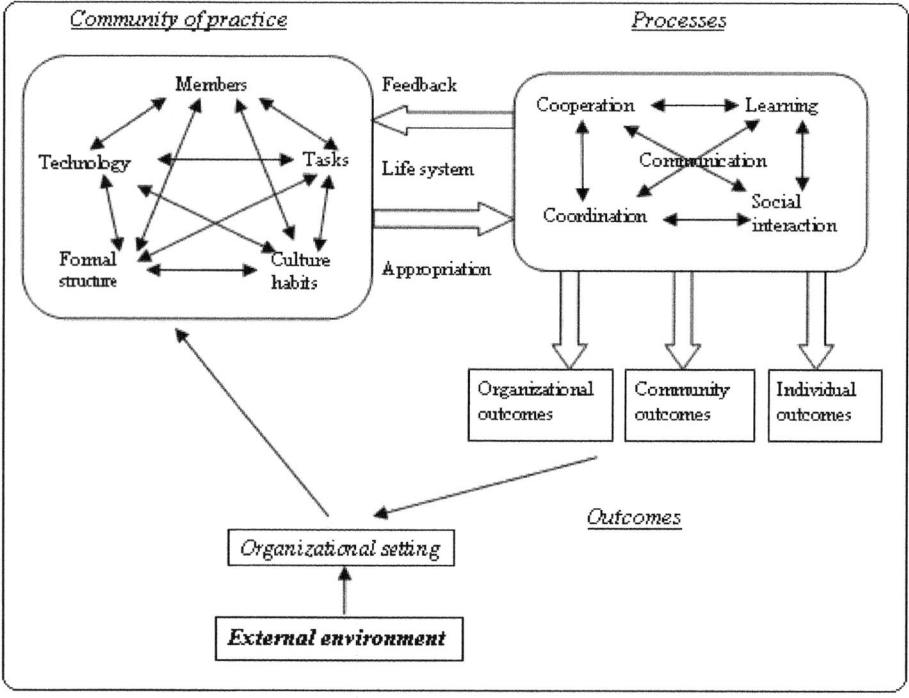

Fig. 1. Dynamic Interaction Model (Source: Adapted from [3])

Communities of practice represent the key for the functioning of any organization, and become critical to those that consider knowledge as a principal asset. An effective organization includes a set of interconnected communities of practice, each of them dealing with specific aspects of the organization competencies. Knowledge is created and shared, organized and revised, and passed on within and among these communities. In this context, collective intelligence represents the capacity of human communities to enable their members to reach the highest potential and to co-evolve toward more complex integrations through collaboration and innovation in mutually supportive relationships.

To describe an agent-based environment for formal modeling of communities of practice, the research in computational organization theory has been used. The computational organization theory is a multidisciplinary field that integrates perspectives from artificial intelligence, organization studies, system dynamics and simulations.

In this framework, a comprehensive interaction model has to fulfill the condition:

- to be a dynamic representation, allowing for change and development over time;
- to have a strong social dimension, whereby members learn, work and interact with others;
- to recognize the existence of general and particular communities of practice associated with particular occupations and organizations.

Symbolic representation and reasoning techniques from research on artificial intelligence are used to develop computational models of theoretical phenomena. Once formalized through a computational model, the symbolic representation can be developed to simulate the dynamics of members' behavior. The empirical validation, reflecting dynamic behavior of organization in communities of practice, determines the results and outcomes of the model to be considered already externally validated and generalized. This approach enables us to integrate qualitative behavior determined by the symbolic models with quantitative dynamics generated through simulations.

Emergent behavior is not attributed to a single individual, but a global result of coordination of individuals. In other words, it is the action of combining simple rules that produces complex results. But the interactions between individuals seem to be the most difficult part to understand. A complex dynamic loop is established when individuals induce behaviors which affect other individuals and their behavior with effect on the initial individual. The complex feedback loop shows the only possible solution: to analyze the emergent phenomena at system level.

As a result, collective intelligence is an emergent phenomenon; it is a synergistic combination of individuals which make the group more capable and intelligent than any individual member.

3   Collective Intelligence

Collective intelligence is a shared intelligence that emerges from the collaboration of individuals. The study of collective intelligence is considered a subfield of sociology, communication or behavior, computer science or cybernetics. The use of new informational technologies should be oriented to collective intelligence field for helping people think, develop and implement ideas collectively.

3.1 Intelligence

"Intelligence is taken here as the ability for attaining goals of for solving problems that puts at work responsiveness of the solver to the situation where the goal or problem arises and use of its previous knowledge and experience." [8]

In this case, intelligence is related to the goal or problem and to the previous knowledge and experience of the solver. But intelligence can be seen from different perspectives: for example, fabricating weapons could be very intelligent from the point of view of a military person, but less intelligent from the point of view of a peace keeper.

3.2 Intelligence of Collectivities

"Collective intelligence is neither a new concept nor a discovery. It is what shapes social organizations – groups, tribes, companies, teams, governments, nations, societies, guilds, etc... - where individuals gather together to share and collaborate, and find an individual and collective advantage that is higher than if each participant had remained alone. Collective intelligence is what we term a positive-sum economy." [23] The presence of collective intelligence has been felt for a long time: families, companies and states are groups of individuals that at least sometimes act intelligent. Bee and ant colonies are examples of groups of insects that are finding food sources acting intelligent. The human brain could be seen as a collection of individual neurons that collectively act intelligent. In the last few years new examples of collective intelligence have been shown up: Google and Wikipedia.

The mathematic measure applied to quantify the collective intelligence is a "collective intelligence quotient". Individual intelligence is evaluated based on external results of behavior during real processes or IQ tests, while elements of collective intelligence, like displacements, actions of beings or exchange of information, can be observed, measured and evaluated. A formal molecular model of computation and mathematical logic for describing the collective intelligence concept has been proposed [28]. The process, random and distributed, is tested in mathematical logics by social structures.

Collective intelligence can be defined as a group ability to solve more problems than its individuals [10]. In order to overcome the individual cognitive limits and the difficulties of coordination, a collective mental map can be used. A collective mental map is represented as an external memory with shared access that can be formalized as a directed graph. The basic mechanism of collective mental map development consists of averaging the individual preferences, amplifying the weak links through positive feedback and integrating specialized sub-networks through division of labor. The efficiency of mental problem-solving depends on the problem representation in the cognitive system. Intelligent agents are characterized by the quality of their mental maps, knowledge and understanding of their environment, capacities for action or goals.

Collective intelligence is trying to offer a new perspective to different phenomena. This concept is trying to suggest another way of thinking about effectiveness, profitability, teamwork or leadership. The formal hierarchies of traditional organizations need to be replaced by self-organizing communities of practice. Why? Because "most fields of expertise are now too complex for any one person to master and thus collective intelligence must be brought to bear to solve important problems".

3.3 Collective Intelligence within Organizations

Collective intelligence has evolved from a "natural collective intelligence", the intelligence developed when the collective has a small number of people, to a "pyramidal collective intelligence", a type of social intelligence developed in the hierarchical mode of social organization. The recent development of the communication technologies has determined an evolution towards a "global collective intelligence", a recreation of natural collective intelligence in groups, collectives and societies, many times bigger [23].

Therefore, the intellectual capital of the organization should be turned into a goal-oriented system, in which the multiple individual competences should be taken into consideration. The base of knowledge management needs to be established by designing an organizational intelligence of inter-connected multiple individual expertise.

Communities of practice exist in any organization. While membership is based on participation not on official status, these communities are not bound by organizational affiliations, and they can span institutional structures and hierarchies. Thus, communities of practice can be found:

• Within businesses: communities of practice arise when people address recurring sets of problems together. So claims processors within an office form communities of practice to deal with the constant flow of information they need to process. By participating in such a communal memory, they can do the job without having to remember everything themselves.

• Across business units: important knowledge is distributed in different business units and people who work in cross-functional teams form communities of practice to keep in touch with their peers in various parts of the company and maintain their expertise.

• Across company boundaries: in some cases, communities of practice become useful by crossing organizational boundaries. For instance, in fast-moving industries, engineers who work for suppliers and buyers may form a community of practice to keep up with constant technological changes.

The key of developing collective intelligence consists of permanent learning on an individual as well as on a collective. Collective intelligence is not an "a priori" condition but "a posteriori" phase, the result of permanent training and learning. Communities of practice structure the learning potential of an organization, both through the knowledge they develop at their core and through the interactions at their boundaries. The core is the center of expertise, but the new insights often arise at the boundary between communities. Therefore, communities of practice truly become organizational assets when their core and their boundaries are active in complementary ways.

People belong to communities of practice in the same way as they belong to other organizational structures. In business units they shape the organization, in teams they take care of the projects, in networks they form relationships. And inside the communities of practice they develop the knowledge that lets them do the other tasks. This informal fabric of communities and shared practices makes the organization effective and profitable.

Inter-organizational formation and utilization of expert knowledge, of social relationships, of knowledge flows are explored through means of social network analysis. The community building represents an effective measure to overcome organizational boundaries and the informal inter-organizational network structures.

4 Trust and Reputation

Computational collective intelligence is a multidisciplinary field that tries to understand human collective intelligence and its augmentation by the means of distributed techniques.

In this context, collective intelligence represents the capacity of human communities to enable their members to reach the highest potential and to co-evolve toward more complex integrations through collaboration and innovation in mutually supportive relationships. Developing and reaching a high level of collective intelligence has become the core that maintains the survival in organizations affected by new technologies and markets.

Communities of practice are relying on the existence of trust relationships among the members. Members have to adapt their behavior to the evolution of the common environment. Thus, trust represents and efficient coordinating device by allowing a certain degree of flexibility in the behaviors. The main characteristic of communities of practice is the specialization of knowledge and tasks between members. In this situation, members interact only with a few other individuals and have a restrictive knowledge of the community as a system.

In this part a selection of computational trust and reputation models will be presented and their main characteristics will be described, clarifying first what the concepts of trust and reputation means in our context. This field is quite recent, but in the last years there have been proposed interesting models with direct implementation in different domains. Then we will propose a mechanism to evaluate the reputation of the members within communities of practice.

4.1 Trust

Trust is important to human society due to its social component. The concept of trust has different meanings, but Gambetta's point of view is the most significant due to its empirical support: "… trust (or, symmetrically, distrust) is a particular level of the subjective probability with which an agent assesses that another agent or group of agents will perform a particular action, both before he can monitor such action (or independently of his capacity ever to be able to monitor it) and in a context in which it affects his own action". [7]

There are significant characteristics of trust mentioned in the above definition:

- trust is subjective;
- trust is related to the actions that cannot be monitored;
- the level of trust is dependent on how our actions are affected by the other agent's actions.

In a socio-cognitive perspective [6], trust represents an explicit reason-based and conscious form. While trust means different things, the concept can be seen as:

- a mental attitude towards another agent, a disposition;
- a decision to rely upon another agent, an intention to delegate and trust;
- a behavior, for example the intentional act of trust and the relation between the trustier and the trustee.

Developing shared communal resources, like styles, vocabulary or artifacts, communities of practice help to create a sense of community that socially binds their members. Trust, empathy and reciprocity bound the relationships among members. They provide behaviors for the knowledge exchange and learning needed to achieve shared goals and to solve problems. The role of trust is complex because sometimes it develops too easily, phenomenon known as hyper-personalization [30]. Hyper-personalization develops when a person offers friendship and support and the other person accepts without questioning or knowing the person.

Communities of practice are relying on the existence of trust relationships among members, mostly due to their commonly evolving environment. Members of the communities have to adapt their behavior to different evolutions. Trust represents the most efficient coordinating tool by allowing a degree of flexibility in their behavior.

The main component of communities of practice is represented by the interactions among agents. While individuals have incomplete information about the other members and their environment, trust plays a central role in facilitating the interactions. In this context, trust can be defined as a subjective probability with which an agent a_1 assesses that another agent a_2 will perform a particular action (adapted from [7]).

In a social manner, trust can evolve from two different perspectives (adapted from [12]):

- An individual perspective – consisted of past experiences of direct interactions between members a_1 and a_2;
- A societal perspective – consisted of observations by the community of past behavior for the member a_2 that are made available to members who have not interacted with a_2 (reputation).

4.2 Reputation

The behavior of a community member can be induced by other members that cooperate, determining a reputation mechanism. The simplest definition of reputation can be the opinion others have of us. Otherwise, reputation represents a perception that a member has of another member's intentions or an expectation about a member's behavior.

Reputation can be defined as an expectation about a community member behavior based on information about or observations of its past behavior [adapted from [1]]. This definition considers reputational information based on member's personal experiences.

4.3 Computational Trust and Reputation Models

In the last few years new approaches have been proposed, with direct implementation in different domains, in order to determine the level of trust.

Marsh has introduced a computational trust model in the distributed artificial intelligence [18]. An artificial agent can absorb trust and then he can make trust-based decisions. This model proposes a representation of trust as a continuous variable over the range [-1, +1). But the model has problems at extreme values and at 0. There are differentiated three types of trust: basic trust (calculated from all agent's experiences), general trust (the trust on another agent without taking into account a specific situation) and situational trust (the trust on another agent taking into account a specific situation). There are proposed three statistical methods to estimate general trust, each determining a different type of agent: the maximum method leads to an optimistic agent (takes the maximum trust value from the experiences he has), the minimum method leads to a pessimistic agent (takes the minimum trust value from the experiences he has) and the mean method that lead to a realistic agent (takes the mean trust value from the experiences he has). Trust values are used in agents' decision whether to cooperate or not with another agent.

Zacharia has proposed two reputation mechanisms (Sporas and Histos) in online communities based on collaborative ratings that an agent receives from others [34]. Sporas takes into consideration only the recent ratings between agents, and users with very high reputation values have smaller rating changes after updates than users with a low reputation. Histos comes as a reply, taking into consideration both direct information and witness information. The reputation value is subjectively assigned by each individual, so reputation mechanisms could generate social changes in users' behavior. A successful mechanism ensures high prediction rates, robustness against manipulability and cooperation incentives of the online community.

Abdul-Rahman and Hailes have suggested a model that allows agents to decide which other agent's opinion they trust more [1]. In their view trust can be observed from two perspectives: as direct trust or as recommender trust. Direct trust can be represented as one of the values: "very trustworthy", "trustworthy", "untrustworthy" or "very untrustworthy". For each partner, the agent has a panel with the number of past experiences in each category, and trust on a partner is given by the degree corresponding to the maximum value in the panel. The model takes into account only the trust coming from a witness, the recommender trust, which is considered "reputation". This approach could not differentiate agents that are lying from those that are telling the truth, but think different, so the model gives more importance to the information coming from agents with similar point of view.

Sabater and Sierra have proposed a modular trust and reputation model (ReGreT) to e-commerce environment [26]. This model takes into consideration three different types of information sources: direct experiences, information from third party agents and social structures. Trust can be determined combining direct experiences with the reputation model. Direct trust is built from direct interactions, using information perceived by the agent itself, and trust is determined from direct experiences. The reputation model is composed of specialized types of reputation: witness reputation (calculated from the reputation coming from witness), neighborhood reputation (calculated from the information regarding social relations between agents) and system reputation (calculated from roles and general properties). Witness reputation is determined based on information from other agents of the community. Neighborhood reputation is expressed based on social environment of the agent and the relations between the agent and that environment. System reputation is considered as objective features of the agent (for example, agent's role in the society). Those components merge and determine a trust model based on direct knowledge and reputation.

5 Trust and Reputation Mechanism in Communities of Practice

The FIRE, coming from "fides" (Latin for "trust") and "reputation", trust and reputation model [12] proposes four main sources that provide trust-related information:

- Direct experiences – member a_1 uses its past experiences in interacting with member a_2; this type of trust is called Interaction Trust.
- Witness information – assuming that members are willing to share their direct experiences, member a_1 collects members' experiences with member a_2; this type of trust is called Witness Reputation.
- Role-based rules – member a_1 can use different relationships with member a_2 or the knowledge about its domain (legislation, norms); this type of trust is called Role-based Trust.
- Third-party references – evaluations produced by members that have interacted with member a_2 certifying its behavior; this type of trust is called Certified Reputation.

The model integrates all four sources of information, being able to provide trust metrics in diverse situations and also to enhance the precision of the trust model. In addition, two assumptions about community members have been made:

Assumption 1: Members are willing to share their experiences with others.
Assumption 2: Members are honest in exchanging information with others.

On the basis of FIRE model, the components determine trust from the information about member a_2 behavior, except the role-based trust component. To capture trust from the information about member a_2, a rating system has been proposed. Ratings are tuples in the form:

$$r = (a_1, a_2, t, i, v) \qquad (1)$$

Where a_1 and a_2 are members participating in the interaction i and v is the rating value member a_1 gave member a_2 for the task t (quality, price, honesty, which represent the outcome of the interaction i).

The rating value v is a variable between [-1, 1], where -1 means absolutely negative, +1 means absolutely positive and 0 means neutral. The ratings will be stored in a local rating database and will be retrieved for trust evaluation or for sharing with other agents.

Trust Value
The trust value of a member is calculated as the weighted mean of interaction trust and role-based trust ratings, and the reputation value as the weighted mean of witness reputation and certified reputation:

$$T(a_1, a_2, t) = \frac{\sum_{r_i \in R_T(a_1, a_2, t)} \omega_T(r_i) \cdot v_i}{\sum_{r_i \in R_T(a_1, a_2, t)} \omega_T(r_i)} \qquad (2)$$

Where $T(a_1, a_2, t)$ is the trust value that member a_1 has in member a_2 with respect to task t, which is calculated by the trust component T (one of the interaction trust or role-based trust), $R_T(a_1, a_2, t)$ is the set of ratings collected by component T for calculating the trust value, $\omega_T(r_i)$ is the rating weight function that calculates the reliability of the rating r_i and v_i is the value of the rating r_i.

The rating weight function ω_T determines the quality of reliability:

Interaction Trust
Interaction trust is composed from direct experiences of a member and models trust resulted from the direct interactions between the members. Member a_1 has to interrogate the database for all the ratings for the member a_2, when the interaction trust value is calculated. The rating weight function for interaction trust has the following form:

$$\omega_I(r_i) = e^{-\frac{\Delta t(r_i)}{\lambda}} \tag{3}$$

Where $\omega_I(r_i)$ is the weight for the rating r_i, $\Delta t(r_i)$ is the time difference between the current time and the time when the rating r_i is recorded and the parameter λ is randomly selected for a particular application depending on the time unit used: for instance, if the time unit is day and the rating for five days earlier needed to be half the effect of the today rating then

$$\lambda = -\frac{5}{\ln(0.5)} \tag{4}$$

Role-based Trust
Role-based trust is resulting from the role-based relationships between two members. In order to determine the role-based trust of member a_2 with respect to task t, the member a_1 has to take the relevant rules from the local rule database, formalized as $R_{RT}(a_1, a_2, t)$. Since the form of a rule is similar to that of a rating, the weight function is calculated as:

$$\omega_R(r_i) = e_i \tag{5}$$

Where $\omega_R(r_i)$ is the weight for the rating r_i and e_i represent the default level of influence of the rule and is a variable between $[0, 1]$.

To summarize, the trust value represents the sum of all the available ratings weighted by the rating reliability and normalized to the range of $[-1, 1]$.

Reputation Value
In the same context, the reputation value of a member is calculated as the weighted mean of witness reputation and certified reputation:

$$R(a_1, a_2, t) = \frac{\sum_{r_i \in R_R(a_1, a_2, t)} \omega_R(r_i) \cdot v_i}{\sum_{r_i \in R_R(a_1, a_2, t)} \omega_R(r_i)} \tag{6}$$

Where $R(a_1, a_2, t)$ is the reputation value that member a_1 has for member a_2 with respect to task t, which is calculated by the reputation component R (one of the witness reputation or certified reputation), $R_R(a_1, a_2, t)$ is the set of ratings collected by component R for calculating the reputation value, $\omega_R(r_i)$ is the rating weight function that calculates the reliability of the rating r_i and v_i is the value of the rating r_i.

Witness Reputation
Witness reputation of member a_2 is built on observations about member's behavior by other agents. Member a_1 needs to find witnesses that have interacted with member a_2

to be able to evaluate the witness reputation. In respect with the assumption that all members are honest, the weight function for witness reputation is similar to the weight function for interaction trust:

$$\omega_W(r_i) = \omega_I(r_i) \tag{7}$$

Certified Reputation

Certified reputation of member a_2 is composed from a number of certified references about member's behavior on particular tasks by other members. The information is stored by member a_2 and is made available to any other member that wishes to evaluate member's trustworthiness for further interactions. Similar to the previous case, the weight function for certified reputation has the same form with the weight function for interaction trust:

$$\omega_C(r_i) = \omega_I(r_i) \tag{8}$$

The reputation value represents the sum of all the available ratings weighted by the rating reliability and normalized to the range of [-1, 1].

An Overall Value

The trust and reputation overall values are given by the following formulas:

$$T_f(a_1, a_2, t) = \frac{\sum_{T\in\{I,R\}} \omega_T \cdot T(a_1,a_2,t)}{\sum_{T\in\{I,R\}} \omega_T} \tag{9}$$

$$R_f(a_1, a_2, t) = \frac{\sum_{R\in\{W,C\}} \omega_R \cdot R(a_1,a_2,t)}{\sum_{R\in\{W,C\}} \omega_R} \tag{10}$$

The FIRE model has been designed and implemented in open multi-agent systems. We have proposed a new approach, an adapted model, in order to determine the level of trust and reputation within communities of practice.

In this context, community members can decide which components to use for trust and reputation evaluation according to the current situation. Since each component produces trust and reputation values from different information sources, combining the components and also the information sources, a higher level of reliability of the trust value will be determined.

6 Evaluation Methodology

A set of experiments and simulations have been designed in order to obtain a formal evaluation of model's performance. The evaluation method is empirical, because trust and reputation are abstract concepts and there is no base for an analytic evaluation. The empirical evaluation allows us to assess the performance of a trust and reputation model in communities of practice based on how much benefit it can bring to its users. Empirical techniques help us to manipulate model's variables, run experiments and simulations, analyze and interpret the results.

In order to evaluate the model we have used hypothesis testing technique. This technique proposes different hypothesis to express intuitions about model's performance under a variety of situations. Then experiments and simulations are run and the results are used in statistical inference to either accept or reject the hypothesis.

Therefore, the performance of the proposed trust and reputation model can be obtained through the difference between the utility of an agent using a trust and reputation model and another one using no trust and reputation model. The performance of an agent, or its utility, is assimilated to the performance of the model. We do not take into consideration other factors that can affect an agent's performance than the trust and reputation model. And by removing these factors, the model is the only differentiating factor in an agent's performance, for instance agents using no trust and reputation model and agents using the trust and reputation model.

Due to the complexity and dynamics of the external environment, there are many factors that can affect model's performance. In order to prevent this, we introduce randomness to evaluate the model. In addition, a community containing 40 agents is evaluated at the same time, in which each agent has a particular situation defined by the environment's randomness. The model is evaluated under a wide range of situations and its performance can be measured as the mean performance of all the agents belonging to the community.

In order to confirm or reject our hypothesis, we compare the performance of agents using the model in comparison to agents using no trust and reputation model and we conduct experiments showing how the model performs with and without a particular component.

6.1 Agents Performance

Usually the trust and reputation models improve their performance through interactions. That is why we need to choose the same test period.

To apply the procedure of hypothesis testing we have to follow certain steps, but first we have to define the variables:

n – The number of interactions chosen for the test period

TRM – The name of the group of agents using the trust and reputation model

N_{TRM} – The number of agents in the group using the trust and reputation model

E_{TRM} – The population mean performance for the agents using the trust and reputation model

μ_{TRM} – The mean performance of a sample of agents using the trust and reputation mode after the n-th interaction

s_{TRM} – The variance of the performance sample of agents using the trust and reputation model

NoTrust – The name of the group of agents using no trust and reputation model

N_{NoTRM} – The number of agents in the group using no trust and reputation model

E_{NoTRM} – The population mean performance for agents using no trust and reputation model

μ_{NoTRM} – The mean performance of a sample of agents using no trust and reputation model after the n-th interaction

s_{NoTRM} – The variance of the performance sample of agents using no trust and reputation model

The first step is to formulate a null hypothesis and an alternative hypothesis, denoted H_0 and H_1:

H_0: $E_{TRM} = E_{NoTRM}$
H_1: $E_{TRM} > E_{NoTRM}$

A sample of performance of agents using the trust and reputation model and another one using no trust and reputation model, in the n-th interaction, is considered and then the mean performance of each group is calculated, denoted μ_{TRM} and μ_{NoTRM}. And N_{TRM} and N_{NoTRM} represent the number of samples in the group of agents using the trust and reputation model and that in the group of agents using no trust and reputation model.

Assuming the null hypothesis is true, that there is no difference between the performance of agents using the trust and reputation model and the performance of agents using no trust and reputation model, the probability of obtaining the sample means μ_{TRM} and μ_{NoTRM} are calculated. This probability is given by the *t-test* function applied to the two samples, determined on the basis of μ_{TRM} and μ_{NoTRM}, N_{TRM} and N_{NoTRM}, and the sample variances of the groups, s_{TRM} and s_{NoTRM}.

If the *t-test* probability is lower than 0.05, the null hypothesis is rejected and the alternative one is accepted. In conclusion, H_1 is true with a confidence level of 95%. This means that the performance of the trust and reputation model is statistically significantly better than the performance of no trust and reputation model.

6.2 Experiments

After an experiment, in the 5-th interaction ($n = 5$), we have obtained the following data:

- TRM Group: $\mu_{TRM} = 7.2856$, $N_{TRM} = 500$, $s_{TRM} = 4368.5219$
- NoTRM Group: $\mu_{NoTRM} = -1.7203$, $N_{NoTRM} = 500$, $s_{NoTRM} = 5217.6327$

Assuming H_0 is true, the probability of obtaining this data given by the two sample *t-test* is 2.95×10^{-2}. In conclusion, the performance of the trust and reputation model is significantly better than in the case of using no trust and reputation model with a confidence level of near 100%.

The hypothesis testing procedure can determine that, at the 5th interaction, the utilization of the trust and reputation model will determine a better utility than using no trust and reputation model. However, it is difficult to establish how quickly the model can achieve that performance level and also whether the model can maintain the same performance level at later interactions.

7 Agent-Based Simulations of Communities of Practice Dynamics

Researchers in artificial intelligence have seen distributed artificial intelligence and multi-agent systems more intelligent than single programs [31]. In this respect, multi-agent systems are used to develop and simulate communities of practice. Agents and multi-agent systems offer new possibilities of analyzing, modeling and implementing the complex systems. An agent-based vision offers a wide range of tools, techniques and paradigms, with a real potential in improving the use of informational technologies.

This section presents how the mechanism by which creative teams self-assemble, determines the structure of collaborative networks. Teams are assembled in order to incorporate individuals with different ideas and opinions, different skills and abilities, different resources. A successful team evolves toward a size large enough to enable specialization and effective division of labor among team members, but also small enough to avoid overwhelming costs of group coordination.

The model is based on three parameters: the number of agents in a team, the probability of a team member to be an incumbent and the tendency of incumbents to repeat previous collaborations. Higher the probability of a team member to be an incumbent is fewer opportunities are for newcomers to enter the network. Thus, the emergence of a large community of practice can be described as a transition phase [9].

A team member can be either a newcomer, an agent with little experience who has not previously participated in any team, or an incumbent, an agent with reputation and experience who has previously participated in a team. The differentiation of agents into newcomers and incumbents determines four possible types of links within a team: newcomer-newcomer, newcomer-incumbent, incumbent-incumbent and repeat incumbent-incumbent. The distribution of different types of links determines team's diversity.

The main objective of this paper is to simulate the collective intelligence capacity using agent-based models and to design a group collaborative system that allows a large group of professionals to make decisions better than a single individual. We will use the NetLogo framework [4] for agent-based modeling to run distributed participatory simulations.

7.1   Team Assembly Model

The team assembly model in NetLogo shows how the behavior of the individuals in assembling small teams for short-term projects determines large-scale network structures over time. Therefore, the team assembly mechanism determines both the structure of the collaboration network and the team performance.

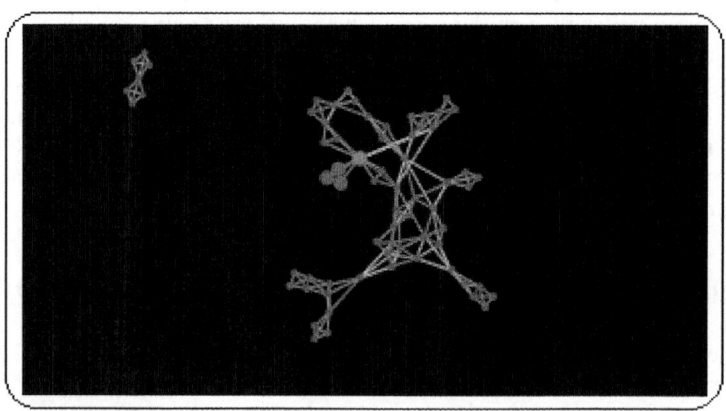

Fig. 2. At each step a new team is assembled and added to the network

The model works with only two parameters: the proportion of the newcomers participating in a team and the propensity for past collaborators to work again with one another. Team size is a constant value between 2 and 10 that can be previously selected. At time zero, team members are newcomers and they become incumbents the first step after being selected in a team. When a team is created all members are linked to one another (Fig. 2). The team members can be either newcomers, or incumbents.

The team assembly model captures basic features of collaboration networks that can influence innovation in creative enterprises. In conclusion, an overabundance of newcomer-newcomer links might indicate that a field is not taking advantage of experienced members, or a multitude of repeated collaborations and incumbent-incumbent links might indicate a lack of in diversity of ideas or experiences.

The main objective of the experiment and the following simulations is to validate and to provide evidence for the "Team assembly" model.

7.2 Simulations

Team size analysis cannot capture the fact that teams are embedded in complex networks. The complex network combines the results of past collaborations with the environment of future collaborations. This network behaves as a repository for the pool of knowledge and the way the agents in the team are embedded in the network affects knowledge accessibility. Therefore, teams formed by agents with large but disparate sets of collaborators can access a more diverse repository of knowledge.

We extended the model by changing the rules so that the number of agents in a team varies random between 2 and 10 (Fig. 3). The links between agents indicate members experience at their most recent time of collaboration: newcomer-newcomer, newcomer-incumbent, incumbent-incumbent or repeated incumbent-incumbent.

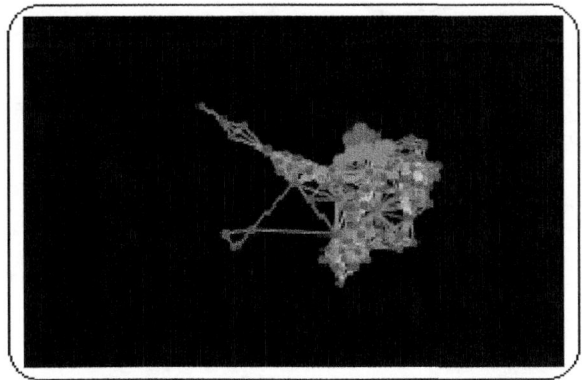

Fig. 3. Team size varies random between 2 and 10

New collaborations among teams naturally tend to the center. Teams or clusters of teams with few connections are naturally isolated. The newcomers always start in the center of the network, while incumbents, could be located in any part of the screen (Fig. 4). Thus, collaborations between newcomers and distant team components tend toward the center, and disconnected clusters are repelled from the centered.

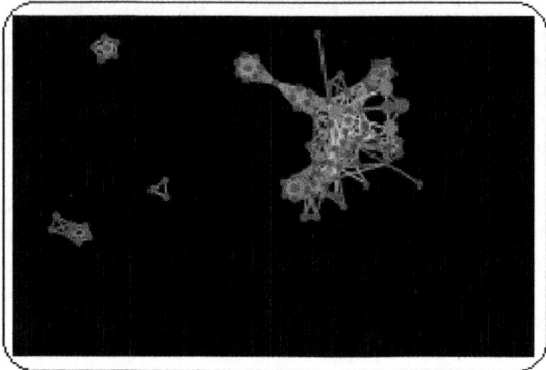

Fig. 4. The newcomers are always in the center of the network, while incumbents can be isolated

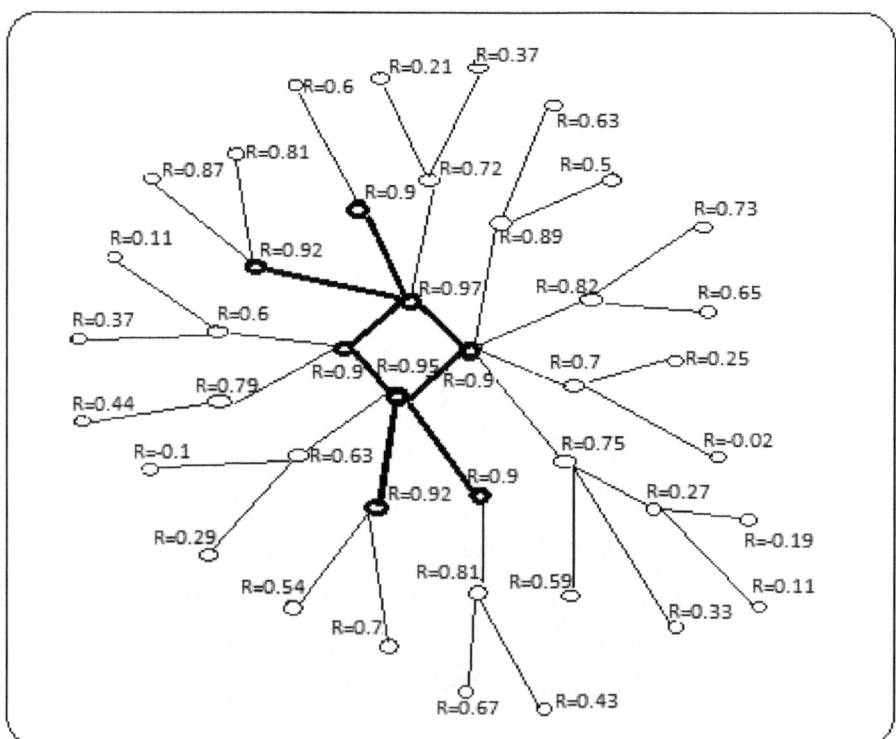

Fig. 5. Reputation values are shown. The maximum reputation value is 1 and the minimum reputation value is -1.

The forthcoming simulations will illustrate agents' behavior assuming that they are endowed with the reputation attribute. This attribute is represented as a variable over the range [-1, 1]. The simulations are averaged over 12 runs.

The reputation of an agent is determined by the number of selections in teams. The more selections an agent has, the reputation value is closer to 1. We can notice that agents prefer to connect to other agents which have a high level of reputation (Fig. 5).

Through participation in a team, agents become part of the complex network. The team assembly mechanism determines the structure of such complex network and the team performance.

8 Conclusions and Future Work

The communities of practice are emerging in knowledge-based organizations. They can enhance the efficiency of production and can improve the innovative processes. In these conditions, both knowledge exchange and knowledge creation processes play an important role. First of all, managers have to understand what the communities of practice are and how they work. Second, we all have to realize that the communities of practice induce knowledge development and define the challenges of the knowledge economy.

Communities of practice are developed around things that matter to people. As a result, their practices reflect the members understanding of what is important. Outside constraints can influence this understanding, but even then, members develop practices that are their own response to these external influences. In this sense, communities of practice are fundamentally self-organizing systems.

To develop the capacities to create and retain knowledge, organizations must understand the process by which learning communities evolve and interact. The role of the communities of practice within organizations is to transfer shared knowledge into organizational knowledge. Organizations of the future are organizations that learn to release the creative power of project communities, knowledge networks, open source teams or new work and learn methods based on free associations of persons passionate about what they do together. In this context, communities of practice represent the center of the innovation movement.

The organizational behavior field is interested in studying organizations as complex social systems. Most of the theories from this field explore individual and collective human behavior within organizations and their central activities try to identify the determinants of intra-organizational cooperation. Managing collective intelligence within an organization implies combining all tools, methods and processes that can lead to connection and cooperation among individual intelligences.

Our research is based on the theoretical approaches presented in the literature, with emphasis on applications in multi-agent systems. The paper indicates how reputation in communities of practice can be evaluated using agent-based models. The simulations explore the complex behavior of individuals in the emergence of collective intelligence within groups. These simulations reveal a need for collaborative systems that allow large group of professionals to make decisions better than single individuals.

Future work in this direction will focus on extending the experiments and simulations in order to establish how quickly the proposed model can achieve a certain performance level and also whether the model can maintain the same performance level at later interactions. Also, we will focus on developing a new model that would lead to an increase on collective intelligence capacity.

Acknowledgement. This article is one of the results of the research activity carried out by the authors under the frame of following projects:

1. PNII - IDEI 810/2008 - "The Development of Theoretical Fundaments of Knowledge Ecosystems and Their Applications on Economy and Healthcare", funded by *CNCSIS –UEFISCSU*, coordinated by Professor Virginia Maracine;
2. "Doctoral Program and Ph.D Students in the education, research and innovation triangle". This project is co-funded by European Social Fund through the Sectorial Operational Programme for Human Resources Development 2007-2013, coordinated by the Academy of Economic Studies, Bucharest.

References

1. Abdul-Rahman, A., Hailes, S.: Supporting Trust in Virtual Communities. In: Proceedings of the Hawaii International Conference on System Sciences, Maui, Hawaii (2000)
2. Ahamed, S.V.: Computational framework for knowledge – Integrated behavior of machines. Wiley, Hoboken (2009)
3. Andriessen, E., Huis, M.: Group dynamics and CoPs. Position paper, ECSCW (2001)
4. Bakshy, E., Wilensky, U.: NetLogo Team Assembly model. Center for Connected Learning and Computer-Based Modeling. Northwestern University, Evanston, IL (2007), http://ccl.northwestern.edu/netlogo/models/TeamAssembly
5. Bedrouni, A., Mittu, R., Boukhtouta, A., Berger, J.: Distributed Intelligent Systems – A coordination perspective. Springer, Heidelberg (2009)
6. Castelfranchi, C., Falcone, R.: Principles of Trust for MAS: Cognitive Anatomy, Social Importance, and Quantification. In: Proceedings of the 3rd International Conference on Multi-Agent Systems (1998)
7. Gambetta, D.: Can We Trust Trust? In: Trust: Making and Breaking Cooperative Relations, ch. 13, pp. 213–237. University of Oxford (2000), http://www.sociology.ox.ac.uk/papers/gambetta213-237.pdf
8. Garrido, P.: Business Sustainability and Collective Intelligence. The Learning Organization 16(3), 208–222 (2009)
9. Guimera, R., Uzzi, B., Spiro, J., Amaral, L.A.N.: Team Assembly Mechanisms Determine Collaboration Network Structure and Team Performance. Science 308(5722), 697–720 (2005)
10. Heylighen, F.: Collective Intelligence and its Implementation on the Web: algorithms to develop a collective mental map. Springer, Netherlands (1999)
11. Hildreth, P., Kimble, C., Wright, P.: Communities of practice in the distributed international environment. Journal of Knowledge Management 4(1), 27–38 (2000)
12. Huynh, T.D., Jennings, N.R., Shadbolt, N.R.: An integrated trust and reputation model for open multi-agent systems. In: Springer Autonomous Agent and Multi-Agent Systems, vol. 13, pp. 119–154 (2006)
13. Juriado, R., Gustafsson, N.: Emergent communities of practice in temporary inter-organizational partnerships. The Learning Organization: The International Journal of Knowledge and Organizational Learning Management 14(1), 50–61 (2007)
14. Lave, J., Wenger, E.: Situated Learning. Legitimate Peripheral Participation. Cambridge University Press, Cambridge (1991)
15. Lévy, P.: Opening the semantic space in the service of collective intelligence. Elect. J. Commun. Inf. Innov. Health (1), 127–137 (2007)

16. Liebowitz, J.: The quick basics of knowledge management. In: Liebowitz, J., Schieber, A.R., Andreadis, J.D. (eds.). CRC Press, Boca Raton (2010)
17. Luck, M., McBurney, P., Preist, C.: Agent Technology: Enabling Next Generation Computing – A Roadmap for Agent Based Computing. Agent Link (2003) ISBN 0854 327886
18. Marsh, S.P.: Formalizing Trust as a Computational Concept. PhD Thesis, Department of Computing Science and Mathematics. University of Stirling (1994)
19. Muller, P.: Reputation, trust and the dynamics of leadership in communities of practice. J. Manage. Governance (2006)
20. Nissen, M.E.: An extended model of knowledge flow dynamics. Communications of the Association for Information System 8, 251–266 (2002)
21. Nissen, M.E., Levitt, R.E.: Agent-based modeling of knowledge flows: Illustration from the domain of information system design. In: Proceedings of 37th Hawaii International Conference on System Sciences (2004)
22. Nonaka, I., Toyama, R., Hirata, T.: Managing flow – A process theory of the knowledge-based firm. Palgrave Macmillan, Hampshire (2008)
23. Noubel, J. F.: Collective intelligence, the invisible revolution. The Transitioner.org (2004), http://www.thetransitioner.org/wen/tiki-list_file_gallery.php?galleryId=1
24. Por, G., van Bukkum, E.: Liberating the Innovation Value of Communities of Practice, Amsterdam (2004)
25. Rutkowski, L.: Computational intelligence – Methods and techniques. Springer, Heidelberg (2008)
26. Sabater-Mir, J., Sierra, C.: REGRET: A Reputation Model for Gregarious Societies (2001)
27. Scarlat, E., Maries, I.: Towards an Increase of Collective Intelligence within Organizations using Trust and Reputation Models. In: Nguyen, N.T., Kowalczyk, R., Chen, S.-M. (eds.) ICCCI 2009. LNCS (LNAI), vol. 5796, pp. 140–151. Springer, Heidelberg (2009) ISSN 0302-9743
28. Szuba, T., Almulla, M.: Was Collective Intelligence before Life on Earth? In: Rolim, J.D.P. (ed.) IPDPS-WS 2000. LNCS, vol. 1800, p. 586. Springer, Heidelberg (2000)
29. Turoff, M., Hiltz, S.R.: The Future of Professional Communities of Practice. LNBIP, vol. 22. Springer, Heidelberg (2009)
30. Walthur, J.B.: Computer-Mediated Communication: Impersonal, Interpersonal and Hyperpersonal Interaction. Communication Research 23(1), 3–43 (1996)
31. Weiss, G.: Prologue – Multiagent Systems and Distributed Artificial Intelligence. In: Multiagent Systems, A Modern Approach to Distributed Modern Approach to Artificial Intelligence, pp. 1–24. The MIT Press, Cambridge (1999)
32. Wenger, E.C., Snyder, W.M.: Communities of practice: the organizational frontier. Harvard Business Review 78(1), 139–145 (2000)
33. Wenger, E., McDermott, R.A., Snyder, W.: Cultivating Communities of Practice: A Guide to Managing Knowledge. Harvard Business School Press, Boston (2002)
34. Zacharia, G.: Collaborative Reputation Mechanisms for Online Communities. Master Thesis, Massachusetts Institute of Technology (1999)
35. Zhang, W., Watts, S.: Online communities as communities of practice: a case study. Journal of Knowledge Management 12(4), 55–71 (2008) ISSN 1367-3270

Loki – Semantic Wiki with Logical Knowledge Representation*

Grzegorz J. Nalepa

Institute of Automatics,
AGH University of Science and Technology,
Al. Mickiewicza 30, 30-059 Kraków, Poland
gjn@agh.edu.pl

Abstract. To fulfill its ambitious promises, Semantic Web needs practical and accessible tools for collective knowledge engineering. Recent developments in the area of semantic wikis show how such tools can be built. However, existing semantic wikis implementations have both conceptual and technological limitations. These limitations are in the areas of knowledge representation, strong reasoning as well as appropriate user interfaces. In this paper a proposal of a new semantic wiki is presented. *Loki* uses a coherent logic-based representation for semantic annotations of the content. The same representation is used for implementing reasoning procedures. The representation uses the logic programming paradigm and the Prolog programming language. The proposed architecture allows for rule-based reasoning in the wiki. It also provides a compatibility layer with the popular Semantic MediaWiki (SMW) platform, directly parsing its annotations. In the paper a prototype implementation called PlWiki is described, and a practical use case is given.[1]

1 Introduction

The Internet has been evolving from a network that stores and massively links human readable information to an information system where machine readable content can be processed by intelligent agents supporting humans in their information interpretation task. The vision of the Semantic Web [2,3] promises interoperable web services that are able to automatically process structured data and perform simple inference tasks. To implement such an architecture the Semantic Web initiative proposed the Semantic Web stack. This layered architecture provided number of data structurization languages such as XML [4], as well as knowledge representation languages of different expressiveness e.g. RDF [5], RDFS [6], and OWL [7], as well as query languages including SPARQL [8]. The new version of OWL [9] supports different perspectives on ontology development with OWL 2 profiles [10]. Current efforts are focused on providing a rule layer

---

* The paper is supported by the *BIMLOQ* Project funded from 2010–2012 resources for science as a research project.

[1] This paper is partially based on the results presented in the paper [1] presented at the ICCCI conference in Wrocław in 2010.

N.T. Nguyen and R. Kowalczyk (Eds.): Transactions on CCI III, LNCS 6560, pp. 96–114, 2011.
© Springer-Verlag Berlin Heidelberg 2011

combined with ontologies. While some different solutions exist, e.g. SWRL [11], or DLP [12], so far they have not been able to overcome all of the challenges [13] of the rules and description logics [14] integration. These methods and technologies, combined with the collective nature of the Web, aim for providing solutions for massively distributed content and knowledge engineering.

To fulfil these promises one needs not just methods and languages, but engineering solutions, practically applicable for a wide number of users, not only experts. So there is a growing pressure for the Semantic Web development to focus on usable tools, not only on conceptual inventions. Recently the so-called semantic wikis proved to be an effective Semantic Web application meeting some of the most important requirements for collective knowledge engineering and querying on the Web. In fact the technology is young and evolving, with number of new solutions being developed and old ones disappearing. Apparently some of the main aspects of the semantic wikis evolution and development are effective and intuitive user interfaces, that help in using the semantic content, expressive knowledge representation [15], as well as reasoning and inference [16]. Even though there has been a rapid development in these areas in recent years, the technology still needs to address its current limitations in these areas to become a successful collective knowledge engineering solution.

The main contribution of this paper is a proposal of a new semantic wiki architecture. It uses a strong, logic-based representation for knowledge processing in the wiki. Such an approach allows for expressive knowledge engineering including decision rules. As the low-level knowledge representation language Prolog is used. However, a dedicated rule engine supporting decision tables and trees is also provided. In the paper a proof of concept implementation of this idea is discussed using an example.

In the rest of the paper the semantic wikis technology is described in Sect. 2. Then, the drawbacks of the current solutions, as well as development trends give motivation for the research as presented in Sect. 3. The proposal of *Loki*, a wiki based on a logical knowledge representation, is introduced in Sect. 4. The system has a prototype implementation called PlWiki presented in Sect. 5. The evaluation of the approach is given in Sect. 6. Directions for the future development and the summary of the paper are contained in the final section.

2 Semantic Wikis Technology

2.1 Wiki Systems

A wiki can be simply described as a collection of linked webpages Wikis appeared in the mid 90s to provide a conceptually simple tool for massively collaborative knowledge sharing and social communication. Some important features of wiki include: remote editing using a basic web browser, simplified text-based syntax for describing context (wikitext), rollback mechanism, thanks to built in versioning, diversified linking mechanism (including internal, interwiki, and external links), access control mechanisms (from simple ones, to regular ACL (Access Control Lists) solutions.) A comprehensive comparison of different wiki systems can be found on http://www.wikimatrix.org.

While wiki systems provide an abstract representation of the content they store, as well as standard searching capabilities, they lack facilities helping in expressing the semantics of the stored content.[2] This is especially important in the case of collaborative systems, where number of users work together on the content. This is why wikis became one of the main applications and testing areas for the Semantic Web technologies.

2.2   Semantic Wikis

The so-called *semantic wikis* enrich standard wikis with the semantic information expressed by a number of mechanisms. Some basic questions every semantic wiki needs to address are [17]: 1) how to annotate content?, 2) how to formally represent content?, 3) how to navigate content?. In last several years multiple implementations of semantic wikis have been developed, including IkeWiki [18], OntoWiki [19], SemanticMediaWiki [20], SemperWiki [21], SweetWiki [22], and AceWiki [23].

In general, in these systems the standard wikitext is extended with semantic annotations. These include relations (represented as RDF triples) and categories (here RDFS is needed). It is possible to query the semantic knowledge, thus providing dynamic wiki pages (e.g. with the use of SPARQL). Some of the systems also allow for building an OWL ontology of the domain to which the content of the wiki is related. This extension introduces not just new content engineering possibilities, but also semantic search and analysis of the content.

The summary of semantic wiki systems is available[3], some of them are in the development stage, while others have been discontinued.Selected implementations are briefly characterized. IkeWiki [18] was one of the first semantic wikis with powerful features. The Java-based systems offered semantic annotations with RDF and OWL support, with OWL-RDFS reasoning. It had introduced simple ontology editing in the wiki with certain visualization techniques. OntoWiki [19] provided improved visualization of the ontological content and more advanced collaborative editing features. SemperWiki [21] used advanced semantic annotations with explicit differentiation of documents and concepts. SweetWiki [22] was based on the CORESE engine (an RDF engine based on Conceptual Graphs (CG)) and used ontology-based model for wiki organization.

When it comes to active implementations, one of the most popular is Semantic MediaWiki [20] (SMW). It is built on top of the MediaWiki engine, and extends it with lightweight semantic annotations and simple querying facilities. AceWiki [23] uses Attempto Controlled English (ACE) for natural language processing in the wiki. A recent FP7 project Kiwi (http://www.kiwi-project.eu) aims at providing a collaborative knowledge management based on semantic

---

[2] Besides simple tagging mechanisms, that can later be used to create the so-called *folksonomies*.

[3] See http://semanticweb.org/wiki/Semantic_Wiki_State_Of_The_Art

wikis (it is the continuation of IkeWiki effort) [24]. It can be observed that from the knowledge engineering point of view, expressing semantics (i.e. representing knowledge) is not enough. In fact a knowledge-based system should provide both effective knowledge representation and processing methods. In order to extend semantic wikis to knowledge-based systems, ideas to use rule-based reasoning and problem-solving knowledge have been introduced. An example of such a system is the *KnowWE* semantic wiki [25,26]. The system allows for introducing knowledge expressed with decision rules and trees related to the domain ontology. A research aiming at the analysis of social collaborations in such systems is also active [27,28]. Number of new solutions use the so-called Web 2.0 tools and methods to enrich knowledge acquisition and management, e. g. see [29,30].

2.3   Wiki Feature Matrix

A new matrix can help to simplify the selection of a semantic wiki system for a given work task has been introduced by Baumeister in [31]. Main motivation for it was the extension and specialization of the matrix[4] used by the semantic wiki community to track the recent developments of semantic wiki features. That matrix lists number of features such as *editing paradigm, annotation mechanism, programming language* and *license*. However, this categorization seems too general for systems using expressive knowledge formalizations. Therefore, in [31] a supplementary set of feature categories has been proposed. These include:

- Targeted applications, e.g. Community-based ontology engineering, E-learning.
- Underlying knowledge representation, w.r.t.
  - Subject granularity (One/multiple concepts/properties for each wiki page),
  - Knowledge representation language (RDF(S), OWL, other),
  - Additional knowledge sources (SWRL rules, Prolog rules, Model-based knowledge, Text in controlled language),
  - UI for knowledge capture and sharing,
    * Knowledge editing paradigm: e.g. Inline text markup, Semantic forms/ visual editors,
    * Semantic search/knowledge retrieval: Used query language (SPARQL, Datalog-like queries), Query integration (Special-purpose forms, queries embedded into the wiki article), Further capabilities of knowledge use (Generated knowledge-based interviews, Prolog queries).
    * Semantic navigation (Extended links within wiki article, Generation of fact sheets)
  - Connectivity, Import/export facilities (e.g. RFS(S)/OWL, SWRL, RIF),
- Extensibility, including Extension mechanism (e.g. Plug-in mechanism, Code-in mechanism), and Existing extensions/modifications.

This categorization aims at capturing the conceptual properties of semantic wikis. Hopefully it will be adapted (possibly in a modified form) by the community. The features of KnowWe have been summarized in the matrix in [31]. In this work the matrix will be used to summarize the solution proposed herein.

---

[4] http://semanticweb.org/wiki/Semantic_Wiki_State_Of_The_Art

3   Motivation

The semantic wikis technology has been rapidly developing. The growing number of practical applications and regular users helps developers in getting feedback useful in development. New applications also reveal limitations of the existing technology and expose persistent challenges facing it. Some of the main areas of possible improvement include:

1. *user interface*, that allows for effective visualization of the semantically enriched content and supports its customization. It should also help in navigating in the wiki.
2. *knowledge representation*, which should be rich enough to be able to express explicit knowledge of different classes, including rules, but also decision trees and tables.
3. *reasoning* should be stronger than simple classification tasks, possibly rule-based, able to infer new facts and provide answers for complex queries.

Research presented in this paper addresses two of the above areas, namely knowledge representation and reasoning.

The principal idea consists in representing the semantic annotations in a formalized way, and simultaneously enriching them with an expressive rule-based knowledge representation. Semantic annotations should use standard solutions, such as RDF, and RDFS and possibly OWL for ontologies of concepts. Such a knowledge base should be homogeneous from the logical point of view, in order to allow strong reasoning support. The knowledge base is coupled with the contents of the wiki. Moreover, the basic wiki engine is integrated with an inference engine. Practical implementation of these concepts should provide backwards compatibility with important existing semantic wiki implementations. In the next section the design of a wiki system following these principles is given. Then a prototype implementation is described.

4   Loki Proposal

Logic-based Wiki, or *Loki* for short, uses the logic programming paradigm to represent knowledge in the wiki, including semantic annotations and rules.[5] The main design principles are as follows:

- provide an expressive underlying logical representation for semantic annotations and rules,
- allow for strong reasoning support in the wiki,
- preserve backward compatibility with existing wikis, namely SMW.

The design has been based on the use of the Prolog programming language.

---

[5] While the solution presented here allows for processing both ontological information, as well as rules, it does not address directly the well-known problems related to possible integration scenarios of ontologies and rules, for example see [13,32,33].

Prolog [34,35] is an expressive logic programming language. The Prolog system uses a knowledge base to answer queries. From a logical point of view, the knowledge base is composed of Horn clauses and a goal (so in fact it is a subset of First Order Predicate Logic). In Prolog two basic forms of statements are possible: facts and rules. While the default inference strategy is backward-chaining it is trivial to built custom meta-interpreters implementing any inference strategy. While Prolog has been traditionally related to Artificial Intelligence [36], it is a mature and universal programming language. Number of powerful implementations are currently available, e.g. SWI-Prolog[6]. It is a mature implementation widely used in research and education as well as for commercial applications. It provides a fast and scalable development environment, including graphics, libraries and interface packages, portable to many platforms, including Unix/Linux platforms, Windows, and MacOS X. SWI-Prolog provides a rich set of libraries, including the *semweb* library for dealing with standards from the W3C standard for the Semantic Web (RDF, RDFS and OWL). This infrastructure is modular, consisting of Prolog packages for reading, querying and storing Semantic Web documents. Additional modules also support TCP/IP networking and XML parsing. The SWI-Prolog environment is licensed under the LGPL.

To build Loki using Prolog several problems has been solved, namely:

- Prolog representation for the Semantic annotations of SMW,
- RDF and OWL support in Prolog,
- integration of the Prolog engine and a wiki engine,
- support for an expressive knowledge representation with decision tables and decision trees.

The solutions addressing these issues are described in the following subsections.

4.1 SMW Support in Loki

There are three main methods of semantic annotations in SMW [37]:

- categories – a simple form of annotation that allows users to classify pages. To state that article (Wiki page) belongs to the Category `Category1` one has to write `[[Category:Category1]]` within the article.
- relations – there is a possibility to describe relationships between two Wiki pages by assigning annotations to existing links. For example there is a relation `capital_of` between Warsaw and Poland. To express this one has edit the page Warsaw and add `[[capital_of::Poland]]` within the page content.
- attributes – allow to specify relationships of Wiki pages to things that are not Wiki pages. For example, one can state that Wiki page `Page1` was created at April 22 2009 by writing `[[created:=April 22 2009]]`.

Annotations are usually not shown at the place where they are inserted. Category links appear only at the bottom of a page, relations are displayed like normal

---

[6] See `http://www.swi-prolog.org`

links, and attributes just show the given value. A factbox at the bottom of each page enables users to view all extracted annotations, but the main text remains undisturbed (see Fig. 1). After making annotations a factbox is displayed in each article, and this factbox also features quicklinks for browsing and searching. In addition to this users can search for articles using a simple query language that was developed based on the known syntax of the Wiki. For example to display city which is capital of Poland following code may be used:

```
{{#ask: [[Category:city]] [[capital of::Poland]]}}
```

The query functionality of Semantic MediaWiki can be used to embed dynamic content into pages, which is a major advantage over traditional wikis. Several other forms of queries can be found in the online documentation.

Fig. 1. Annotations in Semantic MediaWiki

Loki allows to describe categories, relations and attributes the same way as in SMW. They are represented by appropriate Prolog terms. Examples are as follows, with the SMW syntax gives first, and the corresponding Prolog representation below.

```
[[category:cities]] Warsaw is in Poland.
    wiki_category('cities,'warsaw').

Warsaw is [[capital_of::Poland]].
    wiki_relation('subject_page_uri','capital_of','poland').

[[created:=April 22 2009]]
    wiki_attribute('subject_page_uri','created','pril 22 2009').
```

Loki also provides a direct support for RDF and OWL.

4.2   RDF and OWL Support

Plain RDF annotations are supported and separated from the explicit annotations mentioned above. For compatibility reasons, an RDF annotation can be embedded directly in the XML serialization, then it is parsed by the corresponding Prolog library, and turned to the internal representation, that can also be used directly. Using the *semweb/rdf_db* library SWI-Prolog's represents RDF triples simply as:

```
rdf(?Subject, ?Predicate, ?Object).
```

So mapping the above example would result in:

```
rdf('Warsaw',capital_of,'Poland').
```

RDFS is also supported by the *semweb/rdfs* library, e.g.:

```
rdfs_individual_of('Warsaw',cities).
```

SPARQL queries are handled by the *semweb/sparql_client* The SWI-Prolog RDF storage in highly optimized. It can be integrated with the provided RDFS and OWL layers, as well as with the *ClioPatria* platform[7] that provides SPARQL queries support. SWI-Prolog supports OWL using the Thea [38] library. It is an experimental feature, currently being evaluated.

4.3   Prolog Reasoning

Thanks to the full Prolog engine available in the wiki, the inference options are almost unlimited. Prolog uses backwards chaining with program clauses. However, it is very easy to implement meta-interpreters for forward chaining.

A simple clause finding recently created pages might be as follows:

```
recent_pages(Today,Page) :-
    wiki_attribut(Page,created,date(D,'May',2010)),
    I is Today - D,
    I < 7.
```

Compound queries can also be created easily and executed as Prolog predicates.

One should keep in mind, that the Prolog-based representation is quite close to the natural language. Not only on the semantical level, but to a degree also on the syntactic level. It is possible thanks to the operator redefinition. A simple example might be as follows:

```
:- op(100,xfy,is_capital_of).
```

```
'Warsaw' is_capital_of 'Poland'.
```

The first line defines a new infix operator, that is use to construct a fact in the second line. Such an approach is close to controlled languages such as Attempto [39] used in Ace Wiki mentioned in Sect. 2. However, it is not used in the current implementation of Loki.

---

[7] See http://e-culture.multimedian.nl/software/ClioPatria.shtml

4.4   Rule-Based Reasoning

An optional decision rule layer is also considered with the use of the HeaRT [40] runtime for the XTT2 framework [41,42,43]. XTT2 (*eXtended Tabular Trees v2*) knowledge representation incorporates attributive table format. Similar rules are grouped within separated tables, and the system is split into a network of such tables representing the inference flow – this compromises the visual representation of XTT2. Efficient inference is assured thanks to firing only rules necessary for achieving the goal. It is achieved by selecting the desired output tables and identifying the tables necessary to be fired first. The links representing the partial order assure that when passing from one table to another one, the latter can be fired since the former one prepares an appropriate context knowledge [43,40].

The visual representation is automatically transformed into HMR (HeKatE Meta Representation), a corresponding textual algebraic notation, suitable for direct execution by the rule engine. An example excerpt of HMR is:

```
<hmr>
xschm th: [today,hour] ==> [operation].
xrule th/1:
   [today eq workday, hour gt 17] ==>
   [operation set not_bizhours].
xrule th/4:
   [today eq workday, hour  in [9 to 17]] ==>
   [operation set bizhours].
</hmr>
```

The first line defines an XTT2 table scheme, or header, defining all of the attributes used in the table. Its semantics is as follows: "the XTT table *th* has two conditional attributes: *today* and *hour* and one decision attribute: *operation*". Then two examples of rules are given. The second rule can be read as: "Rule with ID *4* in the XTT table called *th*: if value of the attribute *today* equals ($=$) value *workday* and the value of the attribute *hour* belongs to the range ($\in$) $< 9, 17 >$ then set the value of the attribute *operation* to the value *bizhours*". The code is embedded into the wikitext using the hmr tags.

HeKatE RunTime (HeaRT) is a dedicated inference engine for the XTT2 rule bases [40]. The engine is highly modularized. It is composed of the main *inference module* based on ALSV(FD) logic [42,43]. A proposal of integrating ALSV(FD) with Description logics has been given in [44]. It supports four types of inference process, Data and Goal Driven, Fixed Order, and Token Driven [43]. The engine is implemented in Prolog, using the SWI-Prolog stack. The main HMR parser is heavily based on the Prolog operator redefinition [34]. A dedicated forward and backward chaining meta interpreter is provided, implementing custom rule inference modes.

Following scenarios for rules embedding are considered including: 1) single table for single wiki page, and 2) rules working in the same content present in multiple pages in the same namespace. Rules are extracted by Loki parser and concatenated into a single HMR file corresponding to a wikipage or namespace.

4.5   Loki Architecture

Considering featured mentioned above, the following Loki architecture is given (observe Fig. 2). The wikitext from the regular wiki contains basic semantic annotations as in SMW. Additionally it contains Prolog code and HMR rules. These are separated by the Loki engine and combined into a Loki knowledge base. The main engine is integrated with the HeaRT interpreter. It also supports querying the knowledge base using both generic Prolog queries, as well as SPARQL. This architecture has been partially implemented with a proof-of-concept prototype called PlWiki described in the next section.

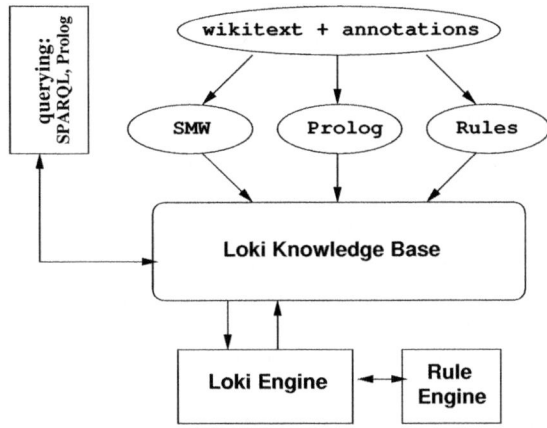

Fig. 2. Loki architecture

5   Prototype Implementation

A prototype implementation of the Loki architecture has been developed. The system is called PlWiki [1,45]. The main goal of the system design is to deliver a generic and flexible solution.

There are tens of wiki engines available. Most of them are similar w.r.t to main concepts and features. However, there are number of differences when it comes to the wikitext syntax, implementation and runtime environment, as well as extra features. This is why, instead of building yet another wiki engine, or modify an existing one, another solution is proposed. The idea is to use a ready, flexible and extensible wiki engine, that could be optionally extended with knowledge representation and processing capabilities. So instead of modifying an existing wiki engine or implementing a new one, a development of an extension of the DokuWiki[8] system was chosen.

DokuWiki is designed to be portable, easy to use and set up. Like number of other solutions DokuWiki is based on PHP. However, it does not require any

---

[8] See www.dokuwiki.org

relational database back-end. It allows for image embedding, and file upload and download. Pages can be arranged into namespaces which act as a tree-like hierarchy similar to directory structure. Its modularized architecture allows the user to extend DokuWiki with plugins which provide additional syntax and functionality. A large number of plugins for DokuWiki is available. The templates mechanism provides an easy way to change the presentation layer of the wiki.

To provide a rich knowledge representation and reasoning for the Semantic Web, the SWI-Prolog environment was selected. The basic idea is to build a layered knowledge wiki architecture, where the expressive Prolog representation is used on the lowest knowledge level. This representation is embedded within the wiki text as an optional extension. On top of it number of layers are provided. These include standard meta-data descriptions with RDF and ontologies specification solutions with RDFS and OWL.

5.1 PlWiki Architecture

The PlWiki architecture can be observed in Fig. 3. The stack is based on a simple runtime including the Unix environment with the Unix filesystem, the Apache web server and the PHP stack. Using this runtime the standard DokuWiki installation is run. The PlWiki functionality is implemented with the use of an optional plugin allowing to enrich the wikitext with Prolog clauses, as well run the SWI-Prolog interpreter. It is also possible to extend the wikitext with explicit semantic information encoded with the use of RDF and possibly OWL representation. This layer uses the Semantic Web library provided by SWI-Prolog.

DokuWiki provides a flexible plugin system, providing several kinds of plugins. These include: *Syntax Plugins*, extending the wikitext syntax, *Action Plugins*, redefining selected core wiki operations, (e.g. saving wikipages), and *Renderer Plugins*, allowing to create new export modes (possibly replacing the standard XHTML renderer) (Admin and Action and Helper Plugins are not mentioned here.) The current version of PlWiki implements both the *Syntax* and *Renderer* functionality. Text-based wikipages are fed to a lexical analyzer (Lexer) which identifies the special wiki markup. The standard DokuWiki markup is extended by a special <pl>...</pl> markup that contains Prolog clauses. The stream of tokens is then passed to the Helper that transforms it to special renderer instructions that are parsed by the Parser. The final stage is the Renderer, responsible for creating a client-visible output (e.g. XHTML). In this stage the second part of the plugin is used for running the Prolog interpreter.

The detailed functionality of the PlWiki Syntax Plugin includes parsing the Prolog code embedded in the wikitext, and generating the knowledge base composed of files containing the Prolog code, where each wikipage has a corresponding file in the knowledge base. The PlWiki Renderer plugin is responsible for executing the Prolog interpreter with a given goal, and rendering the results via the standard DokuWiki mechanism.

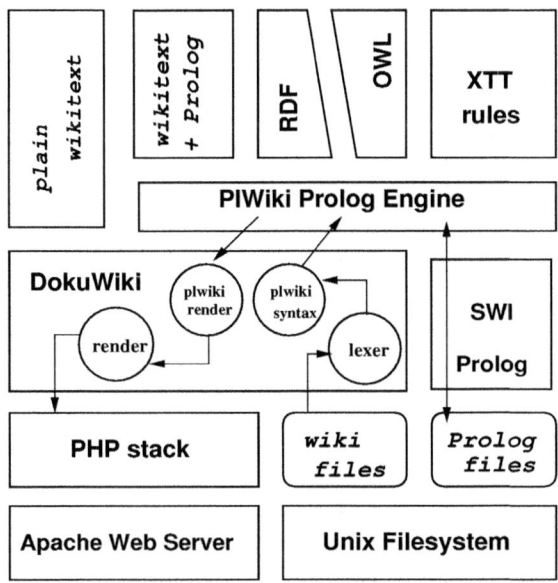

Fig. 3. PlWiki Architecture

There are several options how to analyze the wiki knowledge base (that is Prolog files built and extracted from wiki pages). A basic approach is to combine all clauses. More advanced uses allow to select pages (e.g. given namespace) that are to be analyzed.

On top of the basic Prolog syntax, SMW semantic enhancements are also used. They are directly mapped to Prolog clauses.[9]

5.2 PlWiki in Use

As mentioned previously, PlWiki can directly interpret the SMW syntax. More-over, it allows for embedding any Prolog code, providing more expressive knowl-edge. To do so, a special markup is used, as shown below:

```
<pl>
    capital(poland,warsaw).
    country(poland).
    country(germany).
</pl>
```

This simple statement adds two facts to the knowledge base. The plugin invo-cation is performed using the predefined syntax. To actually specify the goal (query) for the interpreter the following syntax is used:

---

[9] Currently the PlWiki system is under development. See `http://prolog.ia.agh.edu.pl/kwikis/plwiki` user: iccci, password: PlWiki.

```
<pl goal="coutry(X),write(X),nl,fail"></pl>
```

It is possible to combine these two, as follows:

```
<pl goal="country(X),write(X),nl,fail">
    country(france).
    country(spain).
</pl>
```

It is possible to specify a given *scope* of the query (in terms of wiki namespaces):

```
<pl goal="country(X),write(X),nl,fail"
    scope="prolog:examples">
</pl>
```

A bidirectional interface, allowing to query the wiki contents from the Prolog code is also available, e.g.:

```
<pl goal="consult('lib/plugins/prolog/plwiki.pl'),
    wikiconsult('plwiki/pluginapi'),list.">
</pl>
```

These features are presented on an extended example in the next section.

5.3   PlWiki Example

Consider an enhanced bookstore system based on PlWiki, including recommendation mechanism, which informs customer about suggested books [46]. There are four page types:

- genre in bookstore:genre namespace,
- publisher in bookstore:publisher namespace,
- author in bookstore:author namespace,
- book in bookstore:book namespace.

The most important namespace bookstore:book contains information about particular books, and for example bookstore:book:it page source may look like following (rendered page with additional cover photo is presented in Fig. 4):

```
====== Book details: ======
[[category:book]]
**Title**: It [[title:=It]]
**Author**: [[author::bookstore:author:stephen_king]]
**Publisher**: [[publisher::bookstore:publisher:signet]]
**Date**: 1987 [[date:=1987]]
**Language**: English [[language:=english]]
**Genre**: [[genre::bookstore:genre:horror]]
**Pages**: 560
```

```
**Keywords**: horror [[keyword:=horror]],
        thriller [[thriller:=horror]],
        bestseller [[keyword:=bestseller]]

====== Recomentadions: ======
**Books by this author**:  {{#ask: [[category:book]]
        [[author::bookstore:author:stephen_king]] }}
**Books by this publisher**: {{#ask: [[category:book]]
        [[publisher::bookstore:publisher:signet]] }}
**Books in this genre**: {{#ask: [[category:book]]
        [[genre::bookstore:genre:horror]] }}
```

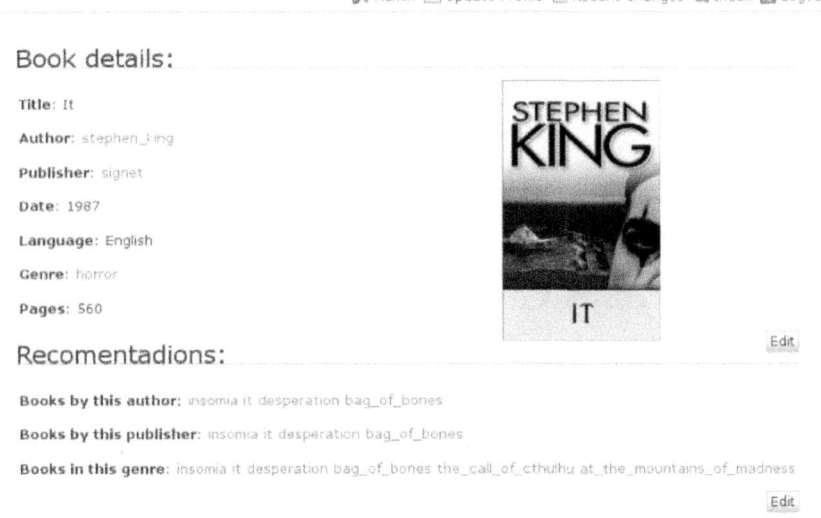

Fig. 4. Bookstore example in PlWiki

Prolog code associated with this page is:

```
wiki_category('bookstore:book:it','book').
wiki_attribute('bookstore:book:it','title','It').
wiki_relation('bookstore:book:it','author',
        ':bookstore:author:stephen_king').
wiki_relation('bookstore:book:it','publisher'
        ,'bookstore:publisher:signet').
wiki_attribute('bookstore:book:it','date','1987').
wiki_attribute('bookstore:book:it','language',
        'english').
```

```
wiki_relation('bookstore:book:it','genre',
        'bookstore:genre:horror').
```

This page contains not only basic information about selected book but it also suggests related books. This mechanism may increase profits and it is very flexible. If a new book is added to the system it will be automatically captured by recommendation mechanism. The only important thing is to define author, publisher and genre of this new book.

Because the fact that PlWiki allows to combine SMW markup with Prolog code more complex recommendations could be defined. For example in December Christmas recommendations are adequate:

```
<pl cache="true">
    custom_recommendations(X) :-
        wiki_attribute(X,'keyword','christmas').
</pl>
```

And on the page with book details:

```
<pl goal="custom_recommendations(X),write(X),nl,fail" scope="*"></pl>
```

Custom recommendations can be easily modified, for example:

```
<pl cache="true">
    custom_recommendations(X) :-
        wiki_attribute(X,'keyword','easter').
</pl>
```

The most important is the fact that only one Wiki page, containing definition of `custom_recommendations/1` has to be updated. SMW markup is not powerful enough to support this functionality. The possibility of combining SMW markup with Prolog code is one of the main advantages of PlWiki.

6 Evaluation

The approach presented in this paper offers a unified expressive knowledge representation for semantic annotations, as well as rules and additional procedures. The features of the Loki prototype – PlWiki – according to the introduced feature matrix (see Sect. 2.3) are presented below (see also [31]).

PlWiki is an experimental development phase. Current applications include special knowledge engineering tasks, including basic rule-based reasoning tasks in the wiki, and teaching knowledge engineering classes to students. Future applications are planned, including dedicated knowledge intensive closed community portals. System development will focus on flexible user interfaces supporting complex knowledge representation features.

A. Targeted applications	
4) Special-purpose system for knowledge engineering tasks	

B. Underlying knowledge representation	
1) Subject granularity	b) Multiple concepts/properties for one wiki page
2) Knowledge repr. lang.	c) Other/combination (Prolog low-level, OWL higher-level)
3) Add. knowledge sources	b) Prolog rules

C. UI for knowledge capture and sharing	
1) Editing paradigm:	a) Inline text markup, d) Other: Prolog editing support
2) Search/Retrieval	a) Prolog queries, b) Queries embedded into the wiki article, c) Further capabilities: Prolog predicates for knowledge processing
3) Semantic navigation	a) Extended links within wiki article, b) Generation of fact sheets

D. Connectivity	
1) Import facilities	a) OWL (planned) d) Proprietary: SMW knowledge format, Prolog, XTT
2) Export facilities	a) OWL (planned) d) Proprietary: Prolog

E. Extensibility	
1) Extension mechanism	(a) Plug-in mechanism, (b) Code-in mechanism
2) Extensions mods	Custom Prolog extensions, SWI Semantic Layer

7   Summary and Outlook

In the paper a proposal of a new semantic wiki system has been presented. Based on a review of important semantic wiki systems, important development directions have been identified. An essential area is a strong rule-based reasoning. The proposed system – Loki – offers such a solutions, thanks to a coherent knowledge representation method used. In Loki standard semantic annotations are mapped to Prolog knowledge base, in which also rule-based reasoning is specified. A custom rule-based engine using decision tables and decision trees is also provided.

Future work includes the full integration of the rule engine, as well as GUIs for ontology editing in the wiki. Compatibility with KnowWE wikimarkup is also planned. A prototype pure-Prolog wikiengine is also considered. As of knowledge processing it is more powerful than the plugin-based PlWiki solution. On top of wiki a knowledge evaluation layer is also considered.

Acknowledgements. The author wish to thank Dr. Joachim Baumeister for his valuable comments on semantic wikis, and the proposal of the name Loki, Dr. Jason Jung for his remarks concerning the PlWiki description, as well as Michał Kotra MSc. for his work on the preliminary PlWiki implementation [46] and Krzysztof Kaczor MSc. for his support with the PlWiki development.

References

1. Nalepa, G.J.: Plwiki - a generic semantic wiki architecture. In: Nguyen, N.T., Kowalczyk, R., Chen, S.M. (eds.) ICCCI 2009. LNCS, vol. 5796, pp. 345–356. Springer, Heidelberg (2009)
2. Berners-Lee, T., Hendler, J., Lassila, O.: The semantic web: Scientific american. Scientific American (May 2001)
3. Hitzler, P., Krötzsch, M., Rudolph, S.: Foundations of Semantic Web Technologies. Chapman & Hall/CRC (2009)
4. Bray, T., Paoli, J., Sperberg-McQueen, C.M., Maler, E. (eds.): Extensible markup language (XML) 1.0, 2nd edn. Technical report, World Wide Web Consortium. W3C Recommendation (2000), http://www.w3.org/TR/REC-xml
5. Lassila, O., Swick, R.R.: Resource description framework (RDF) model and syntax specification. Technical report, World Wide Web Consortium. W3C Recommendation (1999), http://www.w3.org/TR/REC-rdf-syntax
6. Brickley, D., Guha, R.V.: RDF vocabulary description language 1.0: RDF schema. W3C recommendation, W3C (February 2004), http://www.w3.org/TR/2004/REC-rdf-schema-20040210/
7. Patel-Schneider, P.F., Horrocks, I.: OWL 1.1 Web Ontology Language Overview. W3C member submission, W3C (December 2006), http://www.w3.org/Submission/owl11-overview/
8. Seaborne, A., Prud'hommeaux, E.: SPARQL query language for RDF. W3C recommendation, W3C (January 2008), http://www.w3.org/TR/2008/REC-rdf-sparql-query-20080115/
9. Hitzler, P., Krötzsch, M., Parsia, B., Patel-Schneider, P.F., Rudolph, S.: OWL 2 web ontology language — primer. W3C recommendation, W3C (October 2009)
10. Motik, B., Grau, B.C., Horrocks, I., Wu, Z., Fokoue, A., Lutz, C.: OWL 2 web ontology language: profiles. W3C recommendation, W3C (October 2009)
11. Horrocks, I., Patel-Schneider, P.F., Boley, H., Tabet, S., Grosof, B., Dean, M.: SWRL: A semantic web rule language combining OWL and RuleML, W3C member submission, Technical report, W3C (May 21, 2004)
12. Grosof, B.N., Horrocks, I., Volz, R., Decker, S.: Description logic programs: combining logic programs with description logic. In: Proceedings of the Twelfth International World Wide Web Conference, WWW 2003, pp. 48–57 (2003)
13. Horrocks, I., Parsia, B., Patel-Schneider, P., Hendler, J.: Semantic web architecture: Stack or two towers? In: Fages, F., Soliman, S. (eds.) PPSWR 2005. LNCS, vol. 3703, pp. 37–41. Springer, Heidelberg (2005)
14. Baader, F., Calvanese, D., McGuinness, D.L., Nardi, D., Patel-Schneider, P.F. (eds.): The Description Logic Handbook: Theory, Implementation, and Applications. Cambridge University Press, Cambridge (2003)
15. van Harmelen, F., Lifschitz, V., Porter, B. (eds.): Handbook of Knowledge Representation. Elsevier Science, Amsterdam (2007)
16. Brachman, R., Levesque, H.: Knowledge Representation and Reasoning, 1st edn. Morgan Kaufmann, San Francisco (2004)
17. Oren, E., Delbru, R., Möller, K., Völkel, M., Handschuh, S.: Annotation and navigation in semantic wikis. In: SemWiki (2006)
18. Schaffert, S.: Ikewiki: A semantic wiki for collaborative knowledge management. In: Proceedings of the 15th IEEE International Workshops on Enabling Technologies: Infrastructure for Collaborative Enterprises, WETICE 2006, Washington, DC, USA, pp. 388–396. IEEE Computer Society, Los Alamitos (2006)

19. Auer, S., Dietzold, S., Riechert, T.: Ontowiki - a tool for social, semantic collaboration. In: Cruz, I.F., Decker, S., Allemang, D., Preist, C., Schwabe, D., Mika, P., Uschold, M., Aroyo, L. (eds.) ISWC 2006. LNCS, vol. 4273, pp. 736–749. Springer, Heidelberg (2006)
20. Krötzsch, M., Vrandecic, D., Völkel, M., Haller, H., Studer, R.: Semantic wikipedia. Web Semantics 5, 251–261 (2007)
21. Oren, E.: Semperwiki: a semantic personal wiki. In: Proc. of 1st Workshop on The Semantic Desktop - Next Generation Personal Information Management and Collaboration Infrastructure, Galway, Ireland (November 2005)
22. Buffa, M., Gandon, F., Ereteo, G., Sander, P., Faron, C.: SweetWiki: A semantic wiki. Web Semantics: Science, Services and Agents on the World Wide Web (2008) (in press)
23. Kuhn, T.: AceWiki: A Natural and Expressive Semantic Wiki. In: Proceedings of Semantic Web User Interaction at CHI 2008: Exploring HCI Challenges, CEUR Workshop Proceedings (2008)
24. Schaffert, S., Eder, J., Grünwald, S., Kurz, T., Radulescu, M.: Kiwi - a platform for semantic social software (demonstration). In: Aroyo, L., Traverso, P., Ciravegna, F., Cimiano, P., Heath, T., Hyvönen, E., Mizoguchi, R., Oren, E., Sabou, M., Simperl, E. (eds.) ESWC 2009. LNCS, vol. 5554, pp. 888–892. Springer, Heidelberg (2009)
25. Baumeister, J., Puppe, F.: Web-based knowledge engineering using knowledge wikis. In: Proc. of the AAAI 2008 Spring Symposium on "Symbiotic Relationships between Semantic Web and Knowledge Engineering", Stanford University, USA, pp. 1–13 (2008)
26. Baumeister, J., Reutelshoefer, J., Puppe, F.: Knowwe: A semantic wiki for knowledge engineering. In: Applied Intelligence (2010) (to appear)
27. Jung, J.J., Nguyen, N.T.: Collective intelligence for semantic and knowledge grid. J. UCS 14(7), 1016–1019 (2008)
28. Jung, J.J., Nguyen, N.T.: Consensus choice for reconciling social collaborations on semantic wikis. In: Nguyen, N.T., Kowalczyk, R., Chen, S.M. (eds.) ICCCI 2009. LNCS, vol. 5796, pp. 472–480. Springer, Heidelberg (2009)
29. Jung, J.J.: Knowledge distribution via shared context between blog-based knowledge management systems: A case study of collaborative tagging. Expert Syst. Appl. 36(7), 10627–10633 (2009)
30. Razmerita, L., Kirchner, K., Sudzina, F.: Personal knowledge management. the role of web 2.0 tools for managing knowledge at individual and organisational levels. Online Information Review 33(6), 1021–1039 (2009)
31. Baumeister, J., Nalepa, G.J.: Engineering expressive knowledge with semantic wikis. In: Ligęza, A., Nalepa, G.J. (eds.) International Workshop on Design, Evaluation and Refinement of Intelligent Systems (DERIS 2009), Kraków, Poland, November 28, pp. 13–24 (2009)
32. Rosati, R.: DL+log: Tight integration of description logics and disjunctive datalog. In: Proceedings of the Tenth International Conference on Principles of Knowledge Representation and Reasoning (KR 2006), pp. 68–78 (2006)
33. Horrocks, I.: OWL Rules, OK? In: W3C Workshop on Rule Languages for Interoperability (April 27-28, 2005)
34. Bratko, I.: Prolog Programming for Artificial Intelligence, 3rd edn. Addison Wesley, Reading (2000)
35. Covington, M.A., Nute, D., Vellino, A.: Prolog programming in depth. Prentice-Hall, Englewood Cliffs (1996)
36. Russell, S., Norvig, P.: Artificial Intelligence: A Modern Approach, 2nd edn. Prentice-Hall, Englewood Cliffs (2003)

37. Noga, M., Kaczor, K., Nalepa, G.J.: Lightweight reasoning methods in selected semantic wikis. Gdansk University of Technology Faculty of ETI Annals 18(8), 103–108 (2010)
38. Vassiliadis, V., Wielemaker, J., Mungall, C.: Processing owl2 ontologies using thea: An application of logic programming. In: OWLED (2009)
39. Fuchs, N.E., Schwertel, U., Schwitter, R.: Attempto controlled english - not just another logic specification language. In: Flener, P. (ed.) LOPSTR 1998. LNCS, vol. 1559, p. 1. Springer, Heidelberg (1999)
40. Nalepa, G.J.: Architecture of the heart hybrid rule engine. In: Rutkowski, L., Scherer, R., Tadeusiewicz, R., Zadeh, L.A., Zurada, J.M. (eds.) ICAISC 2010. LNCS (LNAI), vol. 6114, pp. 598–605. Springer, Heidelberg (2010)
41. Nalepa, G.J., Ligęza, A.: A graphical tabular model for rule-based logic programming and verification. Systems Science 31(2), 89–95 (2005)
42. Nalepa, G.J., Ligęza, A.: XTT+ rule design using the ALSV(FD). In: Giurca, A., Analyti, A., Wagner, G. (eds.) ECAI 2008: 18th European Conference on Artificial Intelligence: 2nd East European Workshop on Rule-based Applications, RuleApps2008, Patras, University of Patras, July 22, pp. 11–15 (2008)
43. Nalepa, G.J., Ligęza, A.: HeKatE methodology, hybrid engineering of intelligent systems. International Journal of Applied Mathematics and Computer Science 20(1), 35–53 (2010)
44. Nalepa, G.J., Furmańska, W.T.: Proposal of a New Rule-Based Inference Scheme for the Semantic Web Applications. In: Nguyen, N.T., Katarzyniak, R.P., Janiak, A. (eds.) New Challenges in Computational Collective Intelligence. SCI, vol. 244, pp. 15–26. Springer, Heidelberg (2009)
45. Nalepa, G.J.: Collective knowledge engineering with semantic wikis. Journal of Universal Computer Science 16(7), 1006–1023 (2010),
    http://www.jucs.org/jucs_16_7/collective_knowledge_engineering_with
46. Kotra, M.: Design of a prototype knowledge wiki system based on prolog. Master's thesis, AGH University of Science and Technology in Kraków (2009)

Rule Extraction Based on Rough Fuzzy Sets in Fuzzy Information Systems

Ming-Chang Lee[1] and To Chang[2]

[1] Department of Information Management, Fooyin University, Taiwan
151 Chin-Hsueh Rd., Ta-Liao Hsiang Kaohsiung Hsien, 831 Taiwan, ROC
`ming-li@mail2000.com.tw`
[2] Department of Information Management, Shu-Te University, Taiwan
No. 59, Hengshan Rd., Yanchao Kaohsiung County, Taiwan, ROC
`changt@mail.stu.edu.tw`

Abstract. Rough fuzzy sets are an effective mathematical analysis tool to deal with vagueness and uncertainty in the area of machine learning and decision analysis. Fuzzy information systems and fuzzy objective information systems exit in many applications and knowledge reduction in them can't be implemented by reduction methods in Pawlak information systems. Therefore, this paper provides a model for rule extraction in fuzzy information systems and fuzzy objective information systems.

This approach uses inclusion degree to propose and represent a new and low computation complexity way for knowledge discovery and rough fuzzy concept classifier in fuzzy information systems and fuzzy objective information systems. Also, an illustration example in the construction sector is presented.

This approach is a generalization of rough set model for fuzzy information system. Theory and method of attribute reduction under inclusion degree are suggested in this paper. This approach extends the classical rough set theory from complete information to fuzzy information system.

This proposed model is useful for rule extraction in fuzzy information systems and fuzzy objective information systems to figure our knowledge reduction in fuzzy decision systems.

Keywords: Rough sets, Fuzzy sets, Rough fuzzy sets, Inclusion degree.

1 Introduction

The vague concepts of fuzzy sets were introduced in Zadeh [19]. Incorporating fuzziness and uncertainty into decision marking problems can generally generate promising alternatives (Yu [18]), such as fuzzy technique has been applied vague data in approximate reasoning, decision marking, and optimization, control [25].

Theories of fuzzy sets [19] and rough sets [7, 9] are generalizations of classical set theory for modeling vagueness and uncertainty. The theory of rough sets provides rigorous mathematical techniques for creating approximate descriptions of objects for

N.T. Nguyen and R. Kowalczyk (Eds.): Transactions on CCI III, LNCS 6560, pp. 115–127, 2011.

data analysis, optimization and recognition. Rough sets theory belongs to the family of concepts concerning the modeling and representing of incomplete knowledge [4, 8]. Wong et al. [14] presented the probabilistic rough set model, and Wei et al. [12] studied fuzziness in probabilistic rough sets using fuzzy sets. Banerjee and Pal [1] proposed a roughness measure for fuzzy sets, making use of the concept of rough fuzzy sets [2].

One of the key notations in Pawlak's rough set model is the indiscernibility relation [7] (equivalence relation, i.e. reflexive, symmetric and transitive). By using such relation, the equivalence classes are obtained for constructing of the lower and upper approximations. Therefore, such approximations are suitable in the analysis of data presented in terms of the complete information (decision) systems. The Pawlak's rough set theory must be extended in order to overcome this problem, such as [11] proposed a new method to create an intelligent Web search agent based on rough sets and fuzzy sets. Gong et al. [3] deals with an interval valued fuzzy information system [22] by means of integrating the rough sets theory with the interval-valued fuzzy set theory and discusses the basic rough set theory for the interval-valued fuzzy information. Xu et al. [15] presents a novel rough fuzzy set based approach to detect fraud in 3G mobile telecommunication network. Petrosino and Salvi [10] make scale space accordingly to the notation of rough fuzzy sets, realizing a system capable to efficiently cluster data coming from image analysis tasks. Zhang et al. ([20], [21]) proposed similarity measures for measuring the degree of similarity between vague sets and fuzzy rough sets. Liu et al. [6] proposes the model of incomplete and fuzzy objective information systems based on incomplete approximation space and fuzzy objective information system by the tolerance relation. The model is the generalization and fuzzy objective information system in complete space and of rough set model of incomplete information system. There are also similar mistakes in other places, e.g. Yang et al.[16] and Zhang et al.[23] present the distribution reduct, maximum distribution reduct, assignment reduct respectively, and propose the discernibility matrixes computing approaches respect to these reducts. The judgment theorems and discernibility matrices associated with the three reductions were examined, from which we can obtain approaches to knowledge reductions in rough set theory. Yang et al. [17] used dominance-based rough set into the incomplete fuzzy information system. In this paper, we provide a new and low computation complexity way for knowledge discovery and rough fuzzy based fuzzy concept classifier in fuzzy information systems and fuzzy objective information systems.

2   Preliminaries

2.1 Fuzzy Set [19]

Let U be a finite nonempty set of objects. A fuzzy set A is a mapping from U into the unit interval [0, 1]:

$$\mu_A : U \to [0,1], \tag{1}$$

$\mu_A(x)$ is called the membership degree of x in A, which contains $x \in U$.

Given a number $\alpha \in [0, 1]$, the α–cut or α–level set of A is defined as follows:

$$[A]_\alpha = \{x : \mu_A(x) \geq \alpha\} \qquad (2)$$

A strong α–cut set of A is defined as follows:

$$\sigma_\alpha(A) = \{x : \mu_A(x) > \alpha\} \qquad (3)$$

2.2 Rough Sets [6]

Let R be an equivalence relation on a universal set U. Let U / R denote the family of all equivalence classes introduced on U by R. One such equivalence class in U / R, which contains $x \in U$, is designated by $[x]_R$. For any class $A \subseteq U$, we can define the lower approximation (or positive region) and upper approximation (or negative region), defined respectively as follows:

$$\underline{R}(A) = \cup\{[x]_R | [x]_R \subseteq A, x \in X\} \qquad (4)$$

$$\bar{R}(A) = \cap\{[x]_R | [x]_R \cap A \neq \phi, x \in X\} \qquad (5)$$

A rough representation of the given set A is a pair $R(A) = \{\underline{R}(A), \bar{R}(A)\}$ which is called a rough set.

The set BN (A) = $\bar{R}(A)$ - $\underline{R}(A)$ is a rough description of the boundary of A by the equivalence classes of U / R. The approximation is rough uncertainty free if $\underline{R}(A) = \bar{R}(A)$.

2.3 Rough Fuzzy Sets [2]

Let U be a finite nonempty set of objects. R is an equivalence relation on U. A is a fuzzy set. A rough-fuzzy sets is a pair $(\underline{A}, \bar{A})$, where the lower approximation $\underline{A}$ and upper approximations $\bar{A}$ of A are fuzzy sets of U / R, with the membership functions defined by

$$\underline{A}(x) = \inf\{A(x) | \ x \in [x]_R\}, x \in U \qquad (6)$$

$$\bar{A}(x) = \sup\{A(x) | \ x \in [x]_R\}, x \in U \qquad (7)$$

$\underline{A}$ can be comprehended as the membership degree of object x which must belong to fuzzy set A. $\bar{A}$ is the membership degree of object x which may be belong to fuzzy set A.

2.4 Information System

An information system S may be defined as $S = (U, A, V, f)$, where:

U is a finite nonempty set of objects called universal set;

$A = C \cup D$ is a finite nonempty set of attributes, where C is a set of so called conditional attributes, D is a set of so called decision attributes, and $C \cap D = \phi$. For every $a \in A$, such that $f : U \to V_a$, $V = \underset{a \in A}{\cup} V_a$, where V_a is called the value set of attribute a.

3 Fuzzy Decision Information System

3.1 Fuzzy Objective Information System

Definition 1: Fuzzy objective information system (FOIS) [22]

The fuzzy objective information system S is defined as: $S = (U, A, F, V, \tilde{D})$, where:

U is a finite nonempty set of objects, i.e. $U = \{x_1, x_2, .., x_n\}$;

A is a finite nonempty set of condition attributes, i.e. $A = \{a_1, a_2, ..., a_m\}$;

$F = \{f_l : U \to V_l \ (l \le m)\}$ is a set of condition attribute mappings, $f_l : U \to V_l$, $V = \underset{1 \le l \le m}{\cup} V_l$;

$\tilde{D}$ is a finite nonempty set of decision attributes, i.e.
$\tilde{D} = \{\tilde{D}_j : U \to [0,1] \ (j \le r)\}$.

For example, $U = \{x_1, x_2, .., x_4\}$, $A = \{a_1, a_2\}$, $\tilde{D} = \{\tilde{D}_1, \tilde{D}_2\}$, Table 1 is a fuzzy objective information system.

Table 1. Fuzzy decision information system

U	a_1	a_2	$\tilde{D}_1$	$\tilde{D}_2$
X_1	1	1	0.9	0.2
X_2	1	1	1.0	0.3
X_3	1	2	0.8	0.5
X_4	1	1	0.6	0.6

Definition 2: The lower approximation and upper approximation of $\tilde{D}_i$.

$S = (U, A, F, V, \tilde{D})$ is FOIS. Let U be a finite nonempty set of objects. B is an equivalence relation in a universal set U. F (U) is a set of condition attribute mappings, and $B \subseteq U$. One such equivalence class in U / B, which contains $x \in U$, is denoted by $[x]_B$. For any class $B \subseteq U$, A rough-fuzzy sets is a pair $\{\underline{B}(\widetilde{D}_i), \overline{B}(\widetilde{D}_i)\}$, where the lower approximation (or positive region) and upper approximation (or negative region) of U are defined respectively as follows:

$$\underline{B}(\widetilde{D}_i) = \min\{\widetilde{D}_i(y), y \in [x]_B |\} \tag{8}$$

$$\overline{B}(\widetilde{D}_i) = \max\{\widetilde{D}_i(y), y \in [x]_B\}. \tag{9}$$

3.2 Inclusion Degree

Definition 3: $F(U)$ is a set of condition attribute mappings, and $\widetilde{B} \subseteq \widetilde{A} \subseteq F(U)$. D is called the inclusion degree on $F(U)$ If the following expressions hold: [24]

(1) $0 \le D(\widetilde{B}|\widetilde{A}) \le 1$;
(2) $\widetilde{A}, \widetilde{B} \in F(U), \widetilde{A} \subseteq \widetilde{B} \Rightarrow D(\widetilde{B}|\widetilde{A}) = 1$;
(3) $\widetilde{A} \subseteq \widetilde{B} \subseteq \widetilde{C} \Rightarrow D(\widetilde{A}|\widetilde{C}) \le D(\widetilde{A}|\widetilde{B})$

It is easy to prove that the following expressions thereinafter are all inclusion degrees formulae in fuzzy set.

(1) $N(\widetilde{B} / \widetilde{A}) = \bigwedge_{x \in U} (\widetilde{A}^c(x) \vee \widetilde{B}(x))$;

(2) $\Pi(\widetilde{B} / \widetilde{A}) = \bigvee_{x \in U} (\widetilde{A}(x) \wedge \widetilde{B}(x))$;

(3) $M(\widetilde{B} / \widetilde{A}) = \dfrac{\sum_{x \in U}(\widetilde{A}(x) \wedge \widetilde{B}(x))}{\sum_{x \in U} \widetilde{A}(x)}$

Definition 4: In FOIS, let B be an equivalence relation on a universal set U. We define the inclusion degree of $[x_i]_B$ on $\widetilde{D}_k$ and the decision objection of B on $\widetilde{D}_j$ as the following form:

$$D_B(\widetilde{D}_k)(x_i) = N(\widetilde{D}_k / [x_i]_B) = \min\{\widetilde{D}_k(x)| \ x \in [x_i]_B\}, k \le r \tag{10}$$

$$M_B(x_i) = M(\widetilde{D}_k / [x_i]_B) = \{\widetilde{D}_k| \ D_B(\widetilde{D}_j(x_i)) = \max_{j \le r}\{D_B(\widetilde{D}_j(x_i))\} \tag{11}$$

Definition 5: Lower-compatible set and attributes reduction of FOIS ([13])

In FOIS, Let B be an equivalence relation on a universal set U, and $\widetilde{B} \subseteq \widetilde{A}$.

(1) If $N(\tilde{D}_k / [x_i]_A) = N(\tilde{D}_k / [x_i]_B)$ for every $x_i \in U$, B is called a lower-compatible set of FOIS. If every proper subset of B is not a lower- compatible set of FOIS, B is called the lower-attribute reduction of FOIS (based on the inclusion de-gree $N(\tilde{D}_k / [x_i]_B)$.

(2) If $M_A(x_i) = M_B(x_i)$ for every $x_i \in U$, B is called a compatible set of FOIS. If every proper subset of B is not compatible set of FOIS, B is called the attribute reduc-tion of FOIS (based on the inclusion degree $M(\tilde{D}_k / [x_i]_B)$).

By definition 5, we principally introduce the primary concept and methods of attribute reduction which ensures the inclusion degree of each objective invariable.

Definition 6: In FOIS, let B be an equivalence relation on a universal set U. The decision objection of B on $\widetilde{D}_j$ is $M_B(x_i)$. The rule believable of B on $M_B(x_i)$ is defined as:

$$m_B(x_i) = \max_{k \le r}\{D_B(\tilde{D}_k)(x_i)|\ M_B(x_i)\} \tag{12}$$

3.3 Proposed Method

Step 1: Create fuzzy decision information system table

Step 2: Calculate an equivalence relation $[x]_B$.

Step 3: Calculate the inclusion degree of $[x_i]_B$ on $\widetilde{D}_k$ (definition 4)

Step 4: Calculate the decision of B on $\widetilde{D}_j$ (definition 4)

Step 5: Calculate the rule believable of B on D_k (definition 6)

Step 6: Rule extraction

3.4 Fuzzy Information System (FIS) [24]

The fuzzy information system S is defined as: $S = (U, A, \tilde{F}, \tilde{D})$, where

$\quad U$ is a finite nonempty set of objects, i.e. $U = \{x_1, x_2, .., x_n\}$;

$\quad A$ is a finite nonempty set of condition attributes, i.e. $A = \{a_1, a_2, ..., a_m\}$;

$\quad D$ is a finite nonempty set of decision attributes

$\quad \tilde{F} = \{\tilde{A}_{jl_j} : U \to [0,1]\ (j \le m, l_j \le r_j)\}$

$\quad \tilde{D} = \{\tilde{D}_l : U \to [0,1]\ (l \le r)\}$

$\quad$ For example, $U = \{x_1, x_2, .., x_5\}$, $A = \{a_1, a_2\}$, $\tilde{D} = \{\tilde{D}_1, \tilde{D}_2\}$, $a_1 = \{\tilde{A}_{11}, \tilde{A}_{12}\}$, $a_2 = \{\tilde{A}_{21}, \tilde{A}_{22}\}$. Table 2 is a fuzzy information system.

Table 2. Fuzzy information system

U	a_1		a_2			
	$\widetilde{A}_{11}$	$\widetilde{A}_{12}$	$\widetilde{A}_{21}$	$\widetilde{A}_{22}$	$\widetilde{D}_1$	$\widetilde{D}_2$
X_1	0.9	0.1	0.8	0.2	0.9	0.4
X_2	0.7	0.8	0.5	0.1	0.6	0.6
X_3	0.4	1.0	0.5	0.9	0.3	0.9
X_4	0.1	0.6	0.5	0.5	0.1	0.5
X_5	0.6	0.1	0.9	0.1	0.8	0.8

Definition 7: The selection of decision conditional attribute

$S = (U, A, \tilde{F}, \tilde{D})$ is FIS, the selection of conditional decision is defined as:

$$\widetilde{A}_{il_i} \cap \widetilde{A}_{jl_j} \quad 1 \le l_i \le r_i, 1 \le l_j \le r_j, i < j \tag{13}$$

The image of the selection conditional decision on set B is defined as:

$$B = \{(\widetilde{A}_{il_i} \cap \widetilde{A}_{jl_j})|1 \le l_i \le r_i, 1 \le l_j \le r_j, i < j\} \tag{14}$$

Definition 8: In FIS, B is equivalence relation on a universal set U. The inclusion degree of B on $\widetilde{D}_k$ and the maximum decision objection of B on $\widetilde{D}_K$ are defined as:

$$\Pi(B|\widetilde{D}_k) = \cup((\widetilde{A}_{il_i} \cap \widetilde{A}_{jl_j}) \cap \widetilde{D}_k) \tag{15}$$

$$M_B(x_i) = M(B|\widetilde{D}_k) = \{\widetilde{D}_k| D_B(\widetilde{D}_k(x_i)) = \max_{j \le r}\{D_B(\widetilde{D}_j(x_i))\} \tag{16}$$

Definition 9: In FIS, The rule believable of B on $\widetilde{D}_K$ is defined as:

$$m_{\tilde{B}} = \max_{k \le r}\{\widetilde{D}_k|\tilde{B} \in (\widetilde{A}_{il_i} \cap \widetilde{A}_{jl_j}), 1 \le l_i \le r_i, 1 \le l_j \le r_j, i < j)\} \tag{17}$$

Definition 10: In FIS, $\widetilde{B} \subseteq \widetilde{A}$

(1) If $\Pi(A|\widetilde{D}_k) = \Pi(B|\widetilde{D}_k)$ for every $x_i \in$ U, B is called upper-compatible set of FIS. If every proper subset of B is not the upper- compatible set of FIS, B is called upper-attribute reduction of FIS (based on the inclusion degree $\Pi(B|\widetilde{D}_k)$).

(2) If $M_A(x_i) = M_B(x_i)$ for every $x_i \in$ U, B is called a compatible set of FIS. If every proper subset of B is not compatible set of FIS, B is called the attribute reduction of FOIS (based on the inclusion degree $M(B|\widetilde{D}_k)$).

By definition 10, we principally introduce the primary concept and methods of attribute reduction which ensures the inclusion degree of each objective invariable.

3.5 Proposed Method of Fuzzy Information System

Step 1: Create fuzzy information system table.

Step 2: Calculate the selection of conditional decision (definition 7).

Step 3: Calculate the image of the selection conditional decision on set B (definition 7).

Step 4: Calculate the maximum decision objection of B in $\widetilde{D_K}$ (definition 8).

Step 5: Calculate the rule believable of B in $\widetilde{D_K}$ (definition 9).

Step 6: Rule extraction.

4 An Illustration Example

4.1 Fuzzy Objective Information System

Step 1

Let $S = (U, A, V, F, \tilde{D})$ be a fuzzy objective information system, $U= \{X_1, X_2, \ldots, X_6\}$ and $A = \{a_1, a_2\}$ and $\tilde{D} = \{\tilde{D}_1, \tilde{D}_2\}$ (see table 3).

Table 3. Fuzzy objective information system

U	a_1	a_2	$\tilde{D}_1$	$\tilde{D}_2$
X_1	1	1	0.9	0.2
X_2	1	1	1.0	0.3
X_3	1	2	0.8	0.5
X_4	1	2	0.7	0.6
X_5	1	2	0.6	0.9
X_6	2	2	0.2	1.0

Step 2

$[x_i]_B = \{x_j | (x_i, x_j) \in R_B\}$ = {(x$_1$, x$_2$), (x$_3$, x$_4$, x$_5$), x$_6$}

Step 3 and Step 4

When B={X$_1$, X$_2$}, we calculate $D_B(\tilde{D}_1(x_i)$ and $D_B(\tilde{D}_2(x_i)$ by using Eq. (9, 10):

$$D_B(\tilde{D}_1(x_i) = N(\widetilde{D_k} / [x_i]_B) = \min \{0.9, 1.0\} = 0.9$$

$$D_B(\tilde{D}_2(x_i) = N(\widetilde{D_k} / [x_i]_B) = \min \{0.2, 0.3\} = 0.2$$

$$M_B(x_i) = \{\tilde{D}_k | D_B(\tilde{D}_j(x_i)) = \max_{j \leq r}\{D_B(\tilde{D}_j(x_i))\} = \tilde{D}_1$$

When B= $\{X_3, X_4, X_5\}$, we calculate $D_B(\tilde{D}_1(x_i)$ and $D_B(\tilde{D}_2(x_i)$ by using Eq. (9, 10):

$$D_B(\tilde{D}_1(x_i) = N(\widetilde{D_k}/[x_i]_B) = \min\{0.8, 0.7, 0.6\} = 0.6$$

$$D_B(\tilde{D}_2(x_i) = N(\widetilde{D_k}/[x_i]_B) = \min\{0.5, 0.6, 0.9\} = 0.5$$

$$M_B(x_i) = \{\tilde{D}_k| \ D_B(\tilde{D}_j(x_i)) = \max_{j \leq r}\{D_B(\tilde{D}_j(x_i))\} = \tilde{D}_1$$

When B = $\{X_6\}$,

$$D_B(\tilde{D}_1(x_i) = N(\widetilde{D_k}/[x_i]_B) = \min\{0.2\} = 0.2$$

$$D_B(\tilde{D}_2(x_i) = N(\widetilde{D_k}/[x_i]_B) = \min\{1.0\} = 1.0$$

$$M_B(x_i) = \{\tilde{D}_k| \ D_B(\tilde{D}_j(x_i)) = \max_{j \leq r}\{D_B(\tilde{D}_j(x_i))\} = \tilde{D}_2$$

Step 5

The result of the fuzzy objective information attribute's reduction is showed as Table 4.

Table 4. The result of fuzzy objective information attributes reduction

B	$D_B(\tilde{D}_1(x_i)$	$D_B(\tilde{D}_2(x_i)$	$M_B(x_i)$	rule believable
X_1, X_2	0.9	0.2	$\tilde{D}_1$	0.9
X_3, X_4, X_5	0.6	0.5	$\tilde{D}_1$	0.6
X_6	0.2	1.0	$\tilde{D}_2$	1.0

Step 6: Rule extraction

From Table 4, we have:

Rule 1 : If (a1 = 1 and a2 =1), then $\tilde{D}_1$ (The rule believable is 0.9)

Rule 2 : If (a1 = 1, a2 =2), then $\tilde{D}_1$ (The rule believable is 0.6)

Rule 3 : If (a1 = 2, a2 =2), then $\tilde{D}_2$ (The rule believable is 1.0)

4.2 Fuzzy Information System

Step 1

Table 5 is fuzzy information system. U = $\{X_1, X_2, ..., X_5\}$ and $A = \{a_1, a_2\}$ and

$$\tilde{D} = \{\tilde{D}_1, \tilde{D}_2\}. \ \tilde{F} = \{(\tilde{A}_{11}, \tilde{A}_{12}), (\tilde{A}_{21}, \tilde{A}_{22})\}$$

Where, $A = \{a_1, a_2\}$, a_1 is a ratio of price to cost, a_2 is market status, $a_1 = \{\tilde{A}_{11}, \tilde{A}_{12}\}$, a2 $= \{\tilde{A}_{21}, \tilde{A}_{22}\}$.

The attribute $\tilde{A}_{11}$ is high ratio of price to cost. The attribute $\tilde{A}_{12}$ is low ratio of price to cost. The attribute $\tilde{A}_{21}$ is large requirement of marketplace. The attribute $\tilde{A}_{22}$ is small requirement of marketplace. $\tilde{D}_1$ is procreation, and $\tilde{D}_2$ is not procreation.

Table 5. Fuzzy information system

U	a_1		a_2		D	
	$\tilde{A}_{11}$	$\tilde{A}_{12}$	$\tilde{A}_{21}$	$\tilde{A}_{22}$	$\tilde{D}_1$	$\tilde{D}_2$
X_1	0.9	0.1	0.8	0.2	0.9	0.4
X_2	0.7	0.8	0.5	0.1	0.6	0.6
X_3	0.4	1.0	0.5	0.9	0.3	0.9
X_4	0.1	0.6	0.5	0.5	0.1	0.5
X_5	0.6	0.1	0.9	0.1	0.8	0.8

Step 2: We calculate all possible compositions of fuzzy condition attributes by using Eq. (13) (see Table 6)

$\tilde{A}_{11} \cap \tilde{A}_{21} = (0.9) \cap (0.8) = 0.8$; $\tilde{A}_{11} \cap \tilde{A}_{22} = (0.9) \cap (0.2) = 0.2$; $\tilde{A}_{12} \cap \tilde{A}_{21} = (0.6) \cap (0.8) = 0.6$; $\tilde{A}_{12} \cap \tilde{A}_{22} = (0.6) \cap (0.2) = 0.2$

Step 3: We calculate the inclusion of all possible compositions of fuzzy condition attributes by using Eq. (15). The Inclusion degree function is $\Pi(\tilde{B} / \tilde{A})$.

Table 6. All possible compositions of conditional attributes

U	$\tilde{A}_{11} \cap \tilde{A}_{21}$	$\tilde{A}_{11} \cap \tilde{A}_{22}$	$\tilde{A}_{12} \cap \tilde{A}_{21}$	$\tilde{A}_{12} \cap \tilde{A}_{22}$	$\tilde{D}_1$	$\tilde{D}_2$
X_1	0.8	0.2	0.6	0.2	0.9	0.4
X_2	0.5	0.1	0.5	0.1	0.6	0.6
X_3	0.4	0.4	0.5	0.9	0.3	0.9
X_4	0.1	0.1	0.5	0.5	0.1	0.5
X_5	0.6	0.1	0.1	0.1	0.8	0.8

When $\tilde{B} = \tilde{A}_{11} \cap \tilde{A}_{12}$, we have

$$\Pi(\tilde{B} / \tilde{D}_2) = \bigcup_{x \in U}(\tilde{D}_2(x) \cap \tilde{B}(x)) = (0.8 \cap 0.4) \cup (0.5) \cap 0.6) \cup (0.4 \cap 0.9) \cup$$
$$(0.1 \cap 0.5)(\cup (0.6 \cap 0.8 = 0.6$$

$$\Pi(\tilde{B}/\tilde{D}_1) = \bigcup_{x \in U}(\tilde{D}_1(x) \cap \tilde{B}(x)) = (0.8 \cap 0.9) \cup (0.5 \cap 0.6) \cup (0.4 \cap 0.3) \cup$$

$$(0.1 \cap 0.1) \cup (0.6 \cap 0.8) = 0.8$$

Step 4 and Step 5: We calculate decision attribute by using Eq. (16, 17).

$$M_B(x_i) = \{\tilde{D}_k \mid D_B(\tilde{D}_j(x_i)) = \max_{j \le r}\{D_{\tilde{B}}(\tilde{D}_j(x_i))\} = \tilde{D}_1$$

$$m_{\tilde{B}} = \max_{k \le r}\{\tilde{D}_k \mid \tilde{B} \in (\tilde{A}_{il_i} \cap \tilde{A}_{jl_j}), 1 \le l_i \le r_i, 1 \le l_j \le r_j, i < j)\} = \max \{0.8, 0.6\} = 0.8$$

In same way, we obtained the inclusion degree and maximal decisions of condition attributes including decision attributes (see Table 7).

Table 7. The result of fuzzy information attributes reduction

$\tilde{B}$	$\tilde{D}_1$	$\tilde{D}_2$	$M_{\tilde{B}}$	rule believable
$\tilde{A}_{11} \cap \tilde{A}_{12}$	0.8	0.6	$\tilde{D}_1$	0.8
$\tilde{A}_{11} \cap \tilde{A}_{22}$	0.3	0.4	$\tilde{D}_2$	0.4
$\tilde{A}_{12} \cap \tilde{A}_{21}$	0.6	0.5	$\tilde{D}_1$	0.6
$\tilde{A}_{12} \cap \tilde{A}_{22}$	0.3	0.9	$\tilde{D}_2$	0.9

Step 6

Rule 1: If (high ratio of price to cost) and (large requirement of marketplace), then we put into production. (The rule believable is 0.8)

Rule 2: If (high ratio of price to cost) and (small requirement of marketplace), then we do not put into production. (The rule believable is 0.4)

Rule 3: If (law ratio of price to cost) and (large requirement of marketplace), then we put into production. (The rule believable is 0.6)

Rule 4: If (law ratio of price to cost) and (small requirement of marketplace), then we do not put into production. (The rule believable is 0.9)

5   Conclusions

Rough set theory is applied for rule extraction and attributes reductions on fuzzy information system. Two types of information tables with fuzzy numbers, called the fuzzy objective information table and the fuzzy information table in which only decision attributes are fuzzy and both condition and decision attributes are fuzzy respectively, are discussed. In this paper, new concepts and ways are introduced to figure our knowledge reduction in consistent decision system. This is a new technique for rule extraction in fuzzy information systems. Thus, the rough fuzzy sets generalized in a new field for decision marking.

Acknowledgements

I would like to thank the anonymous reviewers for their constructive comments on this paper.

References

1. Banerjee, M., Pal, S.K.: Roughness of fuzzy set. Information Science 93, 235–246 (1996)
2. Dubois, D., Prade, H.: Rough fuzzy sets and fuzzy rough sets. International Journal of General Systems 17, 191–209 (1990)
3. Gong, et al.: Rough set theory for the interval-valued fuzzy Information Systems. Information Sciences 178(8), 1968–1985 (2008)
4. Hu, X.T., Lin, T.Y., Han, J.: A new rough sets model based on database systems. In: Wang, G., Liu, Q., Yao, Y., Skowron, A. (eds.) RSFDGrC 2003. LNCS (LNAI), vol. 2639, pp. 114–121. Springer, Heidelberg (2003)
5. Huynh, V.N., Nakamori, Y.: A roughness measure for fuzzy set. Information Sciences 173, 255–275 (2005)
6. Liu, T., Zhang, Z., Xuejuan, L.: Knowledge Reduction in Incomplete and Fuzzy Objective information Systems. In: Proceedings of the 2008 International Conference on Computational Intelligence and Security, vol. 2, pp. 138–141 (2008)
7. Pawlak, A.: Rough set and fuzzy sets. Fuzzy Sets and Systems 17, 99–102 (1985)
8. Pawlak, A.: Rough Sets. International Journal Computer and Information Sciences 11, 341–356 (1982)
9. Pawlak, A.: Rough Classification. International Journal of Man-Machine Studies 20, 469–483 (1984)
10. Petrosino, A., Salvi, G.: Rough fuzzy set based scale space transforms and their use in image analysis. International Journal of Approximate Reasoning 41, 212–228 (2006)
11. Rojanavasu, P., Pinngem, O.: Extended rough fuzzy sets for web search agent. In: Proceedings of the 25th International Information Technology Interfaces, pp. 403–407 (2003)
12. Wei, L.L., Zhang, W.X.: Probabilistic rough characterized by Fuzzy Sets. LNCS (LNAI), vol. 2369, pp. 173–180. Springer, Heidelberg (2003)
13. Wei, D., Tang, L.: Attribute Reduction based on Inclusion degree for incomplete and fuzzy decision information systems. Journal of Communication and Computer 3(5), 22–28 (2006)
14. Wong, S.K.M., Zialo, W., Li, Y.R.: Comparison of rough set and statistical methods in inductive learning. International Journal of Man-Machine Studied 24, 53–72 (1986)
15. Xu, et al.: Fraud detection in telecommunication: A rough Fuzzy set based approach. In: Proceeding of the Seventh International Conference on Machine Cybernetics, Kuming, July 12-15, pp. 1249–1253 (2008)
16. Yang, F., Guan, Y.Y., Yu, Z.X.: Attributes Reduct and Optimal Decision Rules Acquisition in Fuzzy Objective Information Systems. In: Huang, D.-S., Wunsch II, D.C., Levine, D.S., Jo, K.-H. (eds.) ICIC 2008. LNCS (LNAI), vol. 5227, pp. 857–863. Springer, Heidelberg (2008)

17. Yang, X., Wei, L., Yu, D., Yang, J.: Rough fuzzy set in incomplete fuzzy information system based on similarity dominance relation. Recent Patents on Computer Science 2, 68–74 (2009)
18. Yu, P.R.: Dissolution of Fuzziness for Better Decision Perspective and Techniques. Management Sciences 20, 171–207 (1984)
19. Zadeh, L.A.: Fuzzy sets. Information and Control 8(3), 338–353 (1965)
20. Zhang, C., Dang, P.: The measures similarity between vague sets. Computer Engineering Application 39(17), 92–94 (2003) (in Chinese)
21. Zhang, C., Dang, P., Fu, H.: On measures of similarity between fuzzy rough sets. International Journal Pure and Applied Mathematics 10(4), 451–460 (2004)
22. Zhang, M., Wu, W.Z.: Knowledge reduction with fuzzy decision information systems. Chinese Journal of Engineering Mathematics 20(2), 1–7 (2003)
23. Zhang, W.X., Mi, J.S., Wu, W.Z.: Approaches to knowledge reductions in inconsistent Systems. International Journal of Intelligent Systems 18(10), 592–605 (2003)
24. Zhang, W.X., Leung, Y.: Theory of inclusion degrees and its applications to uncertainty inferences. In: Soft Computing in Intelligent Systems and Information Processing, pp. 496–5011. IEEE, New York (1996)
25. Zimmermann, H.J.: Fuzzy Set Theory and Its Applications, 2nd edn. Kluwer Academic Publishers, Dordrecht (1991)

Patterns in World Dynamics Indicating Agency

Tibor Bosse and Jan Treur

Vrije Universiteit Amsterdam, Department of Artificial Intelligence
De Boelelaan 1081, 1081 HV Amsterdam, The Netherlands
{tbosse,treur}@cs.vu.nl
http://www.cs.vu.nl/~{tbosse,treur}

Abstract. In this paper, the question is addressed which patterns in world dynamics are an indication for a conceptualisation of a world's process as an agent. Six criteria are discussed that provide an indication for the world to show a form agency, and allows for suitable agent-based conceptualisation. The criteria take the form of relationships between the occurrence of certain patterns in the world's dynamics, and are expressed as second-order properties of world dynamics. They are formalised in a reified temporal predicate (meta-)logical language and their use is illustrated in a case study, supported by automated support in the form of simulation and verification.

1 Introduction

To conceptualise processes in the world, often an agent-oriented perspective is a useful conceptual tool. By having distinguished a number of agents and their interaction, the overall process can be analysed from a collective intelligence perspective, as emerging from the individual agent processes and their interactions. However, a fundamental question, usually solved implicitly when agent-based modelling is applied, is which parts of the world's process can reasonably interpreted as agents. Whether or not to choose for an agent-based conceptualisation might be considered just a modelling choice, which is to a certain extent a subjective issue for the modeller. However, not just any process can just be considered an agent in a reasonable manner. The patterns shown by the dynamics of the world should not contradict the possibility of an agent-based conceptualisation. At least certain aspects of agency should show themselves in the world's dynamics. In other words, there are certain criteria for the dynamics of the world that indicate a form of agency. This paper addresses the question which properties patterns occuring in the world's dynamics are indications for agency, and enable a modeller to choose for an agent-based conceptualisation in a justified manner.

Dissatisfaction with agents that are modelled in a way isolated from the physical world, not taking into account adequate criteria for agency, has led to recent attention for the question how to embody agents, and how to embed them in the physical world. The perspective taken in this paper, in a sense, starts at the other end: the world's dynamics and patterns that occur in these dynamics. Using such a perspective, an agent emerges from the world's processes, and thus is fully integrated in them in a natural manner.

N.T. Nguyen and R. Kowalczyk (Eds.): Transactions on CCI III, LNCS 6560, pp. 128–151, 2011.
© Springer-Verlag Berlin Heidelberg 2011

In this paper, in Section 2 six agency-indicating criteria are identified and discussed informally: boundary separating internal and external, isolation, modular world dynamics, input-output dynamics relations, internal-interaction dynamics relations, and representation relations. Next, in Section 3 the formal language MetaTTL is introduced. In subsequent Sections 4 to 9 for each of the criteria it is shown how, using this language, it can be formalised as a second-order dynamic properties of the world. After that, in Section 10, a simple case study illustrates the use of the criteria. This case study has been addressed using automated support in the form of simulation and verification. Finally, as Section 11 a discussion is included.

2 Agency Criteria for Patterns in World Dynamics

In this section, both ontological assumptions on the world state ontology and assumptions on the dynamics of the world are explored as indications for agency. Note that these indications are not assumed to be non-overlapping, nor independent. Moreover, different notions of agency can be covered by taking different subsets of them. For example, a world showing a purely reactive deterministic agent with behaviour fully determined by the input states will fulfill a subset of properties different from the subset fulfilled by a world showing an agent with goal-directed behaviour with some degrees of freedom or randomness in its behaviour.

2.1 Boundary Separating Internal and External

A first criterion for agency concerns the often-mentioned issue that there is a *boundary* separating *internal* states and processes for the agent (internal milieu, body) from states and processes *external* to the agent; cf. Bernard (1865), Brewer (1992), Cannon (1932), Damasio (2000), pp. 133-145, Dobbyn and Stuart (2003). The idea is that this boundary can be crossed only by specific processes: from outside to inside by sensor processes (via agent *input states* at the boundary), and from inside to outside by actuator processes (via agent *output states* at the boundary). The rest of the boundary is not affectable (for example, the shell of a sea animal). Abstracting from more precise spatial relations, this is covered here by the assumption that the world state ontology is the union of a collection of sets for areas: internal, external, boundary, input and output. Note that what is external for a given agent, includes the other agents. What is indicated as 'external world' includes both the physical and social environment of the agent.

2.2 Isolation

In addition to the boundary criterion, the fact that the boundary can only be crossed by specific processes via input and output states is formalised by a criterion on patterns in world dynamics called *isolation*. This criterion expresses that (causal) influences between internal and external state properties or processes can only occur in an indirect manner via the input states and output states. As an example, the internal processes for a biological organism are protected against uncontrolled external influences by skin, or bone (protecting the brain), or shell. As another example, a company organised by a 'front office – back office' structure, protects the work going on in the back office against uncontrolled external influences. The front office serves as an interface to the external world, transferring requests for products (input) from external to internal and offers for products (output) from internal to external.

2.3 Modular World Dynamics

Another criterion for agency is that the world's dynamics is composed from dynamics based on two separate but interacting processes, i.e., a purely internal and a purely external process; e.g., Aleksander (1996), Dobbyn and Stuart (2003). Thus, this criterion describes a form of *modularisation of world dynamics*. For a biological organism, the modularisation shows how the internal processes (such as mental processes and digestion) are separated from the external processes. For the company example, the internal back office process is separated from the external processes.

2.4 Input-Output Dynamics Relations

A further criterion is that (by the internal process) in one way or the other the dynamics of the output states relates to the dynamics of the input states. For example, by Kim (1996, pp. 85-91) such a relation is called an *input-output correlation*. For the company example, the output provided by the front office to the external world depends on the input that was received: for example, if a certain type of product was requested, the offer will involve this type of product.

2.5 Internal and Interaction Dynamics Relations

Relations between the dynamics of input states and of output states, (interaction dynamics, for short), depend on the agent-internal processes. By Kim (1996, p. 87) this is expressed as: a formalisation M of internal dynamics (by a Turing machine in his case) 'is a behavioural description of a system S just in case M provides a correct description of S's input-output correlations'. This shows how the system's behaviour as shown by its input and output states depends on its internal mechanisms: *relations between internal dynamics and interaction* dynamics.

2.6 Representation Relations

Finally, *representational content* is a notion that is often related to internal agent states, in particular if a sense of self is at issue; e.g. Kim (1996), Damasio (2000), Dobbyn and Stuart (2003), Stuart (2002), Jacob (1997), Keijzer (2002), Sun (2000). The *relational specification* approach of representational content as introduced by Kim (1996), pp. 200-202, and worked out by Jonker and Treur (2003) and Bosse, Jonker and Treur (2009), is adopted for this criterion. Kim views this as a way to account for a broad or wide content of mental properties:

'The third possibility is to consider beliefs to be wholly internal to the subjects who have them but consider their contents as giving *relational specifications* of the beliefs. On this view, beliefs may be neural states or other types of physical states of organisms and systems to which they are attributed. Contents, then, are viewed as ways of specifying these inner states; wide contents, then, are specifications in terms of, or under the constraints of, factors and conditions external to the subject, both physical and social, both current and historical. (…) These properties are intrinsic, but their specifications or representations are extrinsic and relational, involving relationships to other things and properties in the world. It may well be that the availability of such extrinsic representations are essential to the utility of these properties in the formulation of scientific laws and explanations. (…) … in attributing to persons beliefs with wide content, we use propositions, or content sentences, to represent them, and these propositions (often) involve relations to things outside the persons. When we say that Jones believes that water is wet, we are using the content sentence "Water is wet" to specify this belief, and the appropriateness of this sentence as a specification of the belief depends on Jones' relationship, past and present, to her environment. (…) The approach we have just sketched has much to recommend itself over the other two. It locates beliefs and other intentional states squarely within the subjects; they are internal states of the persons holding them, not something that somehow extrudes from them. This is a more elegant metaphysical picture than its alternatives. What is "wide" about these states is their specifications or descriptions, not the states themselves.' (Kim, 1996), pp. 200-202; italics in the original.

According to this approach, an internal state property has representational content in the sense that a *representation relation* exists that relates the occurrence of this state property to occurrences of certain patterns in the external part of the world. Such patterns may occur in the past and the future. Similarly, the internal state property may be related to interaction states (for *interactivist* representation; cf. Bickhard, 1993), or to other internal states (*second-order* representation; e.g., Damasio, 2000, pp. 168-182). For the company example, for example, a choice made within the back office relates to the (past) input from a certain customer and also to the (future) output to be provided to this customer.

3 Formalising Patterns in World Dynamics and Their Relationships

To formalise the patterns in world dynamics that play a role in the above criteria, as a basis the *Temporal Trace Language* (TTL) to express dynamic properties is used; cf. (Jonker and Treur, 2002; Bosse, Jonker, Meij, Sharpanskykh and Treur, 2009; Sharpanskykh and Treur, 2010). This language can be classified as a sorted reified temporal predicate logic language (see, e.g., Galton, 2003, 2006), in contrast to, for example, modal-logic-based temporal logics as the ones discussed in, e.g., (Fisher, 2005).

The language is briefly introduced here. For more details, including its semantics, see (Bosse, Jonker, Meij, Sharpanskykh and Treur, 2009; Sharpanskykh and Treur, 2010) [1]. Moreover, to express properties (second-order patterns), that have the form of relationships between the occurrence of patterns, by second-order dynamic properties, the language MetaTTL is introduced.

3.1 States and Traces

In TTL, ontologies for world states are formalised as sets of symbols in sorted predicate logic. For any ontology Ont, the ground atoms form the set of *basic state properties* BSTATPROP(Ont). Basic state properties can be defined by nullary predicates (or proposition symbols) such as hungry, or by using n-ary predicates (with n>0) like has_temperature(environment, 7). The *state properties* based on a certain ontology Ont are formalised by the propositions (using conjunction, negation, disjunction, implication) made from the basic state properties; they constitute the set STATPROP(Ont).

In order to express dynamics in TTL, in addition to state properties, important concepts are *states*, *time points*, and *traces*. A *state* S is an indication of which basic state properties are true and which are false, i.e., a mapping S: BSTATPROP(Ont) → {true, false}. The set of all possible states for ontology Ont is denoted by STATES(Ont). Moreover, a fixed *time frame* T is assumed which is linearly ordered. Then, a *trace* γ over a state ontology Ont and time frame T is a mapping γ : T → STATES(Ont), i.e., a sequence of states γ_t (t ∈ T) in STATES(Ont). The set of all traces over ontology Ont is denoted by TRACES(Ont), i.e., TRACES(Ont) = STATES(Ont)^T. Finally, a *temporal domain description* W is a given set of traces over the state ontology (usually in a given application domain), i.e., W ⊆ TRACES(Ont). This set W represents the world that is considered.

3.2 Patterns in World Dynamics as Dynamic Properties

Patterns in world dynamics are described by dynamic properties. The set of *dynamic properties* DYNPROP(Ont) is the set of temporal statements that can be formulated with respect to traces based on the state ontology Ont in the following manner. Traces and time points can be related to state properties via the relation at, comparable to the Holds-predicate in event calculus (Kowalski and Sergot, 1986) or situation calculus (Reiter, 2001). Thus, at(γ, t, p) denotes that state property p holds in trace γ at time t. Here state propererties are considered objects and denoted by term expressions in the TTL language. Likewise, at(γ, t, ¬p) denotes that state property p does not hold in trace γ at time t. Based on these statements, dynamic properties can be formulated in a formal manner in a sorted predicate logic, using the usual logical connectives such as negation, conjunction, disjunction, implication (denoted by ¬, &, ∨, ⇒ respectively), and universal and existential quantifiers (denoted by ∀, ∃), for example, over traces, time and state properties. An example is the following dynamic property for a pattern concerning belief creation based on observation:

---

[1] Note that in the current paper a slightly different notation is used.

for trace $\gamma \in$ W,

if   at any point in time t1 the agent observes that it is wet outside,

then   there exists a time point t2 after t1 such that at t2 in the trace the agent believes
        that it is wet outside

This property can be expressed as a dynamic property in TTL form (with free variable γ) as follows:

$$\forall t{:}T \ [\ at(\gamma, t, observes(itswet)) \ \Rightarrow \ \exists t' \geq t \ at(\gamma, t', belief(itswet))]$$

The set DYNPROP(Ont, γ) is the subset of DYNPROP(Ont) consisting of formulae in which γ is either a constant or a free variable.

3.3   Past, Future and Interval Patterns

Let two traces γ_1, γ_2 *coincide* on ontology Ont, and interval [t1, t2), denoted by

$$coincide\_on(\gamma_1, \gamma_2, Ont, t1, t2) \ \ or \ \ \gamma_1 =_{Ont, [t1, t2)} \gamma_2$$

if and only if

$$\forall t{:}T \ \forall a{:}BSTATPROP(Ont) \ [\ t1 \leq t < t2 \ \Rightarrow \ [at(\gamma_1, t, a) \Leftrightarrow at(\gamma_2, t, a)]]$$

When no interval is mentioned it is meant that it holds for the whole time frame. Notice that for $\varphi(\gamma)$ in DYNPROP(Ont) it holds that

$$\gamma =_{Ont} \gamma' \Rightarrow [\ \varphi(\gamma) \Leftrightarrow \varphi(\gamma')].$$

An *interval pattern* for the time interval [t1, t2) is formalised as a statement that does not depend on time points before t1 or after t2. The subset IPROP(Ont, η, u1, u2) of DYNPROP(Ont, η) (where u1 and u2 are constant parameters for time points and η for traces) is the set of *interval statements* over state ontology Ont with respect to trace η and interval from time point u1 to time point u2. This set is defined by the predicate

interval_statement($\varphi(\eta$, u1, u2), Ont, η, u1, u2) $\equiv$
    $\forall \gamma_1, \gamma_2, t1, t2 \ [\ \gamma_1 =_{Ont, [t1, t2)} \gamma_2 \ \Rightarrow \ [\varphi(\gamma_1, t1, t2) \Leftrightarrow \varphi(\gamma_2, t1, t2)]]$

In principle, instances of this set can be defined by including for every time quantifier for a time variable s restrictions of the form u1 $\leq$ s, or u1 < s and s $\leq$ u2, or s < u2.

Similarly the sets of past statements and future statements are defined by the predicates

past_statement($\varphi(\eta$, u2), Ont, η, u2) $\equiv$ $\forall\gamma_1,\gamma_2$, t2 [$\gamma_1 =_{Ont, <t2} \gamma_2 \Rightarrow$ [$\varphi(\gamma_1$, t2) $\Leftrightarrow$ $\varphi(\gamma_2$, t2)]]

future_statement($\varphi(\eta$, u1), Ont, η, u1) $\equiv$ $\forall\gamma_1,\gamma_2$, t2 [$\gamma_1 =_{Ont, \geq t1} \gamma_2 \Rightarrow$ [$\varphi(\gamma_1$, t1) $\Leftrightarrow$ $\varphi(\gamma_2$, t1)]]

3.4 Formalising Second-Order Dynamic Properties in MetaTTL

The criteria for agency have the form of (second-order) properties of patterns in world dynamics. As patterns in world dynamics are formalised by TTL formulae, formalisation of the criteria for agency take the form of second-order dynamic properties, i.e., properties that refer to dynamic properties expressed within TTL. Such second-order dynamic properties are expressed in MetaTTL: the meta-language of TTL. For more information on how to formalise such a meta-language, see, for example, Attardi and Simi (1984), Bowen and Kowalski (1982), Bowen (1985), Weyhrauch (1980), Vila and Reichgelt (1996). The language MetaTTL includes sorts for DYNPROP(Ont) and its subsets as indicated above, which contain TTL-statements (for dynamic properties) as objects denoted by term expressions. Moreover, a predicate holds on these sorts can be used to express that such a TTL formula is true. When no confusion is expected, this predicate can be left out. To express second-order dynamic properties, in a MetaTTL statement, quantifiers over TTL statements can be used. As TTL-statements are used to formalise patterns in the world's dynamics, quantifiers over TTL statements can be used to express properties about all patterns or about the existence of patterns with certain properties. For example, for $\varphi1$ of sort IPROP(ExtOnt, η, u1, u2) and $\varphi2$ of sort IPROP(IntOnt, η, u1, u2) the MetaTTL formula

$\forall\gamma$:W $\forall$t1,t2:T [[holds($\varphi1(\gamma$, t1, t2)) & t1$\leq$t2] $\Rightarrow \exists$t3,t4:T [t2$\leq$t3$\leq$t4 & holds($\varphi2(\gamma$, t3, t4))]]

expresses that

> for any trace γ and time points t1 and t2, when the pattern $\varphi1(\gamma$, t1, t2) occurs in γ between t1 and t2, then after t2 the pattern $\varphi2(\gamma$, t3, t4) occurs in γ between some t3 and t4.

For this MetaTTL formula the (definable) abbreviation predicate has_effect is used:

has_effect($\varphi1$:IPROP(Ont, η, u1, u2), $\varphi2$:IPROP(Ont', η, u1, u2)) $\equiv$
    $\forall\gamma$:W $\forall$t1,t2:T [[holds($\varphi1(\gamma$, t1, t2)) & t1$\leq$t2] $\Rightarrow$ $\exists$t3,t4:T [t2$\leq$t3$\leq$t4 & holds($\varphi2(\gamma$, t3, t4))]]

In the next sections, the six criteria for agency will be formalised in MetaTTL. This will show various examples where quantifiers over patterns such as $\varphi1$ and $\varphi2$ are used.

4   Boundary Separating Internal and External

To start with the first boundary criterion suppose WorldOnt is the world state ontology used. It is assumed that this set is the union of a collection of subsets, each of which collects the ontology elements within WorldOnt related to a certain location (local ontology). This collection of local ontologies can be considered a set of locations; it is called LOC, so WorldOnt = $\cup$ LOC = $\cup_{L \in LOC}$ L. Based on this, the set of *local basic world state properties* for location L is BSTATPROP(L), and the set of *local world state properties* is STATPROP(L). Finally,

$$WBSTATPROP \quad = \cup_{L \in LOC} BSTATPROP(L)$$
$$WSTATPROP \quad = \cup_{L \in LOC} STATPROP(L)$$

denote the overall sets of (basic) world state properties.

An ontological assumption for agency is that in the world a distinction can be made between sets of locations: *internal* and *external* locations, and a *boundary* that has two specific parts: the part affectable from outside (*input*), and the part affectable from inside (*output*). The rest of the boundary (if any) is not affectable (e.g, a shell). To formalise this, the collection LOC is partitioned into three disjoint subsets INTLOC, EXTLOC, BOUNDLOC. Within BOUNDLOC two disjoint subsets INLOC and OUTLOC are distinguished that may not exhaust BOUNDLOC. The union of INLOC and OUTLOC is INTERACTIONLOC. So, the following relationships between these sets exist:

$$INTLOC \cup EXTLOC \cup BOUNDLOC = LOC \qquad \text{(disjoint union)}$$
$$INLOC, OUTLOC \subseteq BOUNDLOC \qquad \text{(disjoint subsets)}$$
$$INTERACTIONLOC = INLOC \cup OUTLOC$$

According to this, the following ontologies are defined:

$$IntOnt \quad = \cup \; INTLOC \qquad\qquad ExtOnt = \cup \; EXTLOC$$
$$BoundOnt = \cup \; BOUNDLOC \qquad InteractionOnt = \cup \; INTERACTIONLOC$$
$$InOnt \quad = \cup \; INLOC \qquad\qquad OutOnt = \cup \; OUTLOC$$

On this basis also the other sets can be grouped; e.g., BSTATPROP(IntOnt), STAT-PROP(IntOnt), and DYNPROP(IntOnt).

To make the above more concrete, consider the example (static) world description depicted in Figure 1.

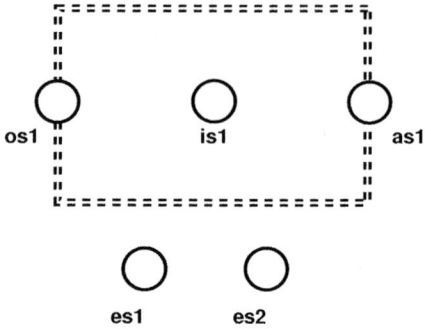

Fig. 1. Example world

This figure describes a process in the world to be considered as an agent and its environment. The box indicates the boundaries of the agent, small circles denote basic state properties. Those within the box are internal state properties, those outside are external, those on the left of the box are input state properties, those on the right output state properties. The following ontologies are used for this example:

IntOnt = {is1} ExtOnt = {es1, es2}   InOnt = {os1} OutOnt = {as1}

Here, is1 stands for 'internal state 1', es1 stands for 'external state 1', es2 stands for 'external state 2', os1 stands for 'observation state 1', and as1 stands for 'action state 1'. The union is WorldOnt. Note that BoundOnt = InteractionOnt in this description.

Now that the assumptions about the (static) world state ontology have been defined, the next five sections will address criteria concerning the world dynamics.

5 Isolation

The isolation principle expresses that influences between internal and external state properties can only occur via the input states and output states. Informally, this criterion for influences from outside to inside can be stated as follows:

> For all dynamic properties $\varphi1$ referring to only external states,
>   and   for all dynamic properties $\varphi3$ referring to only internal states,
> if   for all traces γ, $\varphi1$ implies later $\varphi3$,
> then   there is also a dynamic property $\varphi2$ referring to only input states, such that
> $\varphi1$ implies later $\varphi2$ and $\varphi2$ implies later $\varphi3$ in all traces.

In MetaTTL, this principle can be formalised as follows, using the abbreviation based on the predicate has_effect:

isolation(ExtOnt, InputOnt, IntOnt) ≡

    ∀φ1:IPROP(ExtOnt, η, u1, u2) ∀φ3:IPROP(IntOnt, η, u1, u2)

      has_effect(φ1, φ3) ⇒

      ∃φ2:IPROP(InputOnt, η, u1, u2) [has_effect(φ1, φ2) & has_effect(φ2, φ3)]

This definition can be illustrated by considering Figure 2. This picture shows how possible instances of φ1, φ2 and φ3 are located with respect to an agent. Dotted ovals indicate dynamic properties which are built up from the state properties they contain. Arrows denote (temporal) implications between dynamic properties. The idea of the picture is that, if an instance of the thick arrow exists, then also instances of the thin arrows can be found. The isolation criterion for influences from inside to outside via output states can be defined by interchanging ExtOnt and IntOnt and replacing InOnt by OutOnt in the above formalisation: isolation(IntOnt, OutputOnt, ExtOnt).

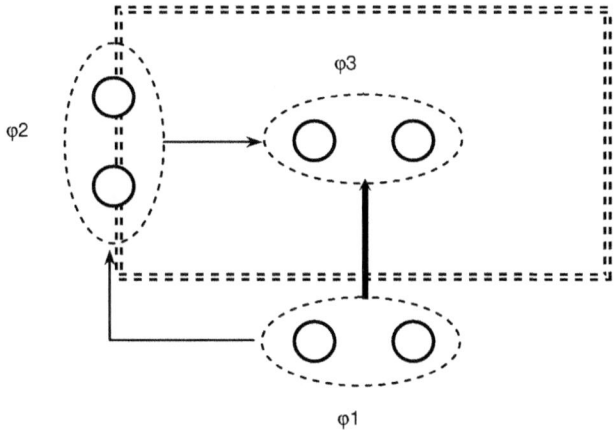

Fig. 2. Isolation Principle

6 Modular World Dynamics

According to the modular world dynamics principle, the dynamics of the world is structured in a modular form, based on dynamic relationships that are purely internal and dynamic relationships that are purely external. Informally, this criterion states the following:

    For all traces γ,

    if   a certain dynamic property ψ over the world ontology holds for γ,

    then there is a dynamic property φ1, referring to only external and interaction states, and there is a dynamic property φ2, referring to only internal and interaction states,

such that φ1 and φ2 hold for γ, and for all traces γ', φ1 and φ2 together imply ψ.

In MetaTTL, this criterion is formalised as follows:

```
modular_world_dynamics ≡
    ∀ψ:IPROP(WorldOnt, η, u1, u2)
    ∀γ:W ∀t1,t2:T [ holds(ψ(γ, t1, t2) ) & t1≤t2  ⇒
        ∃φ1:IPROP(ExtOnt ∪ InteractionOnt, η, u1, u2) ∃φ2:IPROP(IntOnt ∪ InteractionOnt, η, u1, u2)
            holds(φ1(γ, t1, t2)) & holds(φ2(γ, t1, t2)) &
            [∀γ':W [holds(φ1(γ', t1, t2)) & holds(φ2(γ', t1, t2)) ]  ⇒ holds(ψ(γ', t1, t2)) ] ]
```

Also see the (two-dimensional) Figure 3. Again, the three dotted shapes (named ψ, φ1, and φ2) indicate dynamic properties which are built up from the state properties they contain, and arrows denote (temporal) implications between dynamic properties.

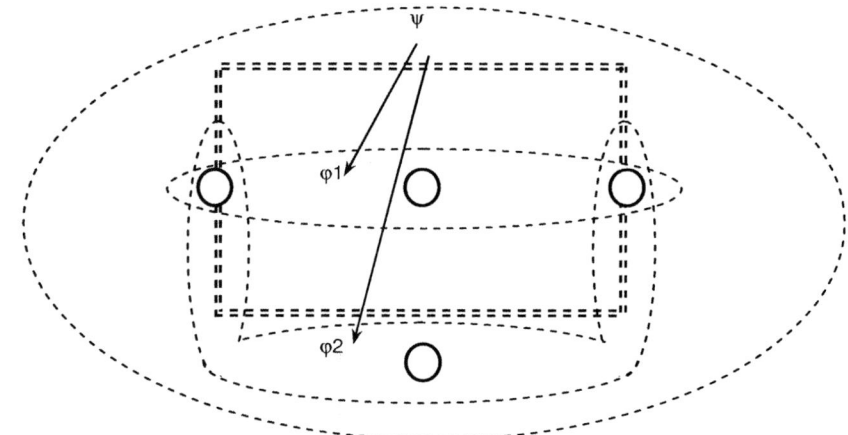

Fig. 3. Modular World Dynamics Principle

7 Input-Output Dynamics Relations

In Kim (1996, pp. 85-91) a relation between input and output is called an input-output correlation. In this paper this is considered a relation between series of input states over time (input traces) and series of output states over time (output traces). This relation may or may not be functional. In case the relation is functional, there is a function mapping input state dynamics (traces) onto output state dynamics (traces). In case the relation is not functional, it has a non-deterministic nature (e.g., a probabilistic relation). This criterion on patterns in world dynamics can be formalised as follows. A first step is as a relation or function between input and output traces, generalising the functionality descriptions in Treur (2002), a relation IOR on the cartesian product of input traces and output traces:

$$\text{IOR} : \text{TRACES(InOnt)} \times \text{TRACES(OutOnt)}.$$

If this relation is functional, i.e., if $\text{IOR}(\gamma_1, \gamma_2)$ and $\text{IOR}(\gamma_1, \gamma_3)$ implies $\gamma_2 = \gamma_3$, then a function IOF exists:

$$\text{IOF} : \text{TRACES(InOnt)} \rightarrow \text{TRACES(OutOnt)}.$$

A further formalisation is by implicit and explicit definability of output traces in terms of input traces, generalising these concepts from Chang and Keisler (1973), and Leemans, Treur, and Willems (2002). For the deterministic, functional case, implicit definability means:

If   for two traces the dynamics of input states is the same,

then   also the dynamics of the output states is the same.

For this functional case, implicit definability is formally expressed by

$$\forall \gamma, \gamma' {:} W \ [\ \gamma =_{\text{InOnt}} \gamma' \Rightarrow \gamma =_{\text{OutOnt}} \gamma' \ ]$$

For the nonfunctional case it can be expressed as:

If   for two traces the dynamics of input states is the same,

then   there is a trace with

the same external and input dynamics of one of these traces

and the same internal and output dynamics as the other trace.

Formally:

$$\forall \gamma, \gamma' {:} W \ \gamma =_{\text{InOnt}} \gamma' \Rightarrow \exists \gamma'' {:} W \ \gamma'' =_{\text{ExtOnt} \cup \text{InOnt}} \gamma' \ \& \ \gamma'' =_{\text{IntOnt} \cup \text{OutOnt}} \gamma.$$

Explicit definability means:

There is a dynamic property expressed in the specification language used that relates the input states over time to output states over time.

For the functional case this is as follows. For $\varphi(\eta)$ in DYNPROP(InteractionOnt), let

$$\text{input\_output\_correlation}(\varphi(\eta))$$

denote

$$\forall\gamma{:}\text{TRACES } [\text{ holds}(\varphi(\gamma)) \Leftrightarrow \exists\gamma'{:}W \ [\gamma =_{\text{InOnt}} \gamma' \ \& \ \gamma =_{\text{OutOnt}} \gamma' \ ] \ \&$$
$$\forall\gamma{:}W \ \exists\gamma'{:}\text{TRACES } [\gamma =_{\text{InOnt}} \gamma' \ \& \ \text{holds}(\varphi(\gamma'))] \ \&$$
$$\forall\gamma,\gamma'{:}\text{TRACES } [\text{holds}(\varphi(\gamma)) \ \& \ \text{holds}(\varphi(\gamma')) \ \& \ \gamma =_{\text{InOnt}} \gamma' \ \Rightarrow \ \gamma =_{\text{OutOnt}} \gamma' \ ] \ ]$$

Then, for the functional case, explicit definability is:

$$\exists\varphi(\eta){:}\text{DYNPROP(InteractionOnt)} \quad \text{input\_output\_correlation}(\varphi(\eta)),$$

see Figure 4. For the nonfunctional case the third conjunct can be left out:

$$\forall\gamma{:}\text{TRACES } [\text{ holds}(\varphi(\gamma)) \Leftrightarrow \exists\gamma'{:}W \ [\gamma =_{\text{InOnt}} \gamma' \ \& \ \gamma =_{\text{OutOnt}} \gamma' \ ] \ \&$$
$$\forall\gamma{:}W \ \exists\gamma'{:}\text{TRACES } [\gamma =_{\text{InOnt}} \gamma' \ \& \ \text{holds}(\varphi(\gamma'))] \ ]$$

φ

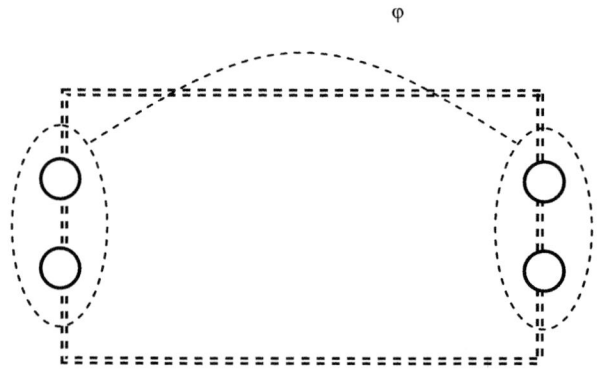

Fig. 4. Input-Output Dynamics Relations

8   Internal and Interaction Dynamics Relations

Given an input-output dynamics relation $\varphi(\eta)$ in DYNPROP(InteractionOnt), this can be related to the internal dynamics described by $\pi(\eta)$ in DYNPROP(IntOnt∪InteractionOnt) as follows:

$\text{internal\_interaction\_relation}(\pi(\eta),\varphi(\eta)) \equiv$

$\forall\gamma{:}W \ [\text{holds}(\pi(\gamma)) \ \Rightarrow \ \text{holds}(\varphi(\gamma))] \ \& \ \forall\gamma{:}W \ [\text{holds}(\varphi(\gamma)) \ \Rightarrow \ \exists\gamma'{:}W \ [\text{holds}(\pi(\gamma')) \ \& \ \gamma' =_{\text{InteractionOnt}} \gamma] \ ]$

Then the criterion is (see also Figure 5):

∀φ(η):DYNPROP(InteractionOnt) [input_output_correlation(φ(η)) ⇒

∃π(η):DYNPROP(IntOnt∪InteractionOnt)   internal_interaction_relation(π(η),φ(η))]

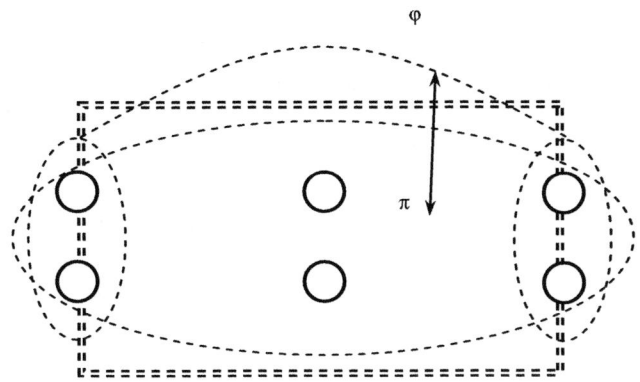

Fig. 5. Internal-Interaction Dynamics Relations

9   Representation Relations

In the literature on Philosophy of Mind different types of approaches to representational content of an internal state property have been put forward, for example the causal/correlational, interactivist and relational specification approach; cf. Bickhard (1993); Kim (1996), pp. 191-193, 200-202. For this paper we adopt the relational specification approach; cf. Kim (1996), pp. 200-202. The formalisation of this approach can be done as follows. Suppose p is an internal state property. A relational specification for p is made by a formula φ(η, u) in DYNPROP(ExtOnt ∪ { p}) that specifies how a certain pattern in the dynamics of external world states relates to p. Here ExtOnt can also be replaced by InteractionOnt to relate p to a pattern in the dynamics of the interaction states. A relational specification can also be obtained in a more specific manner by relating p separately to a past pattern and to a future pattern. Then two formulae φP(η, u) and φF(η, u) exist in DYNPROP(ExtOnt) (or DYN-PROP(InteractionOnt)), where the former is a past formula and the latter a future formula. Based on this, the criterion representation_relations expresses that for all p in STATPROP(IntOnt) there exist formulae φP(η, u) and φF(η, u) that can be related to p by biconditionals (see also Figure 6):

is_past_representation_relation_for($\varphi_P(\eta, u), p$) $\equiv$
        past_statement($\varphi_P(\eta, u)$, ExtOnt, η, u) &
           $\forall\gamma$:W $\forall$t:T [holds($\varphi_P(\gamma, t)$) $\Leftrightarrow$ holds(at(γ, t, p))]
is_future_representation_relation_for($\varphi_F(\eta, u), p$) $\equiv$
        future_statement($\varphi_F(\eta, u)$, ExtOnt, η, u) &
           $\forall\gamma$:W $\forall$t:T [holds($\varphi_F(\gamma, t)$) $\Leftrightarrow$ holds(at(γ, t, p))]
   has_two_sided_representation_relations(p) $\equiv$
       $\exists\varphi_P(\eta, u), \varphi_F(\eta, u)$:DYNPROP(ExtOnt)
       past_representation_relation_for($\varphi_P(\eta, u), p$) & future_representation_relation_for($\varphi_F(\eta, u), p$)

representation_relations $\equiv$ $\forall$p:STATPROP(IntOnt) has_two_sided_representation_relations(p)

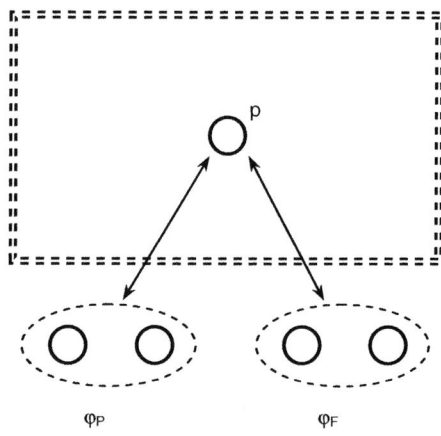

Fig. 6. Representation Relation

10   Case Study

To illustrate how the above criteria for agency apply to a specific example, this section describes a simple case study.

10.1   Boundary Separating Internal and External

In the case study, the following five basic state properties are considered (similar to Figure 1):

    IntOnt = {is1} ExtOnt = {es1, es2}   InOnt = {os1} OutOnt = {as1}

This satisfies the first criterion. The basic dynamical relationships of the case study are represented graphically in Figure 7; this defines the set of traces W for the example.

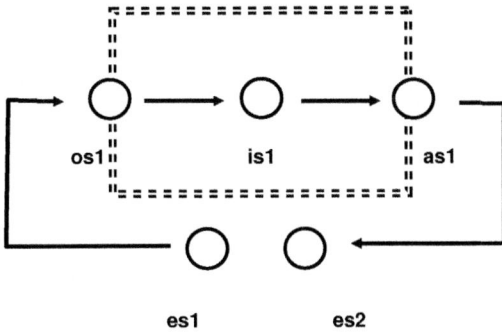

Fig. 7. Relationships within the case study

Circles denote state properties; the arrows denote relationships between state properties. For example, the arrow from os1 to is1 indicates that the occurrence of os1 leads to the occurrence of is1. Furthermore, the state properties are assumed to be non-persistent. Thus, whenever os1 ceases to exists, is1 also ceases to exist.

Based on these relationships, that define the set of traces W, a number of simulation traces have been produced, using the LEADSTO language and its simulation software (Bosse et al., 2005). This language enables to model direct temporal dependencies between two state properties in successive states. This executable format is defined as follows. Let α and β be state properties of the form 'conjunction of atoms or negations of atoms', and e, f, g, h non-negative real numbers. Then the notation $\alpha \twoheadrightarrow_{e, f, g, h} \beta$, means:

If   state property α holds for a certain time interval with duration g

then   after some delay (between e and f) state property β will hold for a certain time interval

of length h.

A trace γ *satisfies* a LEADSTO expression $\alpha \twoheadrightarrow_{e, f, g, h} \beta$ denoted by $\gamma \models \alpha \twoheadrightarrow_{e, f, g, h} \beta$ if

$$\forall t1 \; [\forall t \; [t1-g \leq t < t1 \implies at(\gamma, t, \alpha)] \implies$$
$$\exists d \; [e \leq d \leq f \; \& \; \forall t' \; [t1+d \leq t' < t1+d+h \implies at(\gamma', t, \beta)]]$$

which also can be used as a definition of the LEADSTO format in terms of the language TTL. A specification of dynamic properties in LEADSTO format has as advantages that it is executable and that (besides in textual or formal format), it can often easily be depicted graphically (as in Figure 7). The LEADSTO format has shown its value especially when temporal relations for basic mechanisms in the (continuous) physical world are modelled and simulated; for example, in cooperation with cell biologists, the bacterium *E. coli* and its intracellular chemistry have been modelled as an agent in LEADSTO (Jonker, Snoep, Treur, Westerhoff, and Wijngaards, 2008). The textual specification in LEADSTO format of the example depicted in Figure 7 is as follows:

LP1   es1 $\twoheadrightarrow_{e, f, g, h}$ os1

LP2   os1 $\twoheadrightarrow_{e, f, g, h}$ is1

LP3   is1 $\twoheadrightarrow_{e, f, g, h}$ as1

LP4   as1 $\twoheadrightarrow_{e, f, g, h}$ es2

Here LP2 and LP3 describe the internal process, and LP1 and LP4 describe (part of) the external process. This specification describes the set W characterising the world for the example:

$$W = \{ \gamma \in \text{TRACES(Ont)} \mid \gamma \models \text{LP1 \& LP2 \& LP3 \& LP4} \}$$

Simulation is performed by execution of the LEADSTO rules (similar to executable temporal logic; e.g., Fisher, 2005), thus generating a trace that satisfies all of these rules, and therefore in W. An example of a trace in W as generated by the LEADSTO specification described above is shown in Figure 8 (e, f, g, h all have been taken 1). Here, time is on the horizontal axis, and the state properties are on the vertical axis. A mark on top of a line indicates that a state property is true at that time point.

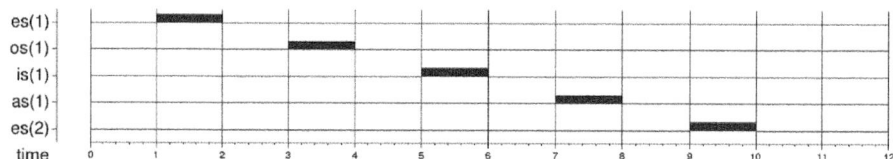

Fig. 8. Example world trace

In the following sections, it is explained in more detail why in addition to the boundary criterion, also the other five criteria for agency hold for these generated traces, which form a representative subset of W.

10.2 Isolation

To start, it is illustrated why the property isolation holds in this case study (also see Figure 2 and the informal description above this figure). Obviously, it is difficult to provide a complete proof for this criterion, since the number of dynamic properties that can be filled in for φ1 and φ3 in principle is large. Therefore, we restrict ourselves to explaining why the criterion holds for some given instances of φ1 and φ3. Suppose, for example, that the following dynamic properties correspond to φ1 in terms of the external state ontology and φ3 in terms of the internal state ontology:

$$\varphi1(\eta, u1, u2) \quad \equiv \quad at(\eta, u1, es1) \ \& \ at(\eta, u2, \neg es1)$$
$$\varphi3(\eta, u1, u2) \quad \equiv \quad at(\eta, u1, is1) \ \& \ at(\eta, u2, \neg is1)$$

Then, as

$$holds(\varphi1(\gamma:W, t1:T, t2:T)) \ \Rightarrow \ \exists t3, t4 \ [\ t2 \leq t3 \leq t4 \ \& \ holds(\varphi3(\gamma:W, t3:T, t3:T))\ ]$$

it holds

$$has\_effect(\varphi1, \varphi3)$$

Therefore, according to the isolation principle, there is a φ2 in terms of the input ontology to be found such that, in all traces, φ1 implies (later) φ2 and φ2 implies (later) φ3, or:

$$has\_effect(\varphi1, \varphi2) \ \& \ has\_effect(\varphi2, \varphi3)$$

Such a φ2 can indeed be found:

$$\varphi2(\eta, u1, u2) \quad \equiv \quad at(\eta, u1, os1) \ \& \ at(\eta, u2, \neg os1)$$

Given this instance of φ2, the property isolation indeed holds for the case study. This can be made more clear by looking at the model described in Figure 7. Intuitively, for all traces in W, which are the traces that can be generated on the basis of this model (such as Figure 8), it is clear that if they satisfy φ1 (i.e., first es1 holds and later es1 does not hold), then later φ3 will hold (i.e., first is1 holds and later is1 does not hold), and that they also will satisfy φ2 in between (i.e., first os1 holds and later os1 does not hold). For the set of traces that have been generated as representative example traces in W, this has been checked automatically, using the TTL checking software described in (Bosse et al, 2006), and found confirmed.

10.3 Modular World Dynamics

Next, the criterion modular_world_dynamics is addressed. Consider the description of this criterion given earlier (also see Figure 3). Again, it is explained why the criterion holds for a given instance of ψ. Thus, as an example for ψ suppose

$\psi(\eta, u1, u2) \equiv$

$\forall t:T [[u1 \leq t < u2 \; \& \; at(\eta, t, es1)] \Rightarrow \exists t' \; [t < t' \leq u2 \; \& \; at(\eta, t', is1)]] \; \&$
$\forall t':T [[u1 < t' \leq u2 \; \& \; at(\eta, t', is1)] \Rightarrow \exists t \; [u1 \leq t < t' \; \& \; at(\eta, t, es1)]]$

Then, according to the modular world dynamics principle, there are $\phi 1$ and $\phi 2$ to be found that hold for γ and such that, in all traces, $\phi 1$ and $\phi 2$ together imply ψ. These $\phi 1$ and $\phi 2$ can indeed be found:

$\phi 1(\eta, u1, u2) \equiv$

$\forall t:T [[u1 \leq t < u2 \; \& \; at(\eta, t, es1)] \Rightarrow \exists t' \; [t < t' \leq u2 \; \& \; at(\eta, t', os1)]] \; \&$
$\forall t':T [[u1 < t' \leq u2 \; \& \; at(\eta, t', os1)] \Rightarrow \exists t \; [u1 \leq t < t' \; \& \; at(\eta, t, es1)]]$

$\phi 2(\eta, u1, u2) \equiv$

$\forall t:T [[u1 \leq t < u2 \; \& \; at(\eta, t, os1)] \Rightarrow \exists t' \; [t < t' \leq u2 \; \& \; at(\eta, t', is1)]] \; \&$
$\forall t':T [[u1 < t' \leq u2 \; \& \; at(\eta, t', is1)] \Rightarrow \exists t \; [u1 \leq t < t' \; \& \; at(\eta, t, os1)]]$

Given these instances of $\phi 1$ and $\phi 2$, the property modular_world_dynamics indeed holds for this ψ in this case.

10.4 Input-Output Dynamics Relation

Next, it is shown that the criterion input_output_correlation (see Figure 4) can be satisfied for the case study. This can be done by choosing the following instance for ϕ:

$\phi(\eta) \equiv \forall t:T [at(\eta, t, os1) \Rightarrow \exists t' > t \; at(\eta, t', as1)] \; \&$
$\forall t:T [at(\eta, t, as1) \Rightarrow \exists t' < t \; at(\eta, t', os1)]$

10.5 Internal-Interaction Dynamics Relation

Next, the case study satisfies the criterion internal_interaction_relation (see Figure 5) with the following instance for π:

$\pi(\eta) \equiv \forall t [at(\eta, t, os1) \Rightarrow \exists t' > t \; at(\eta, t, is1)] \; \&$
$\forall t [at(\eta, t, is1) \Rightarrow \exists t' > t \; at(\eta, t, as1)] \; \&$
$\forall t [at(\eta, t, is1) \Rightarrow \exists t' < t \; at(\eta, t, os1)] \; \&$
$\forall t [at(\eta, t, as1) \Rightarrow \exists t' < t \; at(\eta, t, is1)]$

10.6 Representation Relations

Finally, it is shown that appropriate representation relations can be defined for the internal state properties in the case study. To this end, consider the criterion representation_relations (see Figure 6). Suppose that p corresponds to the state property is1.

Then, for φ_P and φ_F the following dynamic properties yield correct representation relations:

$$\varphi_P(\eta, u) \equiv \exists t':T [t'<u \ \& \ at(\eta, t', es1)]$$
$$\varphi_F(\eta, u) \equiv \exists t':T [t'>u \ \& \ at(\eta, t', es2)]$$

11 Discussion

In this paper, the question is addressed which criteria on patterns in world dynamics indicate an adequate conceptualisation of a world's process as an agent. Here the world can be a physical or social world. Moreover, artificial and cultural worlds such as virtual worlds and economical worlds are covered as well. Also hybrid worlds are possible, including both natural and artificial elements (e.g., a robot on Mars, or a human interacting with a virtual environment). Whatever world is considered, a minimal demand is that the world's dynamics can be analysed and formalised. Among the examples that can be addressed are biological organisms, organisations within society such as a company structured according to the 'front office – back office' principle, and robots.

Six criteria in the form of (second-order) properties of patterns in world dynamics were discussed that indicate when the world shows agency, or at least allows a reasonable agent-based conceptualisation. As a naturalist perspective is taken, the criteria can be used to find out whether a given dynamic phenomenon can be considered an agent in a faithful manner. Such a phenomenon can be, for example, an organisation within society that attempts to behave in a coherent manner to its environment. If every member of this organisation has its own direct interaction with the external world and is affected by this, then an analysis based on the conceptual framework introduced here will show that there is no separate internal process, and hence the criteria 'isolation' and 'modular dynamics' will fail. If log files of the processes of such a company are given, then such an analysis can be supported by automated checking software that has been developed.

Notice that it is not claimed that the criteria are independent or non-overlapping. For example, under certain conditions isolation may entail also modular world dynamics. In future work relations between the criteria will be investigated more extensively.

Our claim is not that the list of six criteria is the one and only truth about agency emerging from world dynamics. An aspect for further investigation is how different notions of agency can be defined on the basis of certain subsets or specialisations or extensions of the criteria mentioned (e.g., purely reactive agents, or agents with beliefs, desires and intentions, or self-aware agents).

Also in Stuart (2002) and Dobbyn and Stuart (2003), criteria for agency are (informally) discussed. Five of their six criteria seem in line with our criteria, except that they claim that a certain richness (e.g., of external world, of input, of output) should be demanded. Moreover, their criterion of representation indicates internal representations of not only external but also internal processes (they aim that an agent is aware of itself). This can be added to the sixth criterion. Their second criterion deals with the possession of self-directed goals. For us, this could be added as a criterion for a more specialised self-aware, goal-directed agent notion.

Our first criterion deals with the possibility to distinguish a boundary separating the internal and external area in the world. Although much literature exists that supports this as an important criterion, there is also literature that casts doubt on whether always a boundary can be found; e.g., Clark and Chalmers (1998). Indeed for the phenomenon of extended mind the boundary seems larger than the skin of an organism. One of the issues to be further investigated is whether such an extended boundary can be defined according to the framework presented in this paper.

A question that may arise is to which extent the criteria as discussed and formalised are internal-external symmetric in the sense that replacing 'internal' by 'external' and 'input' by 'output', and vice versa, obtains the same criteria. Is the external world also an agent according to these criteria? How is the internal area distinguished (as being an agent) by the criteria from the external world (as not being an agent)? Indeed, the first three criteria are internal-external symmetric: boundary separation internal and external, isolation, modular world are all internal-external symmetric. However, the other three criteria are not internal-external symmetric. The fourth criterion on input-output dynamics relations has a direction from input to output, and not in the other direction from output to input. Moreover, there is the fifth criterion on the relation between internal and interaction dynamics, but no criterion on the relation between external and interaction dynamics. Finally, the sixth criterion claims representational relations for internal state properties but not for external state properties.

In how far is it possible to extend the list of criteria in a reasonable manner to obtain internal-external symmetry? It can be imagined that the internal-external mirror image criterion of the fourth criterion on input dynamics relations can also be postulated, thus assuming that the external world can be described in its effects over time on the input states (given the output states over time) by an output-input dynamics relation. In the same line it may be imagined that also for the fifth criterion on relations between internal dynamics and interaction dynamics, the mirror image can be added, claiming a relationship between the external world's dynamics and the output-input dynamics. The two mirror images of the fourth and fifth criterion would imply additional assumptions on in how far the external world is describable in terms of temporal specifications (not necessarily in a deterministic manner). Cases may be considered that these indeed are reasonable assumptions, but also cases may be possible that these assumptions are not fulfilled. For the sixth criterion on representation relations, the situation seems more inherently asymmetric. The mirror image of this criterion would state that the external state properties have representation relations to the internal processes. This does not make sense for almost all situations that can be imagined. It would mean that the internal process would play a role as a kind of almighty power, determining all states in the external world. This could only make sense when the external world is very limited.

Summarising the above deliberations, the background for asymmetry in the criteria is mainly found in these two points:

- The external world may be not fully describable
- Usually not all states in the external world are determined by the internal processes

These seem sufficient reasons to have the criteria asymmetric, which has the positive implication that the criteria do not imply doubt on where the agent is to be found, in the internal area or the external area, or both.

Formalisation of the criteria has been done in the form of second-order dynamic properties expressed in the sorted predicate logic-based language MetaTTL. This approach is comparable to a certain extent to the approach to mental state properties defined as second-order world properties; cf. Kim (2005, pp. 98-102). Here, for example, the mental state 'being in pain' is defined as 'there exists a physical state property p such that tissue damage leads to p and p leads to shouting ouch!'. Mental state properties defined in this manner are called functionalised, as their function is made explicit in this definition, abstracting from their physical realisation. Kim's second-order properties are limited to *state* properties, which is an important difference with our case, as we deal with second-order *dynamic* properties. On the other hand, the idea of functionalisation seems a common aspect, as also in our case the second-order dynamic world properties indicate how the world functions in the sense of its dynamic pattern(s), abstracting from the specific realisation of such dynamic patterns.

Another area of further research is to combine formalisms for causal or probabilistic networks with the formalisation of agency presented here, to have a way of indicating that a certain subgraph in such a network can be considered an agent.

Acknowledgements

The authors are grateful to Catholijn Jonker, Simon McGregor, Alexei Sharpanskykh, Vera Stebletsova and Allard Tamminga for discussions about parts of this work.

References

Aleksander, I.: Impossible Minds: My Neurons, My Consciousness. Imperial College Press, London (1996)

Attardi, G., Simi, M.: Metalanguage and reasoning across viewpoints. In: O'Shea, T. (ed.) Proc. 6th European Conference on AI, ECAI 1984, pp. 413–422. North-Holland, Amsterdam (1984)

Bernard, C.: Introduction a l'etude de la medecine experimentale. J. Baillierre et fils, Paris (1865)

Bickhard, M.H.: Representational Content in Humans and Machines. Journal of Experimental and Theoretical Artificial Intelligence 5, 285–333 (1993)

Bosse, T., Jonker, C.M., van der Meij, L., Treur, J.: A Language and Environment for Analysis of Dynamics by Simulation. International Journal of Artificial Intelligence Tools 16, 435–464 (2007)

Bosse, T., Jonker, C.M., van der Meij, L., Sharpanskykh, A., Treur, J.: Specification and Verification of Dynamics in Agent Models. International Journal of Cooperative Information Systems 18, 167–193 (2009)

Bosse, T., Jonker, C.M., Treur, J.: Representation for Reciprocal Agent-Environment Interaction. Cognitive Systems Research Journal 10, 366–376 (2009)

Bowen, K.A.: Meta-Level Programming and Knowledge Representation. New Generation Computing 3, 359–383 (1985)

Bowen, K., Kowalski, R.: Amalgamating language and meta-language in logic programming. In: Clark, K., Tarnlund, S. (eds.) Logic programming. Academic Press, London (1982)

Brewer, B.: Self-location and agency. Mind 101, 17–34 (1992)

Cannon, W.B.: The Wisdom of the Body. W.W. Norton and Co., New York (1932)

Chang, C.C., Keisler, H.J.: Model theory. North Holland, Amsterdam (1973)

Clark, A., Chalmers, D.J.: The Extended Mind. Analysis 58(1), 7–19 (1998)

Clarke, E.M., Grumberg, O., Peled, D.A.: Model Checking. MIT Press, Cambridge (1999)

Damasio, A.: The Feeling of What Happens: Body, Emotion and the Making of Consciousness. MIT Press, Cambridge (2000)

Dobbyn, C., Stuart, S.: The Self as an Embedded Agent. Minds and Machines 13, 187–201 (2003)

Fisher, M.: Temporal Development Methods for Agent-Based Systems. Journal of Autonomous Agents and Multi-Agent Systems 10, 41–66 (2005)

Galton, A.: Temporal Logic. Stanford Encyclopedia of Philosophy (2003), http://plato.stanford.edu/entries/logic-temporal/#2

Galton, A.: Operators vs Arguments: The Ins and Outs of Reification. Synthese 150, 415–441 (2006)

Jacob, P.: What Minds Can Do: Intentionality in a Non-Intentional World. Cambridge University Press, Cambridge (1997)

Jonker, C.M., Snoep, J.L., Treur, J., Westerhoff, H.V., Wijngaards, W.C.A.: BDI-Modelling of Complex Intracellular Dynamics. Journal of Theoretical Biology 251, 1–23 (2008)

Jonker, C.M., Treur, J.: Compositional Verification of Multi-Agent Systems: a Formal Analysis of Pro-activeness and Reactiveness. International Journal of Cooperative Information Systems 11, 51–92 (2002)

Jonker, C.M., Treur, J.: A Temporal-Interactivist Perspective on the Dynamics of Mental States. Cognitive Systems Research Journal 4, 137–155 (2003)

Jonker, C.M., Treur, J., Wijngaards, W.C.A.: A Temporal Modelling Environment for Internally Grounded Beliefs, Desires and Intentions. Cognitive Systems Research Journal 4, 191–210 (2003)

Keijzer, F.: Representation in Dynamical and Embodied Cognition. Cognitive Systems Research Journal 3, 275–288 (2002)

Kim, J.: Philosophy of Mind. Westview Press, Boulder (1996)

Kim, J.: Physicalism, or Something Near Enough. Princeton University Press, Princeton (2005)

Kowalski, R., Sergot, M.: A Logic-Based Calculus of Events. New Generation Computing 4, 67–95 (1986)

Leemans, N.E.M., Treur, J., Willems, M.: A Semantical Perspective on Verification of Knowledge. Data and Knowledge Engineering 40, 33–70 (2002)

McMillan, K.L.: Symbolic Model Checking: An Approach to the State Explosion Problem. PhD thesis, School of Computer Science, Carnegie Mellon University, Pittsburgh, 1992. Kluwer Academic Publishers, Dordrecht (1993)

Reiter, R.: Knowledge in Action: Logical Foundations for Specifying and Implementing Dynamical Systems. MIT Press, Cambridge (2001)

Sharpanskykh, A., Treur, J.: A Temporal Trace Language for Formal Modelling and Analysis of Agent Systems. In: Dastani, M., Hindriks, K.V., Meyer, J.J.C. (eds.) Specification and Verification of Multi-Agent Systems, pp. 317–352. Springer, Heidelberg (2010)

Stuart, S.: A Radical Notion of Embeddedness: A Logically Necessary Precondition for Agency and Self-Awareness. Journal of Metaphilosophy 33, 98–109 (2002)

Sun, R.: Symbol grounding: a new look at an old idea. Philosophical Psychology 13(2), 149–172 (2000)

Treur, J.: Semantic Formalisation of Interactive Reasoning Functionality. International Journal of Intelligent Systems 17, 645–686 (2002)

Vila, L., Reichgelt, H.: The Token Reificacion Approach to Temporal Reasoning. Artificial Intelligence 83 (May 1996)

Weyhrauch, R.W.: Prolegomena to a theory of mechanized formal reasoning. Artificial Intelligence 13, 133–170 (1980)

Agent-Based Modelling of the Emergence of Collective States Based on Contagion of Individual States in Groups

Mark Hoogendoorn, Jan Treur,
C. Natalie van der Wal, and Arlette van Wissen

Vrije Universiteit Amsterdam, Department of Artificial Intelligence
De Boelelaan 1081, 1081 HV Amsterdam, The Netherlands
{m.hoogendoorn,j.treur,c.n.vander.wal,a.van.wissen}@vu.nl
http://www.few.vu.nl/~{mhoogen,treur,cn.van.der.wal,wissen}

Abstract. This paper introduces a neurologically inspired computational model for the dynamics and diffusion of agent states within groups. The model combines an individual model based on Damasio's Somatic Marker Hypothesis with mutual effects of group members on each other via mirroring of individual states such as emotions, beliefs and intentions. The obtained model shows how this combination of assumed neural mechanisms can form an adequate basis for the emergence of common group beliefs and intentions, while, in addition there is a positive feeling with these common states amongst the group members. A particular issue addressed is how certain types of states may affect other types of states, for example, emotions have an effect on beliefs and intentions, and beliefs may effect emotions.

1 Introduction

To express the impossibility of a task, sometimes the expression 'like managing a herd of cats' is used, for example, in relation to managing a group of researchers. This is meant to indicate that no single direction or decision will come out of such a group, no matter how hard it is tried. As an alternative, sometimes a reference is made to 'riding a garden-cart with frogs'. It seems that such a lack of coherence-directed tendency in a group is considered as something exceptional, a kind of surprising, and in a way unfair. However, as each group member is an autonomous agent with his or her own neurological structures, patterns and states, carrying for example, their own emotions, desires, preferences, and intentions, it would be more reasonable to expect that the surprise concerns the opposite side: how is it possible that so often, groups – even those of researchers – develop coherent directions and decisions, and, moreover, why do the group members in some miraculous manner even seem to feel good with these?

Models of social diffusion focus on the process of change within groups. Examples of social diffusion models found in the area of social sciences are: the diffusion of innovations (see e.g. [35]), social movements such as political interests and parties (see e.g. [22]), and crowd behavior, as for instance seen in emergency evacuation (see e.g. [28]). Diffusion models have also been developed in the domain of multi-agent systems in order to study and simulate the behavior of groups of agents. Hereby,

N.T. Nguyen and R. Kowalczyk (Eds.): Transactions on CCI III, LNCS 6560, pp. 152–179, 2011.

models for the spread of information as well as models for the spread of emotions in agent groups have been expressed (see e.g. [36] and [4], [5], [16], respectively).

In this paper, inspired by the notion of mirroring from the neurological literature (e.g., [14], [23], [24], [31], [32], [33], [30]), first a generic agent-based model is presented for contagion of individual states S such as emotions, beliefs or intentions. The model is a generalization of work on emotion contagion as reported in [4] and [5]. It handles contagion of any individual state S, and takes into account personal characteristics for openness and expressivity for state S, for positive or negative biases for S, and for the extent of amplification for S. Moreover parameters are used for the interaction channels between pairs of agents. The generic model has been used for two more complex models each involving multiple types of internal state S, and involving specific forms of interaction between different types of states. These more complex models are also presented in the paper.

One of these two more complex models is a neurologically inspired computational modelling approach for the emergence of group decisions. It incorporates the ideas of somatic marking as a basis for individual decision making, see [2], [10], [12], [13] and mirroring of both emotions and intentions as a basis for mutual influences between group members, see [14], [23], [24], [31], [32], [33], [30]. The model shows how for many cases indeed, the combination of these two neural mechanisms, via the interaction between emotions and intentions, is sufficient to obtain the emergence of common group decisions on the one hand, and, on the other hand, to achieve that the group members have a positive feeling about these decisions.

The other more complex model presented, formalizes and simulates the spread of different types of emotions and beliefs in a group. In the literature, results have been reported that indicate that the emotional state of a person influences the information processing ability (see e.g. [3], [26]). Hence, the emotions that are spread in a group and experienced by the individuals can influence how beliefs are spread. So, two interactions are considered: the influence of emotions upon spreading of beliefs, and the occurrence of emotions based on the beliefs. In order to exemplify the approach, extensive simulation runs have been performed in an evacuation domain with scenarios that based on varying characteristics of the agents. The model is based on Frederickson's broaden-and-build theory [17], which states that positive emotions broaden people's mind-sets: the scopes of attention, cognition, action and the array of percepts, thoughts, and actions presently in mind are widened. The complementary narrowing hypothesis predicts the reverse pattern: negative emotions shrink people's thought-action repertoires. Support for the broaden and narrowing hypotheses can be found in [18].

The model presented here captures these dynamics between information and emotion. To illustrate, a message containing information about the location and spread of a fire can be expected to elicit fear. Feelings of fear will reinforce the focus of a person towards information relevant to the threat. Furthermore, numerous research studies have shown that information is able to affect emotions. For example, in many psychological experiments fear is elicited by imagery or text to study the process of fear itself or the internal or external signs of fear in humans, see [29]. Another area in psychological research studies fear appeal (persuasive messages that arouse fear) in which it is investigated if fear appeals can motivate behavior change across a variety of behaviors. See for example [37]. In [7] it is argued that the media can influence the perception of fear, via the type of information they spread. Moreover, studies of non-verbal behavior have showed results that emotions can be spread through nonverbal behavior [19]. One can conclude from these many viewpoints and disciplines that emotions, such as fear, can be spread through (non)verbal and textual communications and imagery.

The paper is organised as follows. In Section 2 a brief introduction of the neurological ideas underlying the approach is presented: mirroring and somatic marking. Next, in Section 3 the generic agent-based model is described in detail. Section 4 presents the more complex model for decision making in groups based on an interaction betweeen eomotions and intentions. In Section 5 a number of simulation results are shown and Section 6 addresses verification of the model against formally specified properties describing expected emerging patterns. In Section 7 the more complex model for the interplay between emotion and belief is introduced formally. Section 8 discusses extensive simulation results for this model. In Section 9 a mathematical analysis of the models is discussed. The paper is concluded with a discussion in Section 10.

2   Underlying Neurological Principles

For social interaction, recent neurological findings on the *mirroring function* of certain neurons have turned out to play an important role (e.g., [14], [23], [24], [31], [32], [33], [34], [30]). Mirror neurons are neurons which, in the context of the neural circuits in which they are embedded, show both a function to prepare for certain actions or bodily changes and a function to mirror states of other persons. They are active not only when a person intends to perform a specific action or body change, but also when the person observes somebody else intending or performing this action or body change. This includes expressing emotions in body states, such as facial expressions. For example, there is strong evidence that (already from an age of just 1 hour) sensing somebody else's face expression leads (within about 300 milliseconds) to preparing for and showing the same face expression ([21], p. 129-130). The idea is that these neurons and the neural circuits in which they are embedded play an important role in social functioning and in (empathic) understanding of others; (e.g., [14], [23], [34], [30]). The discovery of mirror neurons is often considered a crucial step for a more solid development of the discipline of social cognition, comparable to the role the discovery of DNA has played for biology, as it provides a biological basis for many social phenomena; cf. [23]. Indeed, when states of other persons are mirrored by some of the person's own states that at the same time are connected via neural circuits to states that are crucial for the own feelings and actions, then this provides an effective basic mechanism for how in a social context persons fundamentally affect each other's actions and feelings.

Given the general principles described above, the mirroring function can take place for different types of individual states. In the first place, via body and face expressions, mirroring of emotional states takes place. This type of mirroring occurs in both more complex models presented below in Section 4 and Section 7. A second way in which a mirroring function can occur is by mirroring of intentions or action tendencies of individuals for the respective decision options. This may work when by verbal and/or nonverbal behaviour, individuals show in how far they tend to choose for a certain option. For example, in [20] action tendencies are described as 'states of readiness to execute a given kind of action, [which] is defined by its end result aimed at or achieved'. ([20], p.70)

This form of mirroring takes place in the model presented in Section 4. A third type of state for which mirroring can take place is for beliefs. Here verbal communication also may occur, but within a group the nonverbal responses may play an even more important role. This type of mirroring takes place in the model presented in Section 7.

Cognitive states of a person, such as sensory or other representations often induce emotions felt within this person, as described by neurologist Damasio, [11], [12]; for example:

'Even when we somewhat misuse the notion of feeling – as in "I feel I am right about this" or "I feel I cannot agree with you" – we are referring, at least vaguely, to the feeling that accompanies the idea of believing a certain fact or endorsing a certain view. This is because believing and endorsing *cause* a certain emotion to happen.' ([12], p. 93)

Damasio's *Somatic Marker Hypothesis*; cf. [2], [10], [12], [13], is a theory on decision making which provides a central role to emotions felt. Within a given context, each represented decision option induces (via an emotional response) a feeling, which is used to mark the option. For example, a strongly negative somatic marker linked to a particular option occurs as a strongly negative feeling for that option. Similarly, a positive somatic marker occurs as a positive feeling for that option. Damasio describes the use of somatic markers in the following way:

'the somatic marker (..) forces attention on the negative outcome to which a given action may lead, and functions as an automated alarm signal which says: beware of danger ahead if you choose the option which leads to this outcome. The signal may lead you to reject, *immediately*, the negative course of action and thus make you choose among other alternatives. (...)   When a positive somatic marker is juxtaposed instead, it becomes a beacon of incentive.' ([10], pp. 173-174)

Usually the Somatic Marker Hypothesis is applied to provide endorsements or valuations for options for a person's actions, thus shaping a decision process. Somatic markers may be innate, but may also be adaptive, related to experiences:

'Somatic markers are thus acquired through experience, under the control of an internal preference system and under the influence of an external set of circumstances which include not only entities and events with which the organism must interact, but also social conventions and ethical rules. ([10], p. 179)

In the computational model introduced in Section 4 somatic marking plays an important role in the spread of intentions in a group. In this model both emotion and intention mirroring effects are incorporated. Mirroring of emotions indicates how emotions felt in different individuals, about a certain considered decision option, mutually affect each other. Assuming a context of somatic marking, in this way they affect how by individuals decision options are valuated based on how they feel about them.

In the model introduced in Section 7, mirroring of emotions and beliefs is addressed. Here another type of interaction between mirroring of two different types of states is addressed. In one direction, for example, emotions may affect the openness and biases of a person. In the other direction the beliefs affect emotions.

3 A Generic Agent-Based Model for Social Diffusion of Individual States

This section introduces the basic agent-based social diffusion model used as a point of departure for this research. This model is a generalization of two existing agent-based emotion contagion models: the absorption model and amplification model (cf. [4], [5]). The model formalizes different aspects and types of social diffusion of mental states, such as absorption, amplification, expressiveness and openness for cognitive and affective (e.g., information and emotion) states, which are inspired by theories on contagion mechanisms. For instance, in [1] Barsade describes an informal model of emotion contagion in which the valence (positive or negative) of the emotion and the energy level with which the emotion is expressed characterize the diffusion.

The basic building block of the model is the definition of the contagion strength between individuals within a group. This contagion strength between agents B and A for any particular state S is defined as follows:

$$\gamma_{SBA} = \varepsilon_{SB} \cdot \alpha_{SBA} \cdot \delta_{SA}. \tag{1}$$

Here ε_{SB} is the personal characteristic *expressiveness* of the sender (agent B) for S, δ_{SA} the personal characteristic *openness* of the receiver (agent A) for S, and α_{SBA} the interaction characteristic *channel strength* for S from sender B to receiver A.

To calculate the level q_{SA} of an agent A for a specific state S the following calculations are performed. First, the overall contagion strength γ_{SA} from the group towards agent A is calculated:

$$\gamma_{SA} = \sum_{B \neq A} \gamma_{SBA} \tag{2}$$

This value is used to determine the weighed impact q_{SA}^* of all the other agents upon state S of agent A:

$$q_{SA}^* = \sum_{B \neq A} \gamma_{SBA} \cdot q_{SB} / \gamma_{SA} \tag{3}$$

How much this external influence actually changes state S of the agent A is determined by two additional personal characteristics of the agent, namely the tendency η_{SA} to absorb or to amplify the level of a state and the bias β_{SA} towards positive or negative impact for the value of the state. The model to update the value of $q_{SA}(t)$ over time is then expressed as a combination of the absorption and amplification models. The result is a more general model of contagion for any state S:

$$q_{SA}(t + \Delta t) = q_{SA}(t) + \gamma_{SA} \cdot [\eta_{SA} \cdot [\beta_{SA} \cdot (1 - (1 - q_{SA}^*(t)) \cdot (1 - q_{SA}(t))) +$$

$$(1 - \beta_{SA}) \cdot q_{SA}^*(t) \cdot q_{SA}(t)] + (1 - \eta_{SA}) \cdot q_{SA}^*(t) - q_{SA}(t)] \Delta t \tag{4}$$

The new value of the state is calculated from the old value, plus the change of the value based upon the contagion. This change is defined as the multiplication of the contagion strength times a factor for the amplification of information plus a factor for the absorption of information. The absorption factor (after $1 - \eta_{SA}$) simply takes the difference between the incoming contagion and the current level. The amplification factor (part of the equation multiplied by η_{SA}) depends on the tendency of the agent towards more positive (part of equation multiplied by β_{SA}) or negative (part of

Table 1. Parameters and states

q_{SA}	level for state S for agent A
ε_{SA}	extent to which agent A expresses state S
δ_{SA}	extent to which agent A is open to state S
η_{SA}	tendency of agent A to absorb or amplify state S
β_{SA}	positive or negative bias of agent A on state S
α_{SBA}	channel strenght for state S from sender B to receiver A
γ_{SBA}	contagion strength for S from sender B to receiver A

equation multiplied by $1 - \beta_{SA}$) information. Table 1 summarizes the most important parameters and states within the model.

4   Modelling the Dynamics of Intentions and Emotions in Groups

In this section a computational model for group decision making is introduced, based on the neurological principles of somatic marking and mirroring discussed Section 2, and the generic model presented in the previous section. To design such a model a choice has to be made for the grain-size. For example, it has to be decided in which level of detail the internal neurological processes of individuals are described. Such a choice depends on the aim of the model. In this case the aim was more to be able to simulate emerging patterns in groups of individuals, than to obtain a more detailed account of the intermediate neurological patterns and states involved. Therefore the choice was made to abstract to a certain extent from the latter types of intermediate processes. For example, the process of mirroring is described in an abstract manner by a direct causal relation from the emotional state shown by an individual to the emotional state shown by another individual, and the process of somatic marking is described by a direct causal relation for any individual from the emotional state for a certain option to the intention for this option (see Fig. 1). The model can easily be refined into a model that also incorporates more detailed intermediate internal processes, for example, based on recursive as-if body loops involving preparation and sensory neuron activations and the states of feeling the emotion, for example, as shown in [25].

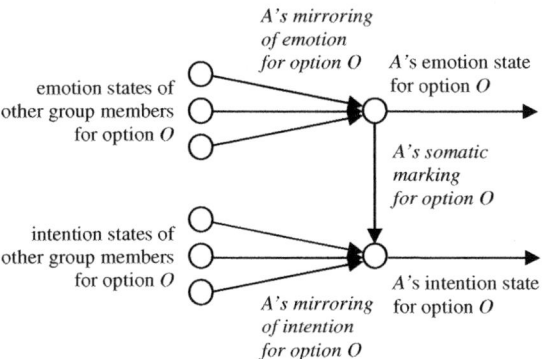

Fig. 1. Abstract causal relations induced by mirroring and somatic marking by person A

The abstract model for mirroring described above applies to both emotion and intention states S or an option O, but does not describe any interplay between them yet. Taking the Somatic Marker Hypothesis on decision making as a point of departure, not only intentions of others, but also one's own emotions affect one's own intentions. To incorporate such an interaction, the basic model is extended as follows: to update $q_{SA}(t)$ for an intention state S relating to an option O, both the intention states of others for O and the $q_{S'A}(t)$ values for the emotion state S' for O are taken into account. These intention and emotion states S and S' for option O are denoted by OI and OE, respectively:

Level of emotion for option O of person A: $q_{OEA}(t)$

Level of intention indication for O of person A: $q_{OIA}(t)$

The combination of the own (positive) emotion level and the rest of the group's aggregated intention is made by a weighted average of the two:

$$q_{OIA}^{**}(t) = (\omega_{OIA}/\omega_{OA})\, q_{OIA}^{*}(t) + (\omega_{OEA}/\omega_{OA})\, q_{OEA}(t)$$
$$\gamma_{OIA}^{*} = \omega_{OA}\, \gamma_{OIA} \tag{1}$$

where ω_{OIA} and ω_{OEA} are the weights for the contributions of the group intention impact (by mirroring) and the own emotion impact (by somatic marking) on the intention of A for O, respectively, and $\omega_{OA} = \omega_{OIA} + \omega_{OEA}$. Then the model for the intention and emotion contagion based on mirroring and somatic marking becomes:

$$q_{OEA}(t + \Delta t) = q_{OEA}(t) + \gamma_{OEA}[\eta_{OEA}(\beta_{OEA}(1 - (1-q_{OEA}^{*}(t))(1-q_{OEA}(t))) + \tag{2}$$
$$(1-\beta_{OEA})\, q_{OEA}^{*}(t)\, q_{OEA}(t)) + (1 - \eta_{OEA})\, q_{OEA}^{*}(t) - q_{OEA}(t)\,]\cdot\Delta t$$

$$q_{OIA}(t + \Delta t) = q_{OIA}(t) + \gamma_{OIA}^{*}\,[\eta_{OIA}(\beta_{OIA}(1 - (1-q_{OIA}^{**}(t))(1-q_{OIA}(t))) + \tag{3}$$
$$(1-\beta_{OIA})\, q_{OIA}^{**}(t)\, q_{OIA}(t)) + (1 - \eta_{OIA})\, q_{OIA}^{**}(t) - q_{OIA}(t)]\cdot\Delta t$$

5   Simulation Results: Interaction between Intentions and Emotions

The model has been studied in several scenarios in order to examine whether the proposed approach indeed exhibits the patterns that can be expected from literature. The investigated domain consists of a group of four agents who have to make a choice between four different options: A, B, C or D. The model has been implemented in Matlab by constructing three different scenarios which are characterized by different relationships (i.e., channel strength) between the agents. The scenarios used, involve two more specific types of agents: leaders and followers. Some agents have strong leadership abilities while others play a more timid role within the group. The general characteristics of leaders and followers as they were used in the experiments, which

Table 2. Parameters and state variables for leaders and followers

	Leader A	Follower B
emotion level	q_{OEA} high for particular O	-
intention level	q_{OIA} high for particular O	-
expressivity	ε_{SA} high	ε_{SB} low
channel strength	α_{SAB} high	α_{SAB} high
	α_{SBA} low	α_{SBA} low

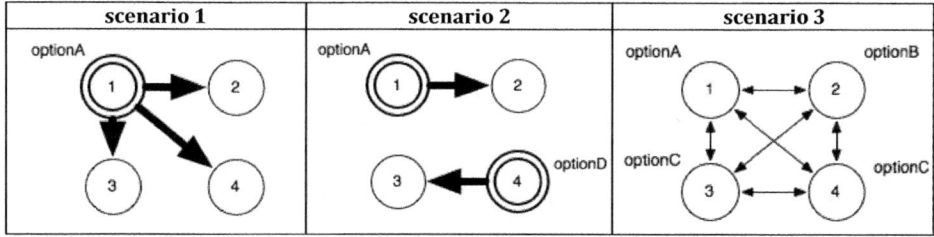

Fig. 2. Scenarios for the presented simulation experiments

can be manifested differently within all agents, can be found in Table 2. The complete settings for the three scenarios can be found in Appendix A.

The different scenarios are depicted in Fig. 2. Scenario 1 consists of a group of agents in which agent1 has strong leadership abilities and high channel strengths to all other agents. His initial levels of emotion and intention for option A, are very high. Scenario 2 depicts a situation where there are two agents with leadership abilities in the group, agent1 and agent4. Agent1 has a strong channel to agent2, while agent4 has a strong connection to agent3. Agent1 has an initial state of high (positive) emotion and intention for option A, while agent4 has strong emotion and intention states for option D. Agent2 and agent3 show no strong intentions and emotions for any of the options in their initial emotion and intention states. In Scenario 3 there are no evident leaders. Instead, all agents have moderate channel strengths with each other. A majority of the agents (agent3 and agent4) prefers option C, i.e., initially they have high intention and emotions states for option C. For both scenarios two variants have been created, one with similar agent characteristics within the group (besides the difference between leader and follower characteristics), and the second with a greater variety of agent personalities. In this section, only the main results using the greater variety in agent characteristics are shown. For the formal verification (Section 6) both have been used.

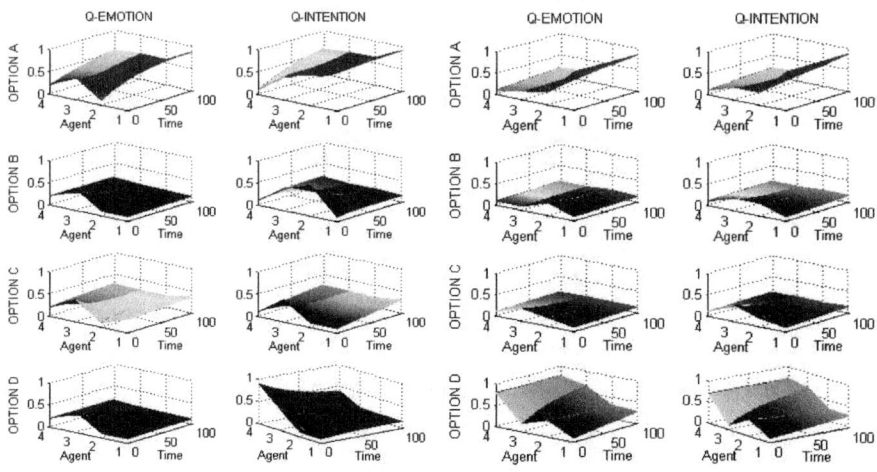

Fig. 3. Simulation results for scenario 1 (column 1 and 2) and scenario 2 (column 3 and 4)

The results of scenario 1 clearly show how one influential leader can influence the emotions and intentions in a group. This is shown in the left graph of Fig. 3, here the z-axis shows the value for the respective states, and the x-and y-axes represent time and the various agents. The emotion and intention of the leader (in this case agent1) spread through the network of agents, while the emotions and intentions of other agents hardly spread. Consequently, the emotions and intentions for option A, which is the preferred option of the leader, develop to be high in all agents. As can be seen in the figure, there are small differences between the developments of emotions and intentions of the agents. This is because they have different personality characteristics, which are reflected in the settings for the scenario (see Appendix A). Depending on their openness, agents are more or less influenced by the states of others. Those agents with low openness (such as agent4) are hardly influenced by intentions and emotions of others.

In scenario 2 (as shown in the right graph of Fig. 3), the leader has somewhat positive emotions about option C as well, which explains the small but increasing spread of emotions (and after a while also intentions) concerning option C through the social network. Even though agent3 and agent2 both have a moderate intention for option B, their only strong channel strength is with each other, causing only some contagion between the two of them. Their intention does not spread because of a low expressive nature and low amplification rate of both agents. The patterns found in the simulation of scenario 2 are similar to the ones of scenario 1, with the addition that both leaders highly dominate the spread of the emotions and intentions. The figure shows that the emotions and intentions of agent2 turn out to depend highly on the emotions and intentions of agent1, whereas the emotions and intentions of agent3 highly depend on those of agent4. As can be seen in the figure, any preferences for option D and C by agent2 and agent3 quickly grow silent.

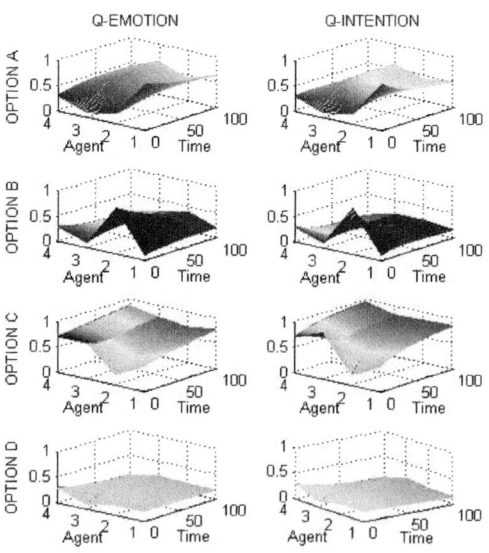

Fig. 4. Simulation results for scenario 3

Scenario 3 shows how a group converges to the same high emotions and intentions for an option when there is no authority. In general, the graphs show that when there is no clear leadership, the majority determines the option with highest emotion and intentions in all agents. Option C, initially preferred by agent4 and agent3, eventually is the preferred option for all. However, the emotions and intentions for option A also spread and increase, though to a lesser extent. This is due to the fact that agent1 has strong feelings and intentions for option A and a high amplification level for these states. Furthermore, he has a significant channel strength with agent3, explaining why agent3 has the most increasing emotions and intentions for option A. However, the majority has the most important vote in this scenario.

Furthermore, some general statements can be made about the behaviour of the model. In case a leader has high emotions but low intentions for a particular option, both the intentions and emotions of all followers will increase for that option. On the other hand, if a leader has high intentions for a particular option, but not high emotions for that option, this intention will not spread to other agents.

6   Verification of Properties Specifying Emerging Patterns

This section addresses the analysis of the group decision making model by specification and verification of properties expressing dynamic patterns that emerge. The purpose of this type of verification is to check whether the model behaves as it should, by automatically verifying such properties against the simulation traces for the various scenarios. In this way the modeller can easily detect inappropriate behaviours and locate sources of errors in the model. A typical example of a property that may be checked, is whether no unexpected situations occur, such as a variable running out of its bounds (e.g., $q_A(t) > 1$, for some time point t and agent A), or whether eventually an equilibrium value is reached, but also more detailed expected properties of the model such as compliance to the theories found in literature.

A number of dynamic properties have been identified, formalized in the Temporal Trace Language (TTL), cf. [6] and automatically checked. The TTL software environment includes a dedicated editor supporting specification of dynamic properties to obtain a formally represented temporal predicate logical language TTL formula. In addition, an automated checker is included that takes such a formula and a set of traces as input, and verifies automatically whether the formula holds for the traces. The language TTL is built on atoms referring to *states* of the world, *time points* and *traces*, i.e. trajectories of states over time. In addition, *dynamic properties* are temporal predicate logic statements that can be formulated with respect to traces based on a state ontology.

Below, a number of the dynamic properties that were identified for the group decision making model are introduced, both in semi-formal and in informal notation (where state(γ, t) |= p denotes that p holds in trace γ at time t). The first property counts the number of subgroups that are present. Here, a subgroup is defined as a group of agents having the same highest intention. Each agent has 4 intention values (namely one for each of the four options that exist), therefore the number of subgroups that can emerge are always: 1, 2, 3 or 4 subgroups.

P1–number of subgroups

The number of subgroups in a trace γ is the number of options for which there exists at least one agent that has an intention for this option as its highest valued intention.

P1_number_of_subgroups(γ:TRACE) ≡ sum(I:INTENTION, case(highest_intention(γ, I), 1, 0)

where

> **highest_intention(γ:TRACE, I:INTENTION)** ≡
> ∃A:AGENT   [∀R1:REAL   state(γ, te) |= has_value(A, I, R1)
> ⇒ ∀I2:INTENTION≠I, ∀R2:REAL [state(γ, te) |= has_value(A, I2, R2) ⇒ R2 < R1]]

In this property, the expression case(p, 1, 0) in TTL functions such that if property p holds it is evaluated to the second argument (*1* in this example), and to the third argument (*0* in this example) if the property does not hold. The sum operator simply adds these over the number of elements in the sort over which the sum is calculated (the intentions in this case). Furthermore, when tb or te are used in the property, they denote the begin or end time of the simulation, whereby in te an equilibrium is often reached. Property P1 can be used to count the number of subgroups that emerge. A subgroup is defined as a group of agents that each have the same intention as their intention with highest value. This property was checked on multiple traces that each belong to one of the three scenario's discussed in the simulation results section. For the traces for both variants of scenario 1, a single subgroup was found. For scenario 2, two subgroups were found, and for scenario 3, a single subgroup was found, which is precisely according to the expectations.

The second property counts the number of agents in each of the subgroups, using a similar construct.

P2–subgroup size

The number of agents in a subgroup for intention I is the number of agents that have this intention as their highest intention.

P2_subgroup_size(γ:TRACE, I:INTENTION) ≡ sum(A:AGENT, case(highest_intention_for(γ, I, A), 1, 0))

where

> **highest_intention_for(γ:TRACE, I:INTENTION, A:AGENT)** ≡
> ∀R1:REAL   [state(γ, te) |= has_level(A, I, R1)
> ⇒ ∀I2:OPTION≠I, ∀R2:REAL [state(γ, te) |= has_level(A, I2, R2) ⇒ R2 < R1]]

In the traces for scenario1 the size of the single subgroup that occurred was 4 agents. For scenario 2 two subgroups of 2 agents were found. Finally, in scenario 3 only a single subgroup combining 4 agents has been found. These findings are correct; they indeed correspond to the simulation results.

The final property, P3, expresses that an agent is a leader in case its intention values have changed the least over the whole simulation trace, as seen from his initial intention values and compared to the other agents (thereby assuming that these agents moved towards the intention of the leader that managed to convince them of this intention).

P3–leader

An agent is considered a leader in a trace if the number of intentions for which it has the lowest change is at least as high as all other agents.

P3_leader (γ:TRACE, A:AGENT) ≡
> ∀A2:AGENT ≠A
> > sum(I:INTENTION, case(leader_for_intention(γ, A, I),1,0)) ≥
> > sum(I:INTENTION, case(leader_for_intention(γ, A2, I),1,0))

where

leader_for_intention(M:TRACE, A:AGENT, I:INTENTION) ≡
∀R1, R2: REAL   [[state(γ, tb) |= has_value(A,I, R1) & state(γ, te) |= has_value(A, I, R2)]
          ⇒   ∀R3, R4: REAL, ∀A2:AGENT ≠A
              [state(γ, tb) |= has_value (A2, I, R4) & state(γ, te) |= has_value (A2, I, R3)
                  ⇒ |R2-R1|< |R3-R4|]]

Using this definition, only agent 1 qualifies as a leader in scenario 1. For scenario 2 only agent 4 is a leader. Finally, in scenario 3 both agent 1 and agent 3 are found to be leaders as they both have equal intentions for which they change the least.

7 Modelling the Dynamics of Beliefs and Emotions in Groups

The agent-based social diffusion model introduced in Section 2 can be applied to both emotion and beliefs, but does not describe any interplay between diffusion of different states. For example, not only emotions of others, but also beliefs may affect emotions. On the other hand, strong emotions may affect personal characteristics for belief diffusion such as openness and expressivity. To incorporate such interactions, the basic model is extended as follows:

1. To update q_{SA} for one state S, also the $q_{S'A}$ values for some other state S' may be taken into account.
2. Some of the personal characteristics for a state S in A may be determined dynamically depending on values $q_{S'A}$ for a certain other state S' in A.

In Section 7.2 the former extension is applied by modelling the effect of belief states on the fear state. In Section 7.1 the latter extension is applied by modelling how the level of fear affects the parameters for personal characteristics involved in the dynamics of belief states.

7.1 The Effect of the Emotion Fear upon Belief

To model the effect of emotions (in particular, fear) on belief diffusion, below the personal characteristics δ_{SA}, η_{SA} and β_{SA} for a belief state S are not assumed constant, but are instead modeled in a dynamic manner, depending on emotions. As can be seen in the adopted model, multiple factors that influence diffusion of a state S have been distinguished. One can divide these into three different categories: state q_{SA}, personal characteristics ε_{SA}, δ_{SA}, η_{SA}, β_{SA} and interaction characteristic α_{BA}. One additional category is introduced here, namely belief state characteristics r_{SA} denoting how relevant, and p_{SA} denoting how positive a belief state S is for agent A. Examples of settings for an evacuation scenario can be found in Table 3.

The intensity of the emotional state of a person will affect his or her ability to believe received information, thereby possibly affecting individual agent characteristics involved in the dynamics of belief states S. In this case the focus is on one type of emotion state for fear: $S' = fear$. A high level of fear contributes to the levels of β_{SA}, η_{SA} and δ_{SA}. However, if fear is low, the value of the parameters should be dominated by their initial values that represent the personal characteristics of the agent instead. First the effect of fear upon the openness for a belief state S (characterized by a relevance r_{SA} and a positiveness p_{SA} for A) is expressed:

$$\delta_{SA}(t+\Delta t) = \delta_{SA}(t) + \mu \cdot (1/(1+ e^{-\sigma(q_{fear,A}(t) - \tau)})) \cdot [(1-(1-r_{SA}) \, q_{fear,A}(t)) - \delta_{SA}(t)] \cdot \Delta t \quad (8)$$

Table 3. Types of Information

		positivity of information (p) [0-1]	
		0	1
relevance for survival (r) [0-1]	0	"The toilets are out of order"	"Local authorities have been informed"
	1	"All rear exits are obstructed"	"The front emergency exit is clear"

If $q_{fear,A}$ is lower than threshold τ (on the interval [0,1]), it will not contribute to the value of δ_{SA}. If $q_{fear,A}$ has a value above τ, the openness will depend on the relevance of the information: when the relevance is high, openness will increase, while if the relevance is low, openness will decrease. In all formulae, μ is an adaptation parameter. This proposed model corresponds to theories of emotions as frames for selective processing, as described in [17], [27]. A distinction between amplification values for different types of information is also made, depending on the emotional state fear. The dynamics for the characteristic $\eta_{SA}(t)$ that model the amplification or absorption of belief state S are described as follows:

$$\eta_{SA}(t+\Delta t) = \eta_{SA}(t) + \mu \cdot (1/(1+e^{-\sigma(q_{fear,A}(t)-\tau)})) \cdot [r_{SA} \cdot (1-p_{SA}) \cdot (q_{fear,A}(t) - \eta_{SA}(t))] \cdot \Delta t \quad (9)$$

The emotion of fear only has an influence when it is above the threshold. In that case the parameter only changes for relevant, non-positive information for which the parameter starts to move towards the value for the emotion of fear (meaning this type of belief will be amplified). This property represents an interpretation of [8] on how emotion can result in selective processing of emotion-relevant information in belief formation and update.

The bias of an agent on a belief state S is influenced by its emotion fear, but in addition depends on the content of the information in S, which can be either positive or negative:

$$\beta_{SA}(t+\Delta t) = \beta_{SA}(t) + \mu \cdot (1/(1+e^{-\sigma(q_{fear,A}(t)-\tau)})) \cdot [q_{fear,A}(t) \cdot ((1-p_{SA}) - \beta_{SA}(t))] \cdot \Delta t \quad (10)$$

Again, the bias is not influenced by fear if its value is low. In case fear is high, p_{SA} has a high impact on the bias: a low positiveness increases the bias, while a high positiveness inhibits the bias. The agent thus has a bias towards negative belief in case it has a high level of fear, which corresponds with the narrowing hypothesis from Frederickson's broaden-and-build theory in [17].

The Effect of Belief upon Emotion

After modeling the influence of emotion upon the belief contagion in the previous section, the opposite direction is investigated in this section: the emotion state for fear being influenced by belief states S. This influence is modeled by altering the overall weighed impact of the contagion of the emotional state for fear based in the relevant belief states S. This is expressed as follows:

$$q_{fear,A}^{*} = v \cdot (\Sigma_{B \neq A} \gamma_{fearBA} \cdot q_{fearB} / \gamma_{fearA}) + (1-v) \cdot (\Sigma_S \omega_{SA} \cdot (1-p_{SA}) \cdot r_{SA} \cdot q_{SA}) \quad (11)$$

Table 4. Six scenarios for diffusion

Initial settings	emotion → info	emotion ↔ info
high fear levels	scenario 1	scenario 4
low fear levels	scenario 2	scenario 5
mixed fear levels	scenario 3	scenario 6

Here the influence depends on the impact from the emotion fear by others (the first factor, with weight v) in combination with the influence of the belief present within the agent. In this case, belief has an increasing effect on fear if it is relevant and non positive.

8   Simulation Results: Interaction between Beliefs and Emotions

In order to see whether the approach indeed exhibits the patterns that can be expected from literature, a case study has been conducted in the domain of emergency evacuation. The states as shown in Table 2 have been used in combination with the emotion of fear. Furthermore, the value of the channel strength α_{SBA} has been made dependent upon the distance:

$$\alpha_{SBA} = 1 - (1/(1 + e^{-4\sigma(d_{AB} - \tau)}))$$ (12)

This formula expresses that a belief is only perceived in case the distance between agent A and B (d_{AB}) is below the distance threshold (τ). The full model has been implemented in Matlab, and six different scenarios have been created. The complete settings of parameters and initial values for the three scenarios can be found in Appendix B.

In the scenarios, the emotional levels have been varied. The influence of belief upon emotion has been left out to allow the sole analysis of the influence of emotions upon belief contagion. In each scenario, 4 agents have been used. The most important results are discussed below. Note that for all scenarios the value for the maximum distance ($\tau_{distance}$) has been set to 4, which represents that one can not hear or see a (non)verbal communication properly anymore when it is farther than the distance of 4. The threshold value for fear (τ_{fear}) is set to 0.5.

Scenario 1. First the general scenario and the interpretation of the values of the parameters is briefly described. In scenario 1, all agents initially are unaware of any danger and thus have low fear ($q_{fear} = 0.1$). Each agent has access to one out of four types of information (the four types can be made out of the four combinations of high/low relevance versus high/low positiveness of information). That is, agent 1 is located near the front exit and observes it is clear. Agent 2 just read on his phone that local authorities have been informed that there is smoke emerging from the building. Agent 3 just received information that all rear exits are blocked and agent 4 noticed that the toilets are out of order.

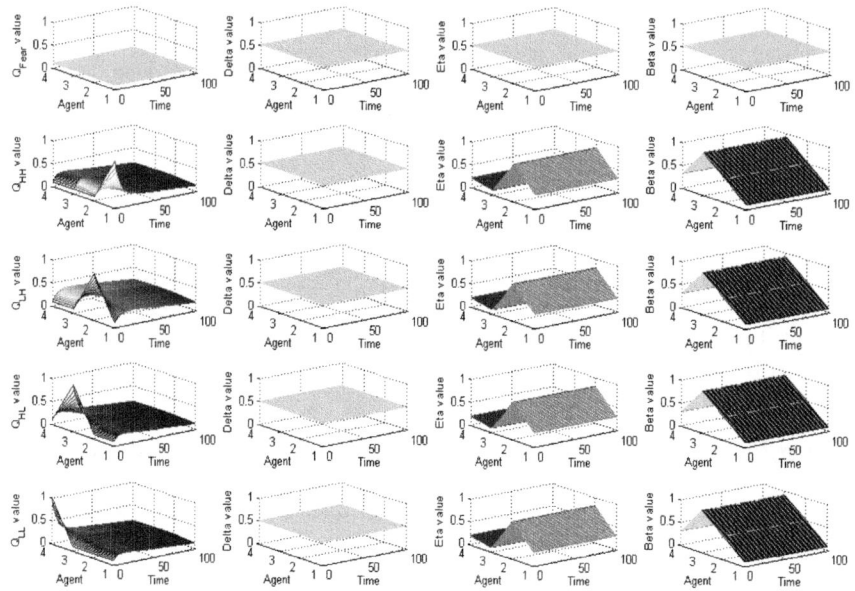

Fig. 5. Simulation results of scenario 1

In order to clearly demonstrate the functioning of the model, all agents in this scenario have the same openness for all information and fear states (0.5) and they have the same amplification rate for fear (0.5). However, they differ in their amplification rate for information they receive. Agent 1, agent 3 and agent 4 all have relatively low amplification rates for all belief states, while agent 2 is more expressive and has a strong amplification for all belief states. In this scenario, agent 1 and agent 3 have a low bias for all types of belief and are not easily primed by it. Agent 2 has an average bias for all belief states and agent 3 is easily primed by any kind of belief. Details on the translation of this information into parameter settings can be found in Appendix B. Fig. 5 shows the simulation results for scenario 1. The rows in the figure represent the various states: the first row shows values for the state fear (q_{fear}), row 2 represents the belief state for highly relevant, positive information (q_{HH}), row 3 of low relevant, positive information (q_{LH}), row 4 of highly relevant, negative information (q_{HL}) and row 5 shows values for the belief state for low relevant, negative information (q_{LL}). The columns represent the values for the belief state itself, and those for the openness, amplification, and bias for that belief state. Analysis of the simulation results leads to the following conclusions. First, the perceived fear remains constant for all agents, since this scenario does not capture the influence of belief on emotion. The same holds for the individual values for openness, amplification and bias due to the fact that fear is so low that it does not influence the contagion of the belief. Second, all types of information are quickly relayed to the other agents but after some time there is a slow decay of all types of belief.

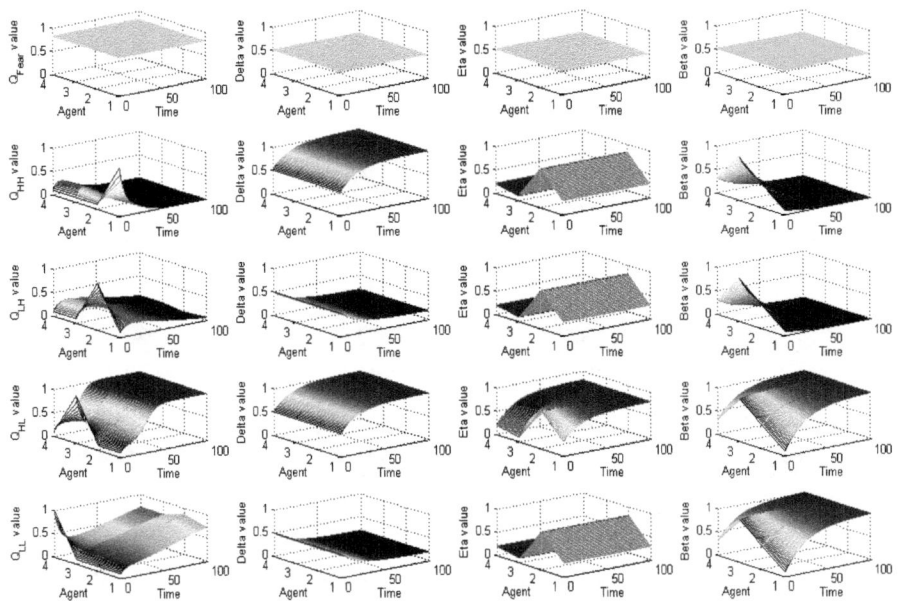

Fig. 6. Simulation results of scenario 2

Scenario 2. The only difference between scenario 1 and 2 is the initial level of fear, which is low for all agents in scenario 1, but high for all agents in scenario 2. In the simulation of scenario 2, which can be found in Fig. 6, different patterns emerge. Although the fear is still a constant factor, the high state of fear of all agents affects their values of openness, amplification and bias for particular belief states. For example, all values increase of the parameters for beliefs concerning highly relevant, negative information. While the levels for beliefs in positive information decrease or stay constant over time, the levels for beliefs in negative information show a significant increase due to these changes of the parameters.

Scenario 3. In scenario 3 the agents all have different personalities and different levels of fear and belief, represented by different personal settings for all parameters. Simulation results show that due to the personal settings, some agents develop higher fear levels over time than others. See Fig. 7.

Scenario 4, 5, and 6. Simulations 4, 5 and 6 also take the influence of belief upon the level of fear into account. In these scenarios, the value for the weights of the influence of the belief state upon fear is set to 0.1, 0.7, 0.1, and 0.1 for q_{HH}, q_{LH}, q_{HL} and q_{LL} respectively. Furthermore, the value for v has been set to 0.5. The initial settings of scenario 4, 5 and 6 are the same as scenario 1, 2 and 3, respectively. Since in the presented model the belief directly affects the emotion (and not the openness, amplification and bias), only the q-values will be discussed. They are displayed in Fig. 8. For the scenario with low fear (scenario 4) the q_{fear} increases slightly for all agents due to availability of belief. However, just as the belief levels decay, the q_{fear} levels decrease again after some time. More interesting are the results from scenario 5 and 6.

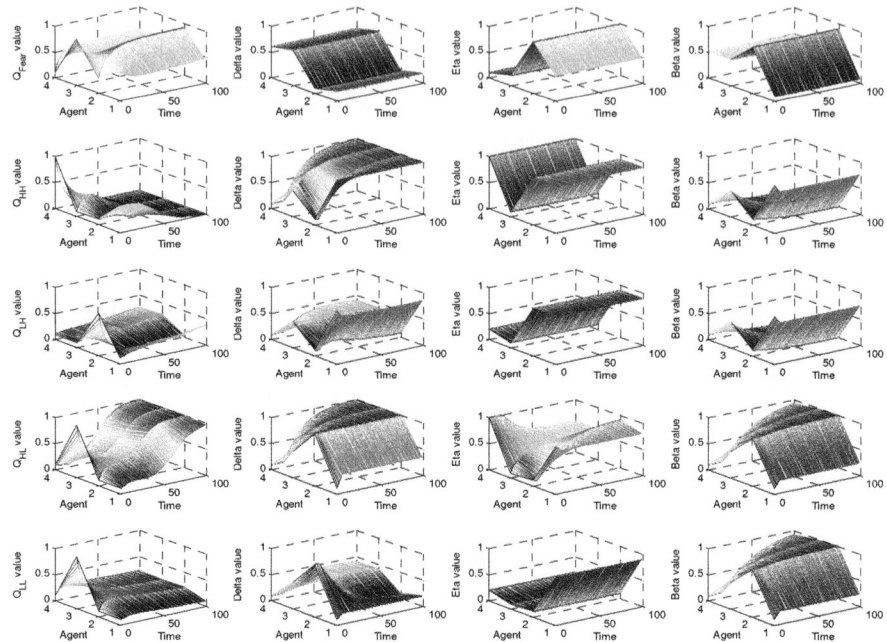

Fig. 7. Simulation results of scenario 3

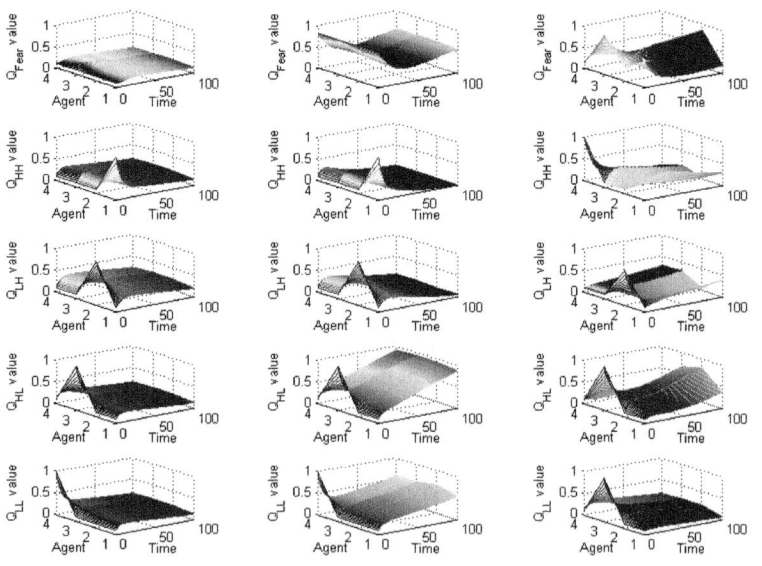

Fig. 8. The q-values for scenario 4 (leftmost column), 5 (center column), and 6 (rightmost column)

The results of the simulation of scenario 5 show that (i) negative information - in particular relevant negative information - spreads quickly through the network of agents, and (ii) the spread of q_{fear} first decreases and then spreads again causing an increase of this level for each of the agents. Note that the increase of q_{HL} and, in a somewhat lesser extent, q_{LL} cause the higher levels of q_{fear}. Looking at the simulation results of scenario 6 two main observations can be made. First, the q_{fear} of agent1, agent 3 and agent 4 does not increase as much as it did in scenario 5, due to the fact that they have lower values for negative information states than agent 2. Second, q_{fear} is reduced as the agents obtain more positive information and soon after increases when the obtained information has a less positive content.

9 Mathematical Analysis of Equilibria and Monotonicity

In this section for the presented models a mathematical analysis will be discussed of equilibria, and monotonicity.

9.1 Mathematical Analysis for the First Model

During simulations it turns out that eventually equilibria are reached: all variables approximate values for which no change occurs anymore. Such equilibrium values can also be determined by mathematical analysis of the differential equations for the model:

$$dq_{OEA}(t)/dt = \gamma_{OEA}[\eta_{OEA}(\beta_{OEA} (1 - (1-q_{OEA}*(t))(1-q_{OEA}(t))) + \qquad (4)$$
$$(1-\beta_{OEA}) q_{OEA}*(t) \; q_{OEA}(t)) + (1 - \eta_{OEA}) q_{OEA}*(t) - q_{OEA}(t)] \cdot \Delta t$$

$$dq_{OIA}(t)/dt = \gamma_{OIA}* [\eta_{OIA} (\beta_{OIA} (1 - (1-q_{OIA}**(t))(1-q_{OIA}(t))) + \qquad (5)$$
$$(1-\beta_{OIA}) q_{OIA}**(t) \; q_{OIA}(t)) + (1 - \eta_{OIA}) q_{OIA}**(t) - q_{OIA}(t)] \cdot \Delta t$$

Putting $dq_{OEA}(t)/dt = 0$ and $dq_{OIA}(t)/dt = 0$ and assuming γ_{OEA} and $\gamma_{OIA}*$ nonzero, provides the following equilibrium equations for each agent A.

$$\eta_{OEA}(\beta_{OEA} (1-(1-q_{OEA}*)(1-q_{OEA})) + (1-\beta_{OEA}) q_{OEA}* \; q_{OEA}) + (1 - \eta_{OEA}) q_{OEA}* - q_{OEA} = 0 \qquad (6)$$

$$\eta_{OIA} (\beta_{OIA} (1-(1-q_{OIA}**)(1-q_{OIA})) + (1-\beta_{OIA}) q_{OIA}** \; q_{OIA}) + (1 - \eta_{OIA}) q_{OIA}** - q_{OIA} = 0 \qquad (7)$$

For given values of the parameters η_{OEA}, β_{OEA}, η_{OIA}, and β_{OIA}, these equations may be solved analytically or by standard numerical approximation procedures. Moreover, by considering when $dq_{OEA}(t)/dt > 0$ or $dq_{OEA}(t)/dt < 0$ one can find out when $q_{OEA}(t)$ is strictly increasing and when strictly decreasing, and similarly for $q_{OIA}(t)$. For example, for equation (2), one of the cases considered is the following.

Case $\eta_{OIA} = 1$ and $\beta_{OIA} = 1$
For this case, equation (2) reduces to $(1-(1-q_{OIA}**)(1-q_{OIA})) - q_{OIA} = 0$. This can easily be rewritten via $(1- q_{OIA}) -(1-q_{OIA}**)(1-q_{OIA}) = 0$ into $q_{OIA}**(1-q_{OIA}) = 0$. From this, it can be concluded that equilibrium values satisfy $q_{OIA}**= 0$ or $q_{OIA} = 1$, and q_{OIA} is never strictly decreasing, and is strictly increasing when $q_{OIA}** > 0$ and $q_{OIA} < 1$. Now the condition $q_{OIA}** = 0$ is equivalent to

$(\omega_{OIA}/\omega_{OA}) q_{OIA}* + (\omega_{OEA}/\omega_{OA}) q_{OEA} = 0 \Leftrightarrow q_{OIA}* = 0$ if $\omega_{OIA} > 0$ and $q_{OEA} = 0$ if $\omega_{OEA} > 0$

where $q_{OIA}* = 0$ is equivalent to $\Sigma_{B\neq A} \gamma_{OIBA} \cdot q_{OIB} / \gamma_{OIA} = 0 \Leftrightarrow q_{OIB} = 0$ for all $B\neq A$ with $\gamma_{OIBA} > 0$. Assuming both ω_{OIA} and ω_{OEA} nonzero, this results in the following:

equilibrium: $q_{OIA} = 1$ or $q_{OIA} < 1$ and $q_{OEA} = 0$ and $q_{OIB} = 0$ for all $B\neq A$ with $\gamma_{OIBA} > 0$
strictly increasing: $q_{OIA} < 1$ and $q_{OEA} > 0$ or $q_{OIB} > 0$ for some $B\neq A$ with $\gamma_{OIBA} > 0$

Table 6. Equilibria cases for an agent A with both $\omega_{OEA} > 0$, $\omega_{OIA} > 0$, and $\gamma_{OEBA} > 0$ for all B

η_{OEA},β_{OEA}	q_{OEA} condition	$\eta_{OIA}=1$, $\beta_{OIA}=1$: $q_{OIA}=1$	$\eta_{OIA}=1$, $\beta_{OIA}=1$: $q_{OIA}<1$; $q_{OEA}=0$; $q_{OIB}=0$ for all $B\neq A$	$\eta_{OIA}=1$, $\beta_{OIA}=0.5$: $q_{OIA}**=q_{OIA}$	$\eta_{OIA}=1$, $\beta_{OIA}=0$: $q_{OIA}=0$	$\eta_{OIA}=1$, $\beta_{OIA}=0$: $q_{OIA}>0$; $q_{OEA}=1$; $q_{OIB}=1$ for all $B\neq A$
$\eta_{OEA}=1$, $\beta_{OEA}=1$	$q_{OEA}=1$	$q_{OEA}=1$; $q_{OIA}=1$	none	$q_{OEA}=1$; $q_{OIA}**=q_{OIA}$	$q_{OEA}=1$; $q_{OIA}=0$	$q_{OEA}=1$; $q_{OIA}>0$; $q_{OIB}=1$ for all $B\neq A$
	$q_{OEA}<1$; $q_{OEB}=0$ for all $B\neq A$	$q_{OEA}<1$; $q_{OIA}=1$; $q_{OEB}=0$ for all $B\neq A$	$q_{OEC}=0$ for all C; $q_{OIA}<1$; $q_{OIB}=0$ for all $B\neq A$	$q_{OEA}<1$; $q_{OIA}**=q_{OIA}$; $q_{OEB}=0$ for all $B\neq A$	$q_{OEA}<1$; $q_{OIA}=0$; $q_{OEB}=0$ for all $B\neq A$	none
$\eta_{OEA}=1$, $\beta_{OEA}=0.5$	$q_{OEA}*=q_{OEA}$	$q_{OEA}*=q_{OEA}$; $q_{OIA}=1$	$q_{OEC}=0$ for all C; $q_{OIA}<1$; $q_{OIB}=0$ for all $B\neq A$	$q_{OEA}*=q_{OEA}$; $q_{OIA}**=q_{OIA}$	$q_{OEA}*=q_{OEA}$; $q_{OIA}=0$	$q_{OEC}=1$ for all C; $q_{OIA}>0$; $q_{OIB}=1$ for all $B\neq A$
$\eta_{OEA}=1$, $\beta_{OEA}=0$	$q_{OEA}=0$	$q_{OEA}=0$; $q_{OIA}=1$	$q_{OEA}=0$; $q_{OIA}<1$; $q_{OIB}=0$ for all $B\neq A$	$q_{OEA}=0$; $q_{OIA}**=q_{OIA}$	$q_{OEA}=0$; $q_{OIA}=0$	none
	$q_{OEA}>0$; $q_{OEB}=1$ for all $B\neq A$	$q_{OEA}>0$; $q_{OIA}=1$; $q_{OEB}=1$ for all $B\neq A$	none	$q_{OEA}>0$; $q_{OIA}**=q_{OIA}$; $q_{OEB}=1$ for all $B\neq A$	$q_{OEA}>0$; $q_{OIA}=0$; $q_{OEB}=1$ for all $B\neq A$	$q_{OIA}>0$; $q_{OEC}=1$ for all C; $q_{OIB}=1$ for all $B\neq A$

For a number of cases such results have been found, as summarised in Table 6. This table considers any agent A in the group. Suppose A is the agent in the group with highest q_{OEA}, i.e., $q_{OEB} \leq q_{OEA}$ for all $B\neq A$. This implies that $q_{OEA}* = \Sigma_{B\neq A} \gamma_{OEBA} \cdot q_{OEB} / \gamma_{OEA} \leq \Sigma_{B\neq A} \gamma_{OEBA} \cdot q_{OEA} / \gamma_{OEA} = q_{OEA} \Sigma_{B\neq A} \gamma_{OEBA} / \gamma_{OEA} = q_{OEA}$, hence $q_{OEA}* \leq q_{OEA}$. Note that when $q_{OEB} < q_{OEA}$ for some $B\neq A$ with $\gamma_{OEBA}>0$, then $q_{OEA}* = \Sigma_{B\neq A} \gamma_{OEBA} \cdot q_{OEB} / \gamma_{OEA} < \Sigma_{B\neq A} \gamma_{OEBA} \cdot q_{OEA} / \gamma_{OEA} = q_{OEA} \Sigma_{B\neq A} \gamma_{OEBA} \cdot / \gamma_{OEA} = q_{OEA}$. Therefore $q_{OEA}* = q_{OEA}$ implies $q_{OEB} = q_{OEA}$ for all $B \neq A$ with $\gamma_{OEBA} > 0$. Similarly, when A has the lowest q_{OEA} of the group, then always $q_{OEA}* \geq q_{OEA}$ and again $q_{OEA}* = q_{OEA}$ implies $q_{OEB}=q_{OEA}$ for all $B \neq A$ with $\gamma_{OEBA} > 0$. This implies, for example, for $\eta_{OEA} = 1$ and $\beta_{OEA} = 0.5$, assuming nonzero γ_{OEBA}, that always for each option the members' emotion levels for option O will converge to one value in the group (everybody will feel the same about option O).

9.2 Mathematical Analysis for the Second Model

In this section it is analyzed which equilibria values occur. In particular, it is focused on the characteristics in the model and the fear state.

Analysis of $\delta_{Sinfo\,A}(t)$, $\beta_{Sinfo\,A}(t)$ and $\eta_{Sinfo\,A}(t)$

The openness $\delta_{Sinfo,A}$ is described in differential equation format by

$$d\,\delta_{Sinfo,A}(t)/\,dt = \mu_{\delta_{Sinfo,A}}\,(1/1+ e^{-\sigma(q_{fear,A}(t)\,-\,\tau)})\cdot [(1-(1-r_{Sinfo\,A})\,q_{fear,A}(t)) - \delta_{Sinfo\,A}(t)]$$

It is assumed that $\mu_{\delta_{Sinfo,A}} >0$. First of all, it follows that when $q_{fear,A} < \tau$, then always $d\delta_{Sinfo,A}(t)/\,dt = 0$, so for these cases any value for $\delta_{Sinfo,A}$ is an equilibrium. Next, assuming $q_{fear,A} \geq \tau$, it holds:

$\delta_{Sinfo,A}$ is in **equilibrium**	iff	$[(1-(1-r_{Sinfo\,A})\,q_{fear,A}) - \delta_{Sinfo\,A}(t)] = 0$
$\delta_{Sinfo,A}$ is **strictly increasing**	iff	$[(1-(1-r_{Sinfo\,A})\,q_{fear,A}) - \delta_{Sinfo\,A}(t)] > 0$
$\delta_{Sinfo,A}$ is **strictly decreasing**	iff	$[(1-(1-r_{Sinfo\,A})\,q_{fear,A}) - \delta_{Sinfo\,A}(t)] < 0$

From this the following equilibrium values can be determined (see also Table 7, upper part):

$$q_{fear,A} < \tau \quad \text{and any value for } \delta_{Sinfo,A} \text{ or}$$
$$q_{fear,A} \geq \tau \quad \text{and } \delta_{Sinfo,A} = 1-(1-r_{Sinfo\,A})\,q_{fear,A}$$

For example, $q_{fear,A} = 1 \Rightarrow \delta_{Sinfo\,A}(t) = r_{Sinfo\,A}$ and $r_{Sinfo\,A} = 1$ and $q_{fear,A} \geq \tau \Rightarrow \delta_{Sinfo\,A} = 1$. The following monotonicity conditions hold for $q_{fear,A}(t) \geq \tau$

$\delta_{Sinfo\,A}(t)$ is **strictly increasing**	iff	$\delta_{Sinfo\,A}(t) < 1-(1-r_{Sinfo\,A})\,q_{fear,A}(t)$
$\delta_{Sinfo\,A}(t)$ is **strictly decreasing**	iff	$\delta_{Sinfo\,A}(t) > 1-(1-r_{Sinfo\,A})\,q_{fear,A}(t)$

These conditions show that $\delta_{Sinfo\,A}(t)$ is attracted by the value $1-(1-r_{Sinfo\,A})$ $q_{fear,A}(t)$, so when $q_{fear,A}(t)$ is stable, this value is a stable equilibrium for $\delta_{Sinfo\,A}(t)$. Similarly the equilibrium values of the characteristics $\beta_{Sinfo,A}$ and $\eta_{Sinfo,A}$ can be determined as shown in Table 5. Moreover, as above it can be shown that β_{SinfoA} is attracted by the value $1-p_{SinfoA}$, and $\eta_{Sinfo\,A}(t)$ is attracted by the value $q_{fear,A}(t)$, so they both are stable.

Analysis of $q_{Sfear,A}(t)$

The fear state is described by

$$dq_{SfearA}(t)/\,dt = \gamma_A \cdot [\eta_{SfearA}\cdot(\beta_{SfearA}\cdot(1-(1-q_{SfearA}{}^*)\cdot(1-q_{SfearA})) +$$
$$(1 - \beta_{SfearA}) \cdot q_{SfearA}{}^* \cdot q_{SfearA}) +$$
$$(1 - \eta_{SfearA}) \cdot q_{SfearA}{}^* - q_{SfearA}]$$

Then the equilibrium equations become:

$\eta_{SfearA} \cdot (\beta_{SfearA} \cdot (1 - (1-q_{SfearA}{}^*) \cdot (1-q_{SfearA})) + (1 - \beta_{SfearA}) \cdot q_{SfearA}{}^* \cdot q_{SfearA}) +$

$(1 - \eta_{SfearA}) \cdot q_{SfearA}{}^* = q_{SfearA}$

In general the equation is too complex to be solved symbolically, but for some cases it can be solved; see Table 7 (lower part).

Special case $\eta_{SfearA} = 1$ and $\beta_{SfearA} = 1$

This case concerns an amplifying agent for fear with an increasing orientation. For this case the analysis shows that there is a strong tendency for q_{SfearA} to reach value 1. It will not reach 1 only if there are extreme circumstances that there is full absence of negative group impact: none of the other group members transfer any bad information or fear (see Table 7).

Special case $\eta_{SfearA} = 1$ and $\beta_{SfearA} = 0$

This case concerns an amplifying agent for fear with a decreasing orientation. For this case the analysis shows that there is a strong tendency for q_{SfearA} to reach value 0. It will only not reach 0 if there are extreme circumstances in the sense that there is full presence of negative group impact: all other group members do transfer bad information and fear. See Table 5.

Special case $\eta_{SfearA} = 0$

This case concerns an absorbing agent for fear. For this case the analysis shows that there is a strong tendency for q_{SfearA} to reach some value between 0 and 1. It will only reach 0 or 1 if there are extreme circumstances that not any of the other group members does transfer any bad information or fear, or if all of them transfer both in a maximal sense. The value reached between 0 and 1 is some form of average of the values of the other group members.

Table 7. Equilibrium values. UPPER: values for $q_{fear,A}$. LOWER: values for $\delta_{Sinfo\,A}$, $\beta_{Sinfo\,A}$, η_{Sinfo}

	$q_{fear,A} = 0$	$0 < q_{SfearA} < 1$	$q_{fear,A} = 1$
$\eta_{SfearA}=1$ $\beta_{SfearA}=1$	any value < 1 for q_{SfearA} iff there is full absence of negative group impact		$q_{fear,A} = 1$
$\eta_{SfearA}=1$ $\beta_{SfearA}=0$	$q_{fear,A} = 0$	any value > 0 for q_{SfearA} iff there is full presence of negative group impact	
$\eta_{SfearA} = 0$	$q_{fear,A} = 0$, and there is full absence of negative group impact	$q_{SfearA}{}^* = q_{SfearA}$	$q_{fear,A} = 1$, and there is full presence of negative group impact
	$q_{fear,A} = 1$	$\tau \le q_{SfearA} < 1$	$q_{SfearA} < \tau$
$\delta_{Sinfo\,A}$	$\delta_{Sinfo\,A} = r_{Sinfo\,A}$	$\delta_{Sinfo\,A} = 1 - (1 - r_{Sinfo\,A}) \, q_{fear,A}$	any value for $\delta_{Sinfo\,A}$
$\beta_{Sinfo\,A}$	any value for $\beta_{Sinfo\,A}$	$\beta_{Sinfo\,A} = 1 - p_{Sinfo\,A}$	any value for $\beta_{Sinfo\,A}$
$\eta_{Sinfo\,A}$	$r_{Sinfo\,A} > 0$ and $p_{Sinfo\,A} < 1$ and $\eta_{Sinfo\,A} = q_{fear,A}$	any value for $\eta_{Sinfo\,A}$	

Equilibria for q_{SfearA}

The equilibrium equation: $q_{SfearA}{}^* = q_{SfearA}$. For the cases $q_{SfearA}{}^* = q_{SfearA} = 0$ and $q_{SfearA}{}^* = q_{SfearA} = 1$ the terms of the double summation for $q_{SfearA}{}^*$ can be handled as above, thus providing the conditions as depicted in Table 7.

10   Discussion

The presented agent-based modelling approach models contagion of different types of individual agent states, which may have mutual interaction. The underlying generic model for contagion of a single type of state was inspired by the neurological concept of mirroring (see e.g. [24], [30]). The generic model generalises emotion contagion models as described in [4], [5], [15], [16]. Emotion contagion, has been shown to occur in many cases varying from emotions in small groups to panicking crowds (cf. [1]). The generic model introduced unifies the models for emotion contagion and generalises to contagion of any type of individual state. The agent-based approach used, differs from the approach of the computational models from social science such as in ([35], [22], [28]), which model the complex spread of innovations as diffusion that is asymmetric in time, irreversible, and nondeterministic. The two more specialised and more complex models presented, involve contagion of multiple types of states for which mutual interaction takes place.

The first more complex model presented addresses the emergence of collective decision making in groups. In this model contagion of emotions and intentions and their interaction play a main role. The model has been based not only on the neurological concept of mirroring (see e.g. [24], [30]) but also on the Somatic Marker Hypothesis of Damasio (cf. [2], [10], [12], [13]). This provides an interaction between the two types of states, in the form of influences of emotions upon intentions. Several scenarios have been simulated by the model to investigate the emerging patterns, and also to look at leadership of agents within groups. The results of these simulation experiments show patterns as desired and expected. In order to be able to make this claim more solid, a formal verification of the simulation traces have been performed, showing that the model indeed behaves properly. By a mathematical analysis, equilibria of the model have been determined.

The second more complex model presented, incorporates the effect of emotions upon the spreading of belief as well as the effect of belief upon emotions. This work has been inspired by a number of theories and observations as found in literature (cf. [1], [7], [8], [17], [27], [37]). The model has been evaluated by a case study in the domain of emergency evacuations, and was shown to exhibit the patterns that could be expected based upon the literature. Also for this model by a mathematical analysis, equilibria have been determined.

For future work, an interesting element will be to scale up the simulations and investigate the behaviour of agents in larger scale simulations. Furthermore, modelling a more detailed neurological model is also part of future work, thereby defining an abstraction relation mapping between this detailed level model and the current model. As part of further work it can also be considered to model how mood can affect (systematic) information processing, for example in case of a depression. In [9] such mechanisms are discussed. Other ideas for future work consist of extending the current model for multiple emotions affecting each other and beliefs as well and vice versa. Moreover, models addressing contagion of more than two different types of states and their interaction will be addressed.

Acknowledgements. This research has partly been conducted as part of the FP7 ICT Future Enabling Technologies program of the European Commission under grant agreement No 231288 (SOCIONICAL).

References

1. Barsade, S.G.: The ripple effect: Emotional contagion and its influence on group behavior. Administrative Science Quarterly 47(4), 644–675 (2002)
2. Bechara, A., Damasio, A.: The Somatic Marker Hypothesis: a neural theory of economic decision. Games and Economic Behavior 52, 336–372 (2004)
3. Bodenhausen, G.V., Sheppard, L., Kramer, G.: Negative affect and social judgment: The differential impact of anger and sadness. European Journal of Social Psychology 24, 45–62 (1994)
4. Bosse, T., Duell, R., Memon, Z.A., Treur, J., van der Wal, C.N.: A Multi-agent Model for Mutual Absorption of Emotions. In: Otamendi, J., et al. (eds.) Proceedings of the 23rd European Conference on Modelling and Simulation, ECMS 2009, pp. 212–218 (2009)
5. Bosse, T., Duell, R., Memon, Z.A., Treur, J., van der Wal, C.N.: A Multi-Agent Model for Emotion Contagion Spirals Integrated within a Supporting Ambient Agent Model. In: Yang, J.-J., et al. (eds.) PRIMA 2009. LNCS (LNAI), vol. 5925, pp. 48–67. Springer, Heidelberg (2009)
6. Bosse, T., Jonker, C.M., van der Meij, L., Sharpanskykh, A., Treur, J.: Specification and Verification of Dynamics in Agent Models. International Journal of Cooperative Information Systems 18, 167–193 (2009)
7. Boulahanis, J., Heltsley, M.: Perceived Fears: The Reporting Patterns of Juvenile Homicide in Chicago Newspapers. Criminal Justice Policy Review 15(132) (2004)
8. Chen, E., Lewin, M., Craske, M.: Effects of state anxiety on selective processing of threatening information. Cognition and Emotion 10, 225–240 (1996)
9. Côté, S.: Reconciling the feelings-as-information and hedonic contingency models of how mood influences systematic information processing. J. of Applied Soc. Psychology 35(8), 1656–1679 (2005)
10. Damasio, A.: Descartes' Error: Emotion, Reason and the Human Brain. Papermac, London (1994)
11. Damasio, A.: The Feeling of What Happens. Body and Emotion in the Making of Consciousness. Harcourt Brace, New York (1999)
12. Damasio, A.: Looking for Spinoza. Vintage books, London (2003)
13. Damasio, A.: The Somatic Marker Hypothesis and the Possible Functions of the Prefrontal Cortex. Philosophical Transactions of the Royal Society: Biological Sciences 351, 1413–1420 (1996)
14. Damasio, A., Meyer, K.: Behind the looking-glass. Nature 454, 167–168 (2008)
15. Duell, R., Memon, Z.A., Treur, J., van der Wal, C.N.: An Ambient Agent Model for Group Emotion Support. In: Cohn, J., Nijholt, A., Pantic, M. (eds.) Proceedings of the Third International Conference on Affective Computing and Intelligent Interaction, ACII 2009, pp. 550–557. IEEE Computer Society Press, Los Alamitos (2009)
16. Duell, R., Memon, Z.A., Treur, J., van der Wal, C.N.: An Ambient Agent Model for Group Emotion Support. In: Proc. of the Third Intern. Conf. on Affective Computing and Intelligent Interaction, ACII 2009, pp. 550–557. IEEE Computer Society Press, Los Alamitos (2009)
17. Frederickson, B.L.: The role of positive emotions in positive psychology: The broaden-and-build theory of positive emotions. American Psychologist 56, 218–226 (2001)
18. Frederickson, B.L., Branigan, C.: Positive Emotions broaden the scope of attention and thought-action repertoires. Cognition and Emotion 19(3), 313–332 (2005)
19. Friedman, H., Riggio, R.: Effect of Individual Differences in Nonverbal Expressiveness on Transmission of Emotion. Journal of Nonverbal Behavior 6(2) (1981)

20. Frijda, N.H.: The Emotions. Studies in Emotion and Social Interaction. Cambridge University Press, Cambridge (1987)
21. Goldman, A.I.: Simulating Minds: The Philosophy, Psychology, and Neuroscience of Mindreading. Oxford Univ. Press, New York (2006)
22. Hedström, P., Sandell, R., Stern, C.: Mesolevel Networks and the Diffusion of Social Movements: The Case of the Swedish Social Democratic Party. American J. of Sociology 106(1), 145–172 (2000)
23. Iacoboni, M.: Mirroring People. Farrar, Straus & Giroux, New York (2008)
24. Iacoboni, M.: Understanding others: imitation, language, empathy. In: Hurley, S., Chater, N. (eds.) Perspectives on Imitation: from Cognitive Neuroscience to Social Science, vol. 1, pp. 77–100. MIT Press, Cambridge (2005)
25. Memon, Z.A., Treur, J.: On the Reciprocal Interaction Between Believing and Feeling: an Adaptive Agent Modelling Perspective. Cognitive Neurodynamics Journal 4, 377–394 (2010), doi:10.1007/s11571-010-9136-7; Preliminary shorter version in Zhong, N., et al. (eds.): BI 2009. LNCS(LNAI), vol. 5819, pp. 13–24. Springer, Heidelberg (2009)
26. Nabi, R.L.: Anger, fear, uncertainty, and attitudes: A test of the cognitive-functional model. Communication Monographs 69, 204–216 (2002)
27. Nabi, R.L.: Exploring the framing effects of emotion: Do discrete emotions differentiallly influence information accessibility, information seeking, and policy preference? Communication Research 30(224), 224–247 (2003)
28. Pan, X., Han, C., Dauber, K., Law, K.: Human and social behaviour in computational modeling and analysis of egress. Automation in Construction 15(4), 448–461 (2006)
29. Patrick, C., Cuthbert, B., Lang, P.: Emotion in the Criminal Psychopath: Fear Image Processing. Journal of Abnormal Psychology 103(3), 523–534 (1994)
30. Pineda, J.A. (ed.): Mirror Neuron Systems: the Role of Mirroring Processes in Social Cognition. Humana Press Inc., Totowa (2009)
31. Rizzolatti, G.: The mirror-neuron system and imitation. In: Hurley, S., Chater, N. (eds.) Perspectives on Imitation: from Cognitive Neuroscience to Social Science, vol. 1, pp. 55–76. MIT Press, Cambridge (2005)
32. Rizzolatti, G., Craighero, L.: The mirror-neuron system. Annu. Rev. Neurosci. 27, 169–192 (2004)
33. Rizzolatti, G., Fogassi, L., Gallese, V.: Neuro-physiological mechanisms underlying the understanding and imitation of action. Nature Rev. Neurosci. 2, 661–670 (2001)
34. Rizzolatti, G., Sinigaglia, C.: Mirrors in the Brain: How Our Minds Share Actions and Emotions. Oxford University Press, Oxford (2008)
35. Rogers, E.: Diffusion of Innovations. Free Press, New York (1983)
36. Soui, M., Ghédira, K., Hammadi, S.: Proposal of Personalized Multimodal Information Diffusion System. In: Proc. of the 1st Intern. Conf. on ICT & Accessibility, ICTA 2007, pp. 219–224 (2007)
37. Witte, K., Allen, M.: A Meta-Analysis of Fear Appeals: Implications for Effective Public Health Campaigns. Health Educ. Behav. 27(5), 591–615 (2000)

Appendix A   Settings for the Scenarios in Section 5

Scenario 1			agent 1	agent 2	agent 3	agent 4
q (initial state)	emotion	optionA	0.9	0.1	0.5	0.2
		optionB	0.1	0.1	0.5	0.2
		optionC	0.3	0.1	0.5	0.2
		optionD	0.1	0.1	0.5	0.2
	intention	optionA	0.9	0.7	0.5	0.1
		optionB	0.1	0.7	0.5	0.1
		optionC	0.1	0.1	0.5	0.1
		optionD	0.1	0.1	0.5	0.9
δ (openness)	emotion	optionA	0.1	0.9	0.9	0.2
		optionB	0.1	0.9	0.9	0.2
		optionC	0.1	0.9	0.9	0.2
		optionD	0.1	0.9	0.9	0.2
	intention	optionA	0.1	0.9	0.9	0.2
		optionB	0.1	0.9	0.9	0.2
		optionC	0.1	0.9	0.9	0.2
		optionD	0.1	0.9	0.9	0.2
η (amplify/absorb)	emotion	optionA	0.9	0.1	0.2	0.9
		optionB	0.1	0.1	0.2	0.9
		optionC	0.9	0.1	0.2	0.9
		optionD	0.1	0.1	0.2	0.9
	intention	optionA	0.9	0.1	0.2	0.9
		optionB	0.1	0.1	0.2	0.9
		optionC	0.9	0.1	0.2	0.9
		optionD	0.1	0.1	0.2	0.9
β (bias)	emotion	optionA	0.9	0.1	0.5	0.6
		optionB	0.1	0.1	0.5	0.6
		optionC	0.9	0.1	0.5	0.6
		optionD	0.1	0.1	0.5	0.6
	intention	optionA	0.9	0.8	0.5	0.6
		optionB	0.1	0.8	0.5	0.6
		optionC	0.9	0.1	0.5	0.6
		optionD	0.1	0.1	0.5	0.6
ε (expressiveness)			1	0.4	0.1	1
α (connection)		agent1	-	0.1	0.1	0.1
		agent2	1	-	0.9	0.1
		agent3	1	0.9	-	0.1
		agent4	1	0.1	0.1	-

Scenario 2			agent 1	agent 2	agent 3	agent 4
q (initial state)	emotion	optionA	*0.9*	*0.3*	*0.2*	*0.1*
		optionB	*0.1*	*0.3*	*0.1*	*0.1*
		optionC	*0.1*	*0.2*	*0.3*	*0.1*
		optionD	*0.1*	*0.4*	*0.2*	*0.8*
	intention	optionA	*0.9*	*0.3*	*0.3*	*0.1*
		optionB	*0.1*	*0.3*	*0.3*	*0.1*
		optionC	*0.1*	*0.2*	*0.4*	*0.1*
		optionD	*0.1*	*0.4*	*0.1*	*0.7*
δ (openness)	emotion	optionA	*0.1*	*0.8*	*0.9*	*0.3*
		optionB	*0.1*	*0.8*	*0.9*	*0.3*
		optionC	*0.1*	*0.8*	*0.9*	*0.3*
		optionD	*0.1*	*0.8*	*0.9*	*0.3*
	intention	optionA	*0.1*	*0.8*	*0.3*	*0.3*
		optionB	*0.1*	*0.8*	*0.3*	*0.3*
		optionC	*0.1*	*0.8*	*0.3*	*0.3*
		optionD	*0.1*	*0.8*	*0.3*	*0.3*
η (amplify/absorb)	emotion	optionA	*0.9*	*0.5*	*0.2*	*0.7*
		optionB	*0.9*	*0.5*	*0.2*	*0.7*
		optionC	*0.9*	*0.5*	*0.2*	*0.7*
		optionD	*0.9*	*0.5*	*0.2*	*0.7*
	intention	optionA	*0.9*	*0.5*	*0.2*	*0.7*
		optionB	*0.9*	*0.5*	*0.2*	*0.7*
		optionC	*0.9*	*0.5*	*0.2*	*0.7*
		optionD	*0.9*	*0.5*	*0.2*	*0.7*
β (bias)	emotion	optionA	*0.9*	*0.3*	*0.6*	*0.7*
		optionB	*0.9*	*0.3*	*0.5*	*0.7*
		optionC	*0.9*	*0.3*	*0.4*	*0.7*
		optionD	*0.9*	*0.3*	*0.5*	*0.8*
	intention	optionA	*0.9*	*0.3*	*0.6*	*0.7*
		optionB	*0.9*	*0.3*	*0.5*	*0.7*
		optionC	*0.9*	*0.3*	*0.4*	*0.7*
		optionD	*0.9*	*0.3*	*0.5*	*0.8*
ε (expressiveness)			*1*	*0.1*	*0.1*	*0.8*
α (connection)		agent1	-	*0.1*	*0.1*	*0.1*
		agent2	*1*	-	*0.1*	*0.1*
		agent3	*0.1*	*0.1*	-	*0.8*
		agent4		*0.1*	*0.1*	-
			0.1			

Scenario 3			agent 1	agent 2	agent 3	agent 4
q (initial state)	emotion	optionA	0.9	0.2	0.1	0.3
		optionB	0.1	0.9	0.1	0.3
		optionC	0.5	0.2	0.7	0.7
		optionD	0.2	0.2	0.1	0.1
	intention	optionA	0.9	0.2	0.1	0.1
		optionB	0.1	0.9	0.1	0.1
		optionC	0.5	0.2	0.9	0.9
		optionD	0.2	0.2	0.1	0.1
δ (openness)	emotion	optionA	0.5	0.1	0.9	0.3
		optionB	0.5	0.1	0.9	0.3
		optionC	0.5	0.1	0.9	0.7
		optionD	0.5	0.1	0.9	0.3
	intention	optionA	0.5	0.1	0.9	0.3
		optionB	0.5	0.1	0.9	0.3
		optionC	0.5	0.1	0.9	0.7
		optionD	0.5	0.1	0.9	0.3
η (amplify/absorb)	emotion	optionA	0.9	0.5	0.2	0.8
		optionB	0.2	0.5	0.2	0.8
		optionC	0.2	0.5	0.2	0.8
		optionD	0.2	0.5	0.2	0.8
	intention	optionA	0.9	0.5	0.1	0.8
		optionB	0.2	0.5	0.1	0.8
		optionC	0.2	0.5	0.1	0.8
		optionD	0.2	0.5	0.1	0.8
β (bias)	emotion	optionA	0.5	0.5	0.9	0.2
		optionB	0.5	0.5	0.9	0.2
		optionC	0.5	0.5	0.9	0.9
		optionD	0.5	0.5	0.9	0.2
	intention	optionA	0.5	0.5	0.9	0.2
		optionB	0.5	0.5	0.9	0.2
		optionC	0.5	0.5	0.9	0.9
		optionD	0.5	0.5	0.9	0.2
ε (expressiveness)			0.9	0.7	0.1	0.5
α (connection)		agent1	-	0.3	0.5	0.7
		agent2	0.1	-	0.5	0.5
		agent3	0.8	0.8	-	0.2
		agent4	0.6	0.5	0.2	-

Appendix B   Settings for the Scenarios in Section 8

Scenario 1 and 2		Fear sc1 / sc2	Information high r, high p	Information low r, high p	Information high r, low p	Information low r, low p
q (initial state)	Agent1	0.1 / 0.8	1	0.1	0.1	0.1
	Agent2	0.1 / 0.8	0.1	1	0.1	0.1
	Agent3	0.1 / 0.8	0.1	0.1	1	0.1
	Agent4	0.1 / 0.8	0.1	0.1	0.1	1
δ (openness)	Agent1	0.5	0.5	0.5	0.5	0.5
	Agent2	0.5	0.5	0.5	0.5	0.5
	Agent3	0.5	0.5	0.5	0.5	0.5
	Agent4	0.5	0.5	0.5	0.5	0.5
η (amplify/ absorb)	Agent1	0.5	0.3	0.3	0.3	0.3
	Agent2	0.5	0.8	0.8	0.8	0.8
	Agent3	0.5	0.1	0.1	0.1	0.1
	Agent4	0.5	0.2	0.2	0.2	0.2
β (bias)	Agent1	0.5	0.1	0.1	0.1	0.1
	Agent2	0.5	0.5	0.5	0.5	0.5
	Agent3	0.5	0.9	0.9	0.9	0.9
	Agent4	0.5	0.3	0.3	0.3	0.3
Scenario 3						
q (initial state)	Agent1					
	Agent2	0.3	0.1	0.8	0.1	0.1
	Agent3	0.9	0.1	0.1	1	1
	Agent4	0.1	1	0.1	0.1	0.1
δ (openness)	Agent1	0.2	1	1	0.1	0.1
	Agent2	0.1	0.1	0.1	1	1
	Agent3	0.7	0.5	0.5	0.5	0.5
	Agent4	0.6	0.1	0.1	0.1	0.1
η (amplify/ absorb)	Agent1	0.5	0.9	0.9	0.9	0.9
	Agent2	1	0.9	0.9	0.9	0.1
	Agent3	0.2	0.1	0.1	0.1	0.1
	Agent4	0.1	1	0.2	1	0.2
β (bias)	Agent1	0.1	0.9	0.9	0.1	0.1
	Agent2	0.9	0.1	0.1	0.9	0.9
	Agent3	0.5	0.5	0.5	0.5	0.5
	Agent4	0.5	0.1	0.1	0.1	0.1

Head-On Collision Avoidance by Knowledge Exchange under RAF Control of Autonomous Decentralized FMS

Hidehiko Yamamoto, Takayoshi Yamada, and Katsutoshi Ootsubo

Department of Human and Information Systems, Gifu University, Japan
yam-h@gifu-u.ac.jp, yamat@gifu-u.ac.jp, otsubo@gifu-u.ac.jp

Abstract. The author past studies on production planning include agent systems where agents act independently under the real-time control of Reasoning to Anticipate the Future (RAF) in order to realize an autonomous decentralized flexible manufacturing systems (AD-FMS) and achieve high production efficiency. However, RAF did not solve the automated guided vehicles (AGVs) colliding problem. This paper describes the method of cooperation by knowledge exchange in AGVs moving autonomously under the real-time control of RAF in AD-FMSs to avoid AGVs collisions. The method gives the AGV an individual knowledge called AGV-knowledge, and by the exchange of which, each AGV can avoid collisions. This method does not use the conventional control by a host computer but applies communication among AGVs. Head-on collisions were prevented by applying this method to 9 types of FMSs constructed in a computer.

Keywords: Autonomous decentralized system, FMS, AGV, Head-on collision avoidance.

1 Introduction

One approach to the operation of production plants in the 21st century is an Autonomous decentralized flexible manufacturing systems (AD-FMSs) [1]–[5]. In a study on AD-FMS, the author examined the movements of automated guided vehicles (AGVs) in terms of controlling which part should be taken next to which machining center during FMS operation [6]. In this study, a system called reasoning to anticipate the future (RAF) was developed that can determine the next action of the AGV at a given point in time by anticipating the next actions available to the AGV (next action) for several steps into the future and anticipating in advance the FMS operating status that will be produced in the near future.

In this way, the author studies on production planning include agent systems where agents act independently under the real-time control of RAF in order to realize an AD-FMS and achieve high production efficiency [5],[7]. However, for each agent to be able to act independently, the agents require not only the objective of production but also a method to move independently. This means that AGVs in an AD-FMS under the real-time control of RAF must move independently but in coordination with other AGVs. The conventional FMS operates according to the host computers' orders. AGVs also move according to the prescheduled plans made by the host computers. When an FMS becomes more complicated, such that the number of AGVs increase

N.T. Nguyen and R. Kowalczyk (Eds.): Transactions on CCI III, LNCS 6560, pp. 180–198, 2011.

and have two-way routes, AGVs will have a high possibility of colliding if they move according to prescheduled orders. This is because each machining center (MC) of an FMS in a real factory does not always finish its jobs on schedule and AGVs sometimes break down. That is, a few AGVs may close in on the same point at the same time because very few AGVs' actual locations match the prescheduled locations. The author past research did not solve the AGVs' colliding problem.

This paper proposes a method to solve the problem of possible collisions within an AD-FMS by enabling AGVs to exchange knowledge and cooperate with each other. Especially, the four types of AGV knowledge: path-knowledge, self-knowledge, neighbor-knowledge, and emergency-knowledge are proposed to avoid AGVs collisions. The AD-FMS adopts the condition of AGVs' moving in two directions on a guide line. This paper describes the knowledge that AGVs hold, the knowledge that is exchanged between AGVs to cooperate and the method of exchanging that knowledge.

Various methods for controlling AGVs motion have been studied [8],[9]. These include a priori path optimization of right-of-the-way determination and rules control. These are different, however, from our research: controlling AGV motion by knowledge exchange.

2   Factory Infrastructure Conditions and Factory Control

2.1 FMS Construction

The AD-FMS dealt with in this paper consists of internal agents including a parts warehouse for the supply of parts into the AD-FMS, a product warehouse where completed parts are kept, AGVs that transport single parts, and several MCs, as shown in Fig. 1. The AGVs move at a constant speed along the line lattice in the figure. The MCs can process several types of parts, and the machining process and processing time for each are preset. In addition, there are several units of the same type of MC that do the same work. Groups of the same type of MC are called MC groups, and are designated as MC_1, MC_2, and so on. To distinguish between individual MCs in a group, a further designation is made with a hyphenated number after the group name, as MC_{1-1}, MC_{1-2}, and so on.

2.2 Factory Control by RAF

In the AD-FMS in this study, production is carried out with each AGV determining its own actions through the reasoning method called Reasoning to Anticipate the Future (RAF). That is, each AGV includes the function of RAF. RAF can anticipate up to several future steps available to the AGV. Then, through predictions based on discrete production simulations of phenomena that may occur within these several future steps, RAF works backward to the present to decide which of the options the AGV should choose at the present point in time [10][11] just like a hypothetical reasoning [12]~[14].

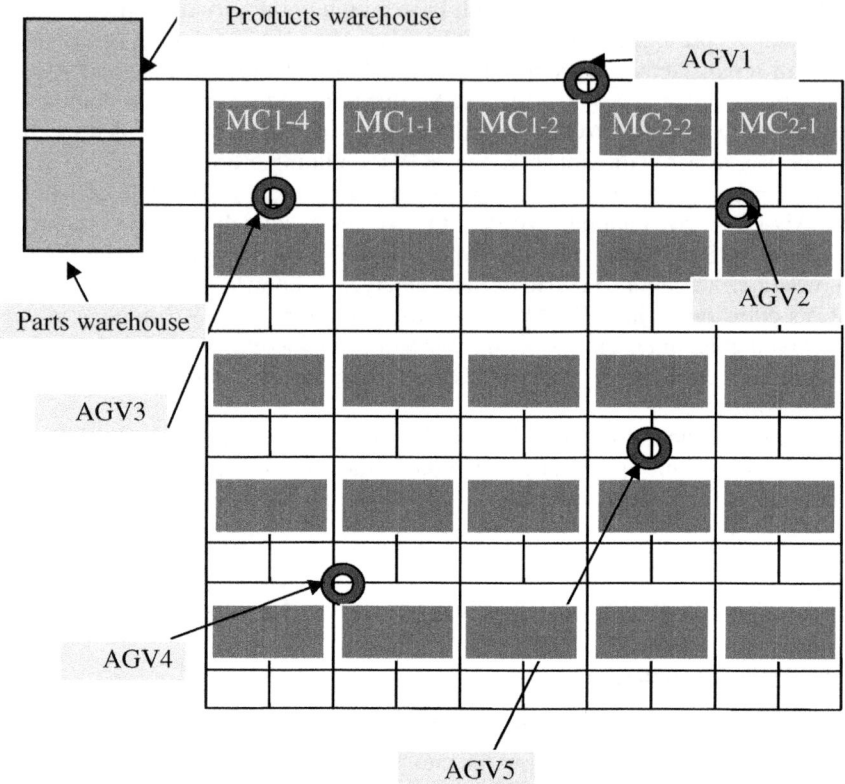

(a) Top view of AD-FMS

(b) 3-D of AD-FMS

Fig. 1. Autonomous decentralized FMS layout

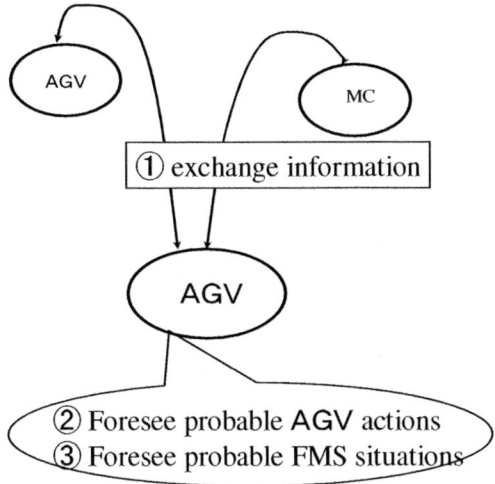

Fig. 2. AGVs real-time control

As shown in Fig.2, the real-time control of AGVs adopts the following process procedure of an real-time communications among each agent when AD-FMS is working : <1>acquiring information by exchanging each agent information , <2> foresee the near future of probable AGVs actions, <3> foresee probable AD-FMS operating situations. Based on the prediction results of <3>, RAF to find the AGVs' next actions is carried out. RAF resembles a chess strategy that moves a piece after anticipating the several alternatives for one move. The real-time communication by RAF decides both where the AGV moves next and which part it carries next. In this way, predetermined parts delivering schedule is not needed.

The probable action (Next Action) that an AGV will take next is not decided as a single action but as many actions. This is because there are Group MCs whose elements are doing the same manufacturing process jointly, maybe the AGV transfers finished parts to the products warehouse, or maybe delivers a new part into AD-FMS from the parts warehouse, and there is a possibility that another AGVs will make the same action, as shown in Fig.3. Hypothetically, if an AGV chooses one of the above actions, in an actual AGV, each agent in AD-FMS keeps doing its chosen operation. When an AGV needs the choice of Next Action again, it chooses a single Next Action from among the probable choices again. In this way, the operating situation of AD-FMS is expressed as the choice process of unending cycle of AGVs Next Actions. That is, it is expressed as a tree construction which includes nodes corresponding to probable AGVs Next Actions. The tree construction can be extended infinitely, as shown in Fig.4. The characteristics of RAF are to consider the probable Next Actions that the AGV will be able to take locally a few steps ahead as a foreseeable range, as well as globally foreseeing phenomena happening in AD-FMS in a near future and, then going back to the present, and finally decide which choice should be chosen at present. In order to do RAF, the hypothetical reasoning [6][15] which considers the choices that the AGV will be able to take as competitive hypotheses and the discrete simulator [16][17] are included into RAF.

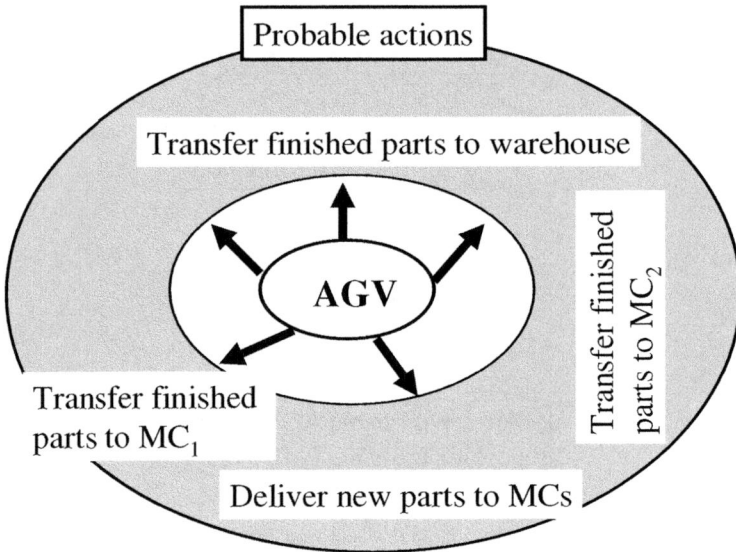

Fig. 3. Probable AGV actions

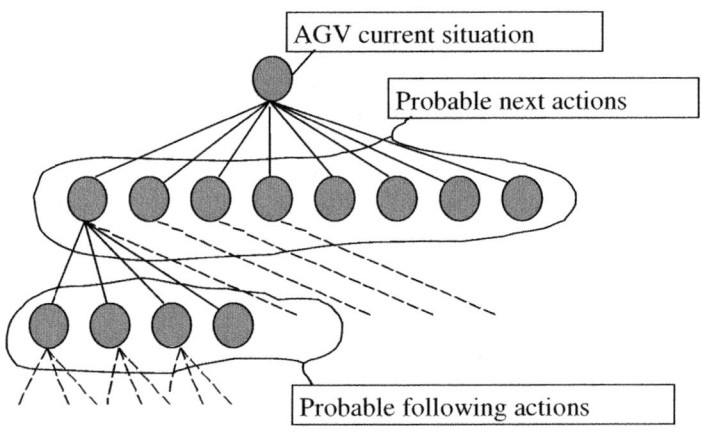

Fig. 4. Tree construction representing probable AGV actions

3   Collision Avoidance by Knowledge Exchange and Cooperation

In present study, each AGV in the AD-FMS works as an agent of the autonomous decentralized system under the control of RAF. Under the real-time control of RAF, AGVs result in the problem of colliding each other. To solve the problem, each agent corresponding to AGVs cooperates by knowledge exchange, as shown in Fig. 5.

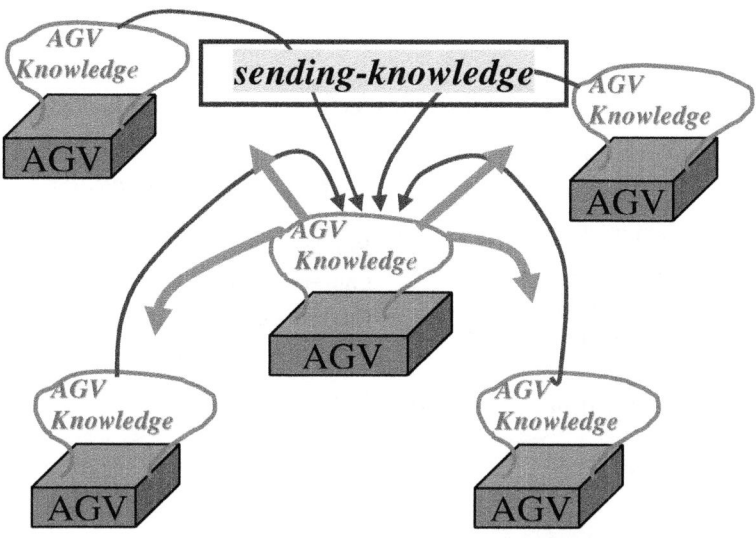

Fig. 5. AGVs' communication by knowledge

The cooperative actions that comprise the following three elements are proposed: AGV-knowledge (knowledge that each AGV holds), sending-knowledge (knowledge that an AGV sends to other AGVs), and each AGV's consultations about the route and avoid collisions by exchanging sending-knowledge.

3.1 AGV Knowledge

AGV-knowledge is a set of knowledge to move independently and has four components, as shown in Fig.6: (1) path-knowledge, (2) self-knowledge, (3) neighbor-knowledge, and (4) emergency-knowledge. Each AGV holds its AGV-knowledge. The four types of knowledge are defined as follows.

[Definition] path-knowledge: path-knowledge expresses a set of elements indicating sequential intersection coordinates along which the AGV moves. For example, when an AGV receives a part, it memorizes the sequential intersection coordinates indicating the shortest route to take the part to the MC.

[Definition] self-knowledge: self-knowledge is knowledge about the AGV itself and consists of four elements: self-name, last-crossing, next-crossing, and following-crossing. Self-name expresses the AGV's own name, last-crossing expresses the coordinates of the intersection that the AGV passed through last, next-crossing expresses the coordinates of the intersection that the AGV moves through next, and following-crossing expresses the coordinates of the intersection to which the AGV moves two points ahead. Self-knowledge is expressed as a list below.

self-knowledge = ((self-name) (last-crossing) (next-crossing) (following-crossing))

(1)

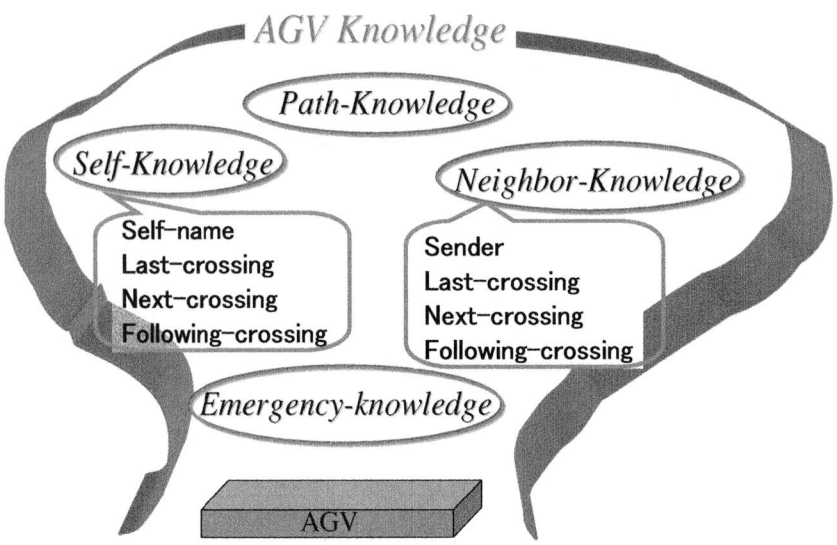

Fig. 6. AGV-knowledge

Each AGV recognizes its current intersection (or path) by checking the second and third elements. Each AGV also recognizes the following-path along which it moves by checking the third and fourth elements. AGVs generate and update their self-knowledge when they pass through an intersection.

[Definition] neighbor-knowledge: It is difficult for AGVs to move independently if they do not hold other AGVs' information. However, it is not feasible for each AGV to hold all information about every other AGV. To solve this problem, AGVs are given the minimum knowledge on the current and subsequent paths of the AGV's. This knowledge is called neighbor-knowledge and consists of four elements. The first element is sender (the name of other AGVs). The second and subsequent elements are expressed as the same intersection coordinates as self-knowledge elements. That is, the four elements for one AGV, as described in Equation (2), are considered as a subset of AGV-knowledge, and each AGV holds as neighbor-knowledge all subsets of other AGVs' knowledge for AGVs moving in the AD-FMS. Neighbor-knowledge is created by the received knowledge as described below.

neighbor-knowledge = (((sender-1) (last-crossing1) (next-crossing1) (following-
                        crossing1)) ((sender-2) ((last-crossing2) (next-crossing2)
                        (following-crossing2))
                        ...)   (2)

[Definition] emergency-knowledge: emergency-knowledge is a set of knowledge that is memorized when emergency sending-knowledge (hereafter, E-sending-knowledge) is received. Each AGV holds the number of received E-sending-knowledge. Except for the empty element of emergency-knowledge, AGVs recognize that a collision avoidance action is being executed somewhere.

As described above, for the AGVs to move independently—in other words, to recognize which passage it (AGV) itself is now on and which paths other AGVs are now on— they hold three types of knowledge: knowledge about whole path from the start to the goal, path-knowledge, self-knowledge, and neighbor-knowledge, and when needed, emergency-knowledge to avoid collisions. By means of these knowledges, AGVs can autonomously move, judge, and avoid collisions when needed.

3.2 Sending-Knowledge and Message-Knowledge

AGVs can move autonomously by sending some of their AGV-knowledge to others. This information is called sending-knowledge and is sent from an AGV to other AGVs in the form of a radio broadcast, as shown in Fig. 5. Most sending-knowledge is intersection coordinates; however, just sending intersection coordinates does not always correspond to agent cooperation. A certain will that an AGV holds has to be sent if we want to consider it agent cooperation. One characteristic of our research is that sending-knowledge includes exchanging wills.

Sending-knowledge is created and sent when one of the following two conditions is satisfied.

Condition 1: AGV passes through the intersection.
Condition 2: AGV receives sending-knowledge from another AGV.

Sending-knowledge created in condition 1 corresponds to informing the AGV of its current location and is particularly called ordinal sending-knowledge (O-sending-knowledge). Sending-knowledge created in condition 2 is formed when a collision is about to occur and is called emergency sending-knowledge (E-sending-knowledge).

As shown in Fig. 7, ordinal sending-knowledge consists of four elements. The first element (sender) is the AGV corresponding to the sending AGV. The second and later correspond to the intersection coordinates. That is, the second indicates the intersection coordinates that the sender has just transmitted, and the intersection is called last-crossing. The third indicates the intersection coordinates that the sender moves to next, and the intersection is called next-crossing. The fourth indicates the intersection coordinates on which the sender will move two intersections later and is called following-crossing. Equation (3) shows the ordinal sending-knowledge. When an AGV receives this ordinal sending-knowledge, the AGV memorizes it as an element of neighbor-knowledge in AGV-knowledge.

O-sending-knowledge = ((sender) (last-crossing) (next-crossing)
(following-crossing))   (3)

As shown in Fig. 8, E-sending-knowledge does not hold information for intersection coordinates but holds certain messages expressing the wills of AGVs, which are as indispensable as the coordinates between AGVs. The first element of the knowledge is sender name, the second is the content to inform (message), the third is the name of the AGV that receives (addressee), and the fourth and the subsequent are the intersection coordinates. Based on the type of message, the coordinates described as the fourth element differ. The second element, message, expresses the will of AGVs, and the following eight terms are the corresponding possible messages: (1) Ask, (2) Answer, (3) Ask-again, (4) Answer-again, (5) Reverse, (6) Clear, (7) After-you, (8) Thanks.

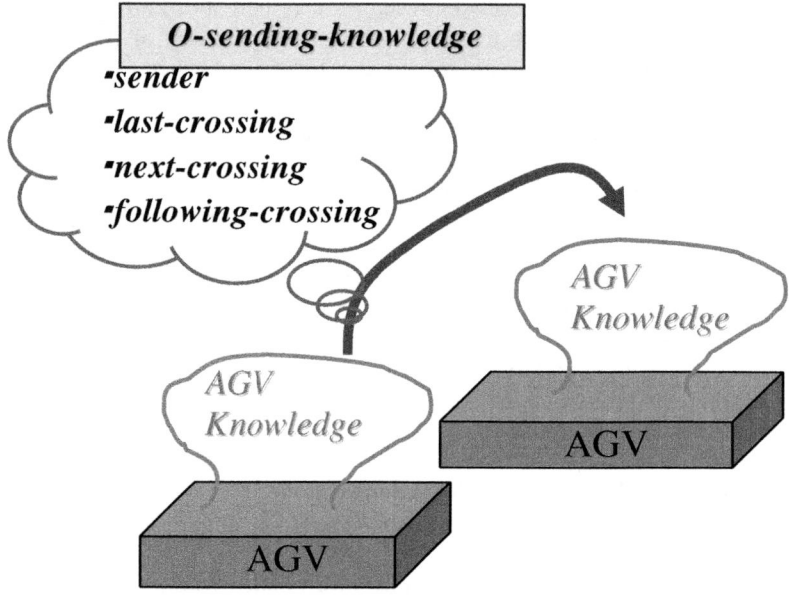

Fig. 7. O-sending-knowledge

Emergency-knowledge describes one of the eight messages that can be sent as emergency-knowledge. Equation (4) expresses emergency-knowledge. Intersection coordinates are described in the blanks of the parentheses and the number of the parentheses depend on the types of messages.

$$\text{E-sending-knowledge} = ((\text{sender}) \,(\text{message}) \,(\text{address}) \,(\quad).......(\quad)) \quad (4)$$

Each message for emergency-knowledge is defined below.

[Definition] Ask: Ask is the message, "What are the three intersections ahead of you?" Usually, AGV store neighbor–knowledge, which includes the last intersection coordinates that other AGVs have passed through, the coordinates of the intersection immediately ahead, and those of the intersections two points ahead. As a result of this memory, AGVs can recognize the current paths of other AGVs and the next paths that other AGVs will move on. In addition, when needed, the message Ask can express the will to know the following path. For example, E-sending-knowledge = ((AGV-1) (Ask) (AGV-2)) is sent and the meaning is AGV-1 asks AGV-2 which intersection AGV-2 passes three intersections ahead.

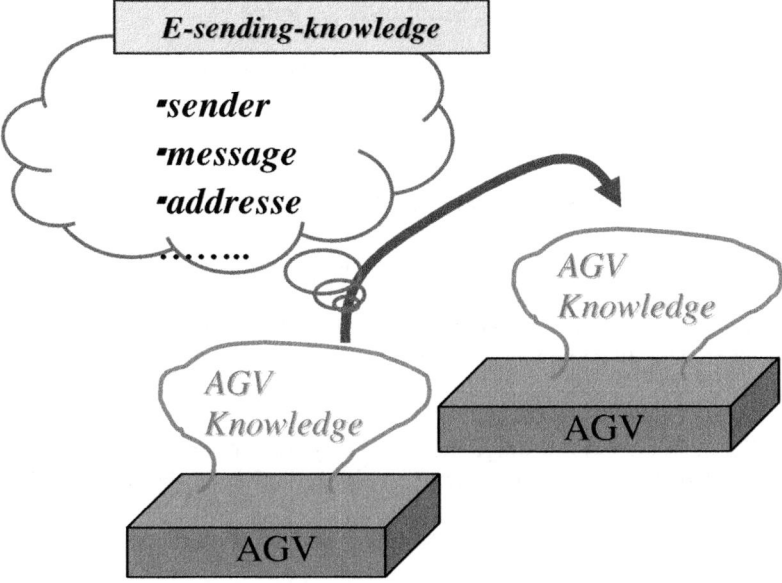

Fig. 8. E-sending-knowledge

[Definition] Answer: Answer holds the message that expresses the coordinates of the third intersection ahead. When an AGV receives the message whose addressee is the AGV itself, the AGV returns the message as Answer. For example, when E-sending-knowledge = ((AGV-2) (Answer) (AVG-1) (1, 3)) is sent, it means that AGV-2 informs AGV-1 that the coordinates of the third intersection ahead of AGV-2 are (1, 3).

[Definition] Ask-again: Ask-again is the message to ask for the coordinates of an intersection one intersection ahead of the intersection asked for with Ask.

[Definition] Answer-again: When an AGV receives the message with Ask-again and the addressee that the message includes is itself, the AGV returns the message as Answer-again. The message Ask-again gives the coordinates the intersection one point ahead of the intersection at which the Ask message is sent.

[Definition] Reverse: Reverse is the message to inform others, "I'm moving backward to avoid a collision." The message Reverse is the most urgent message, and if an AGV receives the message, other AGVs must not interfere with its movement.

[Definition] Clear: Clear is the message to inform others, "Please move backward because there is no problem."

[Definition] After-you: After-you is the message to inform others, "You can move first."

[Definition] Thanks: Thanks is the message to inform others that "The situation is over" as the reverse movement is finished. This means that when Thanks is received, all AGVs return to their normal situation.

3.3 Cooperation by Exchanging Sending-Knowledge

AGVs always repeat their basic and fixed processes to execute cooperation actions. These processes are called routine AGV processes (RAP) and the following are the details.

[RAP]

Step1-1: When an AGV updates its self-knowledge, go to Step1-2, and when it receives emergency-knowledge, go to Step1-3.

Step1-2: The AGV compares its self-knowledge with its neighbor-knowledge and judges the possibility of collision in the following manner. Judge whether the third and the fourth elements of self-knowledge are the same as the fourth and third elements of each neighbor-knowledge, and if the same is found, go to Step 1-2-2; if not, go to Step 1-2-1.

Step1-2-1: The AGV finishes RAP.

Step1-2-2: The AGV, to judge the possibility for a collision, stops at the middle of the current path, creates emergency-knowledge including the message Ask, sends it, and finishes RAP.

Step 1-3: The AGV creates emergency-knowledge according to the received message, sends it, and finishes RAP.

In this manner, AGVs check the possibility for a collision by performing RAP whenever they update self-knowledge and receive sending-knowledge. Foreseeing a possible collision in Step 1-2, AGVs start to exchange emergency-knowledge. Here, we use the term foreseeing since a collision does not always occur at this step.

3.4 Message Exchange for Head-On Collisions

AGVs foresee the possibility for a collision by RAP described in Section 3.3. Several patterns for collisions are considered, such as head-on collisions and flank collisions. This section deals with a head-on collision, the most popular collision pattern, and explains how messages are exchanged to avoid collisions. The strategy for collision avoidance involves two processes: [a] an AGV remains stationary there if the other AGVs get into its current path, and [b] in the case where the other AGVs get into its current path, the AGV moves backward and waits till the other AGVs pass through. The strategy carries out the two processes in the sequence [a]→[b].

In Step1-2-2 of RAP, when an AGV foresees the possibility of collision, it starts to exchange emergency-knowledge based on the following rules of exchange (ROE) for avoiding head-on collisions. Priority AGV and Concessive AGV are determined. The former means the AGV that is given the priority to move in order to avoid collisions, and the latter means the AGV that makes way for the Priority AGV to avoid collisions. To be specific, the AGV that has updated self-knowledge in Step 1-2-2 of RAP will be changed to the Concessive AGV. Then, part of ROE adopts certain terms as well as the eight messages described in Section 3.2. The terms are defined as below.

[Definition] description style {[S] → [V] [O]}: The letter in the parenthesis before "→" corresponds to subject and the letters in the parenthesis after "→" correspond to verb and object. The composition SVO has several permutations of verb and object. Further, the symbol "+" expresses additional actions. For example, {[A] → ([message-1] [B] + [Act-1])} means A sends message-1 to B and executes the action, Act-1.

[Definition] Stay-1: Move onto the middle of the current path and wait.

[Definition] Check-1: Check whether the two intersections ahead of the current path of the Concessive AGV and the path of the Priority AGV are the same or not. To be specific, check whether the third and the fourth elements of the Concessive AGV's self-knowledge and the coordinates of the Priority AGV's two intersections ahead and three intersections ahead, which are the intersection coordinates included in the message Answer, are the same.

[Definition] Find-1: Find the path that is different from the path three intersections ahead of the Priority AGV. The path found corresponds to an evacuated path.

[Definition] Check-2: Check whether the evacuated path and the one intersection ahead path are the same or not. If same, wait on the middle of the current path.

[Definition] Move-1: Move on the middle of an evacuated path and stay there.

[Definition] Move-2: Move out as scheduled.

[ROE]

Rule-1: *if* {an AGV foresees the possibility of a collision}, *then* {[Concessive AGV] → [Ask] [Priority AGV] + [Stay-1]}

Rule-2: *if* {an AGV receives Ask}, *then* {[Priority AGV] → [Answer] [Concessive AGV] + [Stay-1]}

Rule-3: *if* {an AGV receives Answer}, *then* {[Concessive AGV] → [Check-1] + [Ask-again] [Priority AGV]} *or*
          {[Concessive AGV] → [Check-1] + [After-you] [Priority AGV]}

Rule-4: *if* {an AGV receives Ask-again}, *then* {[Priority AGV] → [Answer-again] [Concessive AGV]}

Rule-5: *if* {an AGV receives Answer-again}, *then* {[Concessive AGV] → [Find-1] + [Reverse] [all AGVs]}

Rule-6: *if* {an AGV receives Reverse}, *then* {[all AGVs] → [Check-2] + [Clear] [Concessive AGV]}

Rule-7: *if* {an AGV receives Clear}, *then* {[Concessive AGV] → [Move-1] + [After-you] [Priority AGV]}

Rule-8: *if* {an AGV receives After-you}, *then* {[Priority AGV] → [Move-3] + [Thanks] [all AGVs]}

Fig. 9 shows the relationship between RAP and ROE. The detailed procedures of ROE are described below.

Explanation of Rule-1: The Concessive AGV asks the Priority AGV the intersection coordinates three points ahead. In the situation shown in Fig. 10, AGV-1 updates its self-knowledge soon after passing the intersection (1, 2) and foresees the possibility of the collision with AGV-2 by matching neighbor-knowledge with the updated self-knowledge. To foresee if the collision will occur between the path (3, 2)–(5, 2), AGV-1 sends an Ask message to AGV-3 and remains stationary at the middle of the current path. AGV-2 already passed the intersection (7, 2) and declared to move onto the path (3, 2)–(5, 2) earlier than AGV-1 does because AGV-2 sent the message to all AGVs by the radio-type method. As a result of early declaring, AGV-2 is given the priority to pass the intersection (5, 2) and becomes the Priority AGV. AGV-1, which sent the Ask message, is declared later than AGV-2 and becomes the Concessive AGV.

Explanation of Rule-2: As the reply for the Ask message, the Priority AGV sends the intersection coordinates three points ahead and an Answer message including emergency-knowledge. The Priority AGV replies with the intersection coordinates that are one point ahead of the following-crossing corresponding to the fourth element of self-knowledge and remains stationary at the middle of the current path till an After-you message is received. At this time, the Priority AGV acquires E-sending-knowledge of an Ask message as one element of emergency-knowledge.

Explanation of Rule-3: As the reply for an Answer message, the Concessive AGV judges whether the third and the fourth elements of the Concessive AGV's self-knowledge and the Priority AGV's coordinates of the two and three points ahead intersections are the same or not. That is, the Concessive AGV compares its current path with the path of the Priority AGV two points ahead and carries out the following.

(1) If the two paths are same, the Concessive AGV generates E-sending-knowledge including Ask-again and sends it. At the same time, the Concessive AGV memorizes E-sending-knowledge included in received an Answer message as one element of emergency-knowledge.

(2) If the two are different, the Concessive AGV generates an After-you message, sends it, and remains stationary on the current position till it receives a Thanks message. After receiving a Thanks message, it starts to move as scheduled because the possibility of collisions has been removed. At the same time, the Priority and the Concessive AGVs update their emergency-knowledge.

Explanation of Rule-4: As the reply for an Ask-again message, the Priority AGV sends an Answer-again message and E-sending-knowledge including intersection coordinates for four points ahead to the Concessive AGV. Now, the Priority AGV memorizes E-sending-knowledge that includes a received Ask-again message as one element of emergency-knowledge.

Explanation of Rule-5: As the Concessive AGV can find the Priority AGV's three points ahead path from the Priority AGV's four points ahead intersection coordinates that are an element of a received Answer-again message, the Concessive AGV selects the path that is different from the three points ahead path corresponding to an evacuated path and sends the coordinates of two intersections expressing the evacuated path and E-sending-knowledge including a Reverse message. At the same time, the Concessive AGV memorizes E-sending-knowledge that includes a received Answer-again message as one element of emergency-knowledge.

Explanation of Rule-6: AGVs that received a Reverse message confirm that their own path one point ahead is different from the evacuated path that the Concessive AGV selected and send E-sending-knowledge including a Clear message informing others that the evacuated path is safe. However, if the points are not different, the AGVs whose one point ahead path is the same as the evacuated path that the Concessive AGV selected remain stationary at the middle of the current path and send E-sending-knowledge including a Clear message. AGVs that receive a Reverse message memorize E-sending-knowledge that includes a received Reverse message as one element of emergency-knowledge.

Explanation of Rule-7: When the Concessive AGV that received a Clear message from all AGVs moves onto the middle of an evacuated path, the AGV sends the Priority AGV E-sending-knowledge including an After-you message expressing, "It's safe and you can go ahead." At the same time, the AGV memorizes a received E-sending-knowledge including a Clear message as one element of emergency-knowledge.

Explanation of Rule-8: As the reply for an After-you message, just after the Priority AGV passes the scheduled path, the AGV sends all AGVs E-sending-knowledge including a Thanks message expressing that the emergency situation for avoiding a collision is over. Receiving the Thanks message, AGVs update emergency-knowledge blanks and return to their scheduled actions.

Although the Reverse message is the highest priority message, some Reverse messages are sent when several collision avoidance situations occur at the same time. In this case, the first received Reverse message is given priority, the collision avoidance action for the effective Reverse message is performed first, and the Reverse message received next becomes effective next. The first come first serve method is adopted.

In this way, each AGV has the minimum information for other AGVs and can acquire their knowledge when necessary by exchanging knowledge. When the possibility of a collision is foreseen during the knowledge exchange, the Concessive AGV moves from the current path and avoids the collision by giving way to the Priority AGV, as shown in Rule-3 and Rule-7. This action of moving is called concessive action. Concessive action and exchanging knowledge correspond to the result of our study on cooperation. Similar to the evacuated path described in Rule-5, one path is randomly selected among the intersection coordinates included in an Answer-again message except for the two points ahead path of the Priority AGV.

"Creates emergency-knowledge according to the received message" described in Step1-3 of RAP Section 3.3 corresponds to the procedures of Rule-2 and the later rules of ROE.

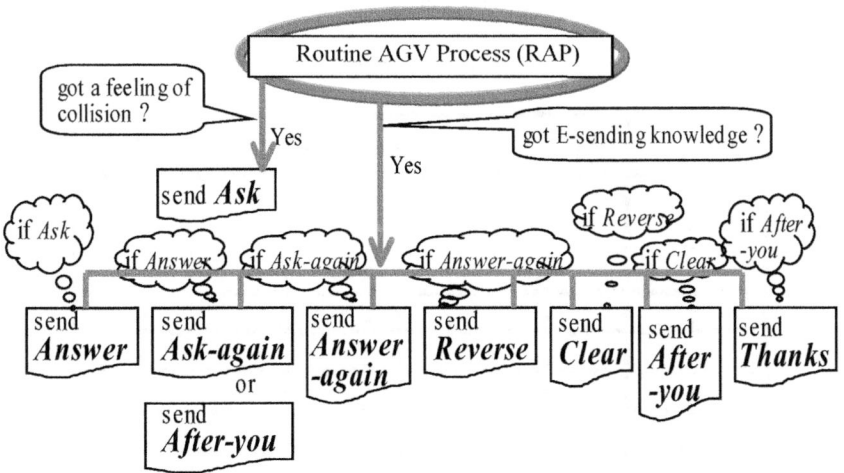

Fig. 9. Routine AGV process and message exchange rules

4   Simulation Examples for Head-On Collisions

The idea of cooperation by exchanging knowledge proposed in Section 3 was programmed and applied for an operating AD-FMS. Nine types of AD-FMSs from Style-1 to Style-9 were adopted and the differences are shown in Table 1. The table lists (from left to right) AD-FMS types (Styles), part types, number of MCs ($_g$MC), and number of AGVs. The number outside the parenthesis in the MC column is the type number of MC and the number inside the parenthesis is the MC number for each type. For example, the part type of Style-9 is 9, MC numbers are 8 and three MCs for each MC type are located in the AD-FMS. Fig. 1 (a) shows the layout of Style-9. The layouts of other FMSs have a smaller number of MCs than Style-9. Each part has a different machining time for each MC. Table 2 shows the machining times and process sequences for each part of Style-4 through Style-9. The sequence from the top to bottom of Table 2 indicates the process sequence of the part being machined. The examples adopted unpredicted troubles in operating the AD-FMS, which were not dealt with by preplanned schedules. The adopted troubles have two conditions. One is

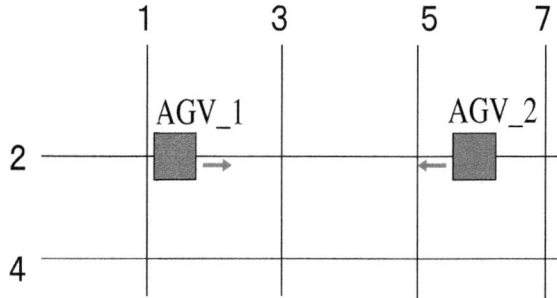

Fig. 10. Example of collision

Table 1. AD-FMS styles

Styles	Parts kinds	gMC(MC)	AGV
1	3	3(1,1,1)	3
2	3	3(1,2,1)	3
3	3	3(2,2,2)	3
4	6	6(1,1,1,1,1,1)	5
5	6	6(2,2,2,2,2,2)	5
6	6	6(3,3,3,3,3,3)	5
7	9	8(1,1,1,1,1,1,1,1)	5
8	9	8(2,2,2,2,2,2,2,2)	5
9	9	8(3,3,3,3,3,3,3,3)	5

Table 2. Machining time and process sequence examples of Style_4~6

Parts	P1	P2	P3
Machining time(second) & Process sequence	gMC1 180	gMC3 120	gMC4 180
	gMC2 120	gMC1 60	gMC1 180
	gMC3 120	gMC5 180	gMC5 120
	gMC4 60	gMC6 120	
	gMC5 180		

Table 3. Simulation results of Style-3

		Developed system	Conventional system
Product output	Part_1	200	221
	Part_2	242	266
	Part_3	80	80
Number to avoid collisions		1,879	-----
Number of collisions		984	1,488

Table 4. Simulation results of Style-5

		Developed system	Conventional system
Product output	Part_1	98	130
	Part_2	117	158
	Part_3	58	78
	Part_4	60	77
	Part_5	38	51
	Part_6	19	25
Number to avoid collisions		3,584	-----
Number of collisions		1,776	3,792

that each AGV breaks down randomly three times in 24 hours and the AGV stops for five minutes each time. The other is that each MC randomly finishes its machining after a delay of 10%.

The AGVs' collision times were examined after operating each AD-FMS for 24 hours. As Due to space limitations, the simulation results of Style-3, Style-6, and Style-9 are shown in Tables 3, 4, and 5. The results correspond to the values of developed system in Tables 3, 4, and 5. The tables also include each part output and the occurrences of collision avoidance. The times indicate how many AGVs change paths and wait to avoid a collision. The results of the conventional system that does not adopt knowledge-exchange cooperation are also described in the right-most column of the tables. For example, the outputs of the developed system of Table 3 are 200 for part_1, 242 for part_2, and 80 for part_3. The collision avoidance times are 1,879, which indicate that a large number of avoidances occurred for 24 hours. Collisions occurred 984 times. On the contrary, the conventional system's outputs are 221 for part_1, 266 for part_2, and 80 for part_3, and collisions occurred 1,488 times. The number of collisions in the developed system, when compared to the conventional system that does not adopt the collision avoidance measures, decreased from 1,488 to 984 owing to the knowledge-exchange cooperation. As for Style-6 and Style-9, the number of collisions reduced from 3,792 to 1,776 and from 3,336 to 1,896, respectively. The other styles that are not shown in the tables had the same reduced results, and all simulation results indicate that the collision times were reduced. The results signify that ROE and the research to adopt knowledge-exchange cooperation are effective.

Although many collisions occurred, after investigations it was found that they did not correspond to head-on collision but to other types of collisions such as flank collisions and rear-end collisions.

Table 5. Simulation results of Style-9

		Developed system	Conventional system
Product outputs	Part_1	50	72
	Part_2	71	86
	Part_3	36	46
	Part_4	35	44
	Part_5	23	29
	Part_6	12	14
	Part_7	46	58
	Part_8	60	73
	Part_9	23	29
	Number to avoid collisions	2,491	-----
	Number of collisions	1,896	3,336

5   Conclusions

The research dealt with the knowledge-exchange cooperation for autonomously moving AGVs, which is essential for operating an AD-FMS with the real-time control RAF. The proposed method avoids collisions by adopting three steps: (1) each AGV is given knowledge, (2) by exchanging knowledge, some AGVs change to AGVs that have the priority to move and some that make concession moves, and (3) between these AGVs, collision avoidance is executed by exchanging knowledge.

This method involves each AGV holding four types of AGV knowledge: path-knowledge, self-knowledge, neighbor-knowledge, and emergency-knowledge. Furthermore, AGV collisions are autonomously avoided by exchanging the sending-knowledge, including the messages of wills of AGVs. The method was applied to nine types of AD-FMSs built in a computer and complete prevention of all head-on collisions was confirmed.

References

1. Laengle, T., et al.: A Distributed Control Architecture for Autonomous Robot Systems. In: Workshop on Environment Modeling and Motion Planning for Autonomous Robots. Series in Machine Perception and Artificial Intelligence, vol. 21, p. 384. World Scientific, Singapore (1994)
2. Moriwaki, T., Hino, R.: Decentralized Job Shop Scheduling by Recursive Propagation Method. International Journal of JSME, Series C 45(2), 551 (2002)
3. Mitrouchev, P., Brun-Picard, D.: A New Model for Synchronous Multiagents Production among Clients and Subcontractors. International Journals of Simulation Model, 141–153 (2007)
4. Nishi, T., et al.: A distributed routing method for AGVs under motion delay disturbance. Robotics and Computer-Integrated Manufacturing 23(5), 517–532 (2007)
5. Yamamoto, H., Ramli, R.B.: Real-time Decision Making of Agents to Realize Decentralized Autonomous FMS by Anticipation. International Journal of Computer Science and Network Security 6(12), 7–17 (2006)
6. Yamamoto, H.: Decentralized Autonomous FMS Control by Hypothetical Reasoning including Discrete Simulator. In: Monostori, L., Váncza, J., Ali, M. (eds.) IEA/AIE 2001. LNCS (LNAI), vol. 2070, pp. 571–581. Springer, Heidelberg (2001)
7. Yamamoto, H., Ramli, R.B.: Real-time control of decentralized autonomous flexible manufacturing systems by using memory and oblivion. International Journal of Intelligent Information and Database Systems 1(3/4), 346–355 (2007)
8. Berman, S., Edan, Y.: Decentralized autonomous AGV system for material handling. International Journal of Production Research 40(15)
9. Wallace, A.: Application of AI to AGV control. International Journal of Production Research 39(4), 709–726 (2002)
10. Berman, S., Edan, Y.: Decentralized autonomous AGV system for material handling. International Journal of Production Research 40(15)
11. Wallace, A.: Application of AI to AGV control. International Journal of Production Research 39(4), 709–726 (2002)
12. Poole, D.: A methodology for using a default and abductive reasoning system. International Journal of Intelligent Systems 5(5), 521 (1990)

13. Provetti, A.: Hypothetical reasoning about actions: from situation calculus to event calculus. Computational Intelligence 12(3), 478 (1996)
14. Baldoni, M., Giordano, L., Martelli, A.: A modal extension of logic programming: Modularity, beliefs and hypothetical reasoning. Journal of Logic and Computation 8(5), 597 (1998)
15. Berger, J.O.: Statistic Decision Theory and Bayesian Analysis, 2nd edn. Springer, Heidelberg (1985)
16. Variant, L.: A Theory of the Learnable. Communication of the ACM 27(11), 1134 (1984)
17. Janetzko, D., Wess, S., Melis, E.: Goal-driven similarity assessment. In: Ohlbach, H.J. (ed.) GWAI 1992. LNCS, vol. 671, p. 283. Springer, Heidelberg (1993)

Quality Assessment of an Expert System: An Instrument of Regular Feedback from Users

Barbara Begier

Institute of Control and Information Engineering, Poznan University of Technology
barbara.begier@put.poznan.pl

Abstract. One of the possible solutions to ensure software quality is to involve users in its development and gradual improvement. In the described approach users provide regular feedback on the considered expert system in a survey by questionnaire. In the presented paper there are given guidelines on how to design and conduct such survey. The devised quality tree reflects the users' point of view. Specifications formulated on the basis of the feedback allow software designers to develop improved versions of the considered intelligent system. The reported empirical research refers to an expert system applied in civil engineering. After six iterations of its assessment and then its related improvements the level of users' satisfaction from the product is currently much better than that at the beginning.

Keywords: evolutional development of an expert system, user involvement, software quality, survey by questionnaire.

1 Introduction

Authors of various intelligent software products concentrate their efforts on innovations built in the developed expert systems. The innovative elements refer to knowledge representation, intercommunication of software agents, inference methods, and other formal models considered in the design of this kind of software. Then software authors are concerned with correct implementation of the devised models and technical problems. This constitutes the basis for software correctness [7] from their point of view. But they often ignore quality aspects especially concerning software usage and users' comfort of work.

First of all, good quality of software is equivalent to a small number of defects, which leads to a minimal amount of avoidable rework [3]. This is a useful criterion from a programmer's point of view; however, low density of defects alone does not satisfy software users any more. Nowadays the quality of a software product is assessed by the users rather than by the developer. And a set of measures is applied rather than a single measure of quality.

The product is being developed evolutionally for years to cover more and more real life cases, functions, constraints, and exceptions. The decision what should be improved during the next iteration of a system development requires an instrument to determine whether the installed software tool meets expectations of its users. From software users'

N.T. Nguyen and R. Kowalczyk (Eds.): Transactions on CCI III, LNCS 6560, pp. 199–214, 2011.

point of view the quality referred to information systems and customer satisfaction are based on a content and format of the presented data and usage aspects of the considered software [5, 14]. A brief review of quality aspects related to software tools and users' involvement in their development, is given in Section 2.

In the presented paper the quality aspects are referred to expert systems. Their users are not professionals in computer science or software engineering. They are experts in their professional domain like civil engineering in the presented case. They often complain the limited number of real life cases considered by the delivered software tool. Correctness of input data is usually far away from researchers' interest but it forms a basis of usefulness of a given product. Defects in input data implicate further failures in software usage. The quality characteristics noticed and cyclically assessed by users of the considered class of software are given in Section 3. Users' impressions and feelings related to the comfort of work, and ethical aspects are added to the set of considered quality criteria in the described approach. Measures of usability include software features observed also by indirect users.

The problem arises how to learn users' opinions and expectations and to measure software quality from the users' point of view. Feedback from users in the software process is recommended to improve software quality. It is in line with agile methodologies [10, 19] and the principles expressed in the Agile Manifesto [18]. Users' involvement in software development definitely brings benefits [15, 20]. On the other hand, user's role may be problematical so some guidance for users is also required [8]. Cooperation with users especially helps defining requirements successfully [16]. But domain experts are often not available for software developers. The described proposal is to reduce users' involvement to the cyclic assessment of each developed software version and then make use of obtained results in the evolutional development of a particular product.

The intended, and confirmed in practice, product assessment makes possible to elicit feedback from software users. The described case study (see Section 4) comes from the civil engineering. The former experiences with a software product assessment [1, 2] show that results of a software cyclic assessment are useful for software developers. This way the developers of expert systems are not completely isolated from software users. The presented paper is focused on guidelines how to design and perform activities referred to software quality assessment, then process their results statistically, and how to make use of these results. Selected results of software assessments conducted in 2005–2009 are included. Specifications of product quality improvements based on the results of the survey are discussed in Section 5.

2   User-Centeredness and Software Quality

The software product is being developed evolutionally for years to cover more and more real life cases, constraints, and exceptions. Software quality bears in the software process. It is the core principle expressed in the family of the ISO 9000 standards and it forms the basis for the CMM model recommended by the Software Engineering Institute [4]. But customers and users on the one side and software developers on the other side often share different views on a project success.

The International Standard ISO 13407 [12] provides guidance on human-centred design activities throughout the life cycle of computer-based interactive systems. There are recommended (but not specified in details) four human-centred design activities which aim to: understand and specify the context of use, specify the users and organizational requirements, produce design solutions, and evaluate designs against requirements.

Propagators of quality standards and enthusiasts of agile methodologies declare with one voice their **user-centeredness**. However, this concept is sometimes overstated. In practice, it has various meanings and dimensions like the following [13]:

- *user focus* limited to specifying goals from a point of view of a fictional user who substitutes for an average user,
- *work-centeredness* as a focus on effective work of an average (but still abstract) user whose actions are supported by the intended system,
- *user participation* usually limited to small software projects and observed mainly during the design and testing user interface; students of computer science may act in users' name, for example,
- involving the diversity of real users in the design process to provide an adaptable *personalization* (adaptability allows a user to change the system according to his/her preferences); it involves user's learning when using the system.

User involvement in the software process is an important and promising way of improving software quality. On the other hand there are also empirical results that user participation can negatively influence project performance which can become more time-consuming and less effective. The notion of a software project success from the perspective of developers is at the first sight different than that from software users' point of view. But in a long time perspective the satisfied customer and users are the primary measure of a project success. So there is the question of when user participation is actually helpful and when it might negatively impact project performance. The survey data from 117 software development projects and 746 respondents [25] confirm that the highest level of software authors' satisfaction takes place in the case of a high user involvement in new software projects although at the same time users' expectations are excessively growing. In turn, users were most happy by engaging minimal time in the development process. Thus the recommended forms of user involvement cannot be too time-consuming.

Some works are focused on integration of humans into workflows to increase software quality and reduce development effort. Such model-driven development requires some extensions [17] of the UML standard. The *User-centred design* (UCD) approach has been applied also to the development of large ERP systems. The U-CEI (*User-Centred ERP Implementation*) has been described in [26]. This methodology aims at improving human working conditions and realizes it by early user involvement in the system design. All success factors presented there are in fact the human factors. Vilpola focuses the need to involve *real users* to meet requirements of an entire organization because only those people ensure the desired feedback on a software system to software designers. The author has done it earlier.

The Web era shows that software users may abandon those applications which are too difficult or simply boring for them and may switch to other pages. The quality criteria related to software available via Web do not much differ from those formulated for other products. Mostly primary features are emphasized – software product should be technically complete, testable, maintainable, structured, efficient, secure, etc. [24]. To keep users' attention, the quality criteria for Website excellence have been formulated

[22], starting from the necessary *functionality* (including accessibility, speed, and easy navigation) which constitutes however only 20% of the entire excellence. But the devised set of quality criteria still does not consider user's comfort of work, his/her likings, and atmosphere at workplace, for example. The derived measures, devised for a particular software product, are then applied in its quality assessment. But it is not obvious who is predisposed to assess the product – its developers, domain experts, quality engineers, quality auditors, users? The presented approach confirmed an importance of a feedback from software users.

In the described approach the close cooperation of developers and users is not limited to the requirements phase. User-based evaluation of software quality can be used to provide feedback from users. Some experience in this area is presented in this paper.

3 Guidance to Develop Quality Characteristics of an Expert System from Its Users' Point of View

Authors of expert systems especially addressed for real organizations should accept some general statements considered during development of various software applications:

- Software system is evolutionally developed till its withdrawal; the iterative-incremental model is applied in the relatively long product life cycle.
- Clerks, officials, lawyers, doctors, etc. but not programmers are the direct users.
- The provided quality of services for indirect users (applicants, patients, customers, etc.) depends deeply on solutions implemented in the software tool.
- New requirements are born after the basic needs are satisfied.
- Correctness of the input data conditions proper results including the correct content of generated documents.
- The existing data have to be incorporated and applied in the new system.
- Maintained records support communication across an organization.
- Privacy is a problem of great importance and no more can be ignored.

Strategies and tactics have been analyzed how to manage end user expectations and to address the risk of failure in this area. The notion of consumer satisfaction applied in marketing has been extended to software development [9, 14, 21]. Software production is not only a product development but is a combination of product and service delivery to offer a solution to the users. Working *with* users (not only *for* them) and letting them make tough choices, and, in general, keeping users involved throughout the project are considered the successful tactics [23].

An expert system (ES) is an open system – it interacts with its environment where users are its primary elements. Its operation is context-dependent; for example, 39 socio-technical dimensions of ES quality have been specified [6]. There are needed useful criteria to assess software quality. Then they are decomposed into a set of measures. There are usually followed the basic quality attributes formulated in the ISO 9126: *functionality*, *reliability*, *usability*, *efficiency*, *maintainability*, and *portability*. This set can be decomposed and expanded to include other important quality attributes from software user's point of view. Then it is used as a checklist in software development and its quality assessment.

The devised the author set of quality attributes to represent quality of expert systems from their users' point of view is shown in Figure 1. This set is an extension of quality characteristics recommended in the ISO 9126. Let us explain their meaning starting from quality attributes on the left side of the presented quality tree.

General usefulness of an expert system for an entire organization of software purchaser and its customers has been introduced as the important criterion – users are employees and they are domain experts who know the needs better than system developers. Civil engineers are the domain experts in the reported case.

It is been assumed that basic *Functionality* and *Safety* (presence, suitability, and accuracy of the implemented functions) have been already confirmed during the testing phase in accordance with functional requirements. The user evaluates mainly: the variety of the considered types of real life cases (building constructions and their loads, for example), convenient cooperation of the analyzed software product with other applied software tools (the AutoCAD system in the presented case), and data verification and correction facilities suitable for particular types of data and cases of usage. Therefore, *Functionality* is decomposed into at least three subsets of measures to assess the *Variety of* considered *real life cases*, required *Cooperation with other software tools*, and *Data correctness* facilities. The last criterion has been introduced to emphasize the problem of reliable data. Since the real life expert, like a civil engineer, makes a number of intermediate (design) decisions on the base of partial results, the software product should have the properties of granularity and *visualization of subsequent steps of calculations*, i. e. it should consists of modules or other units which generate partial results visible for the user. Specialists must be able to trace calculations, change the input data at any point and resume calculations from that point. Also an ability to repeat calculations from a selected point is often expected. *Safety* refers mainly to the maintained data.

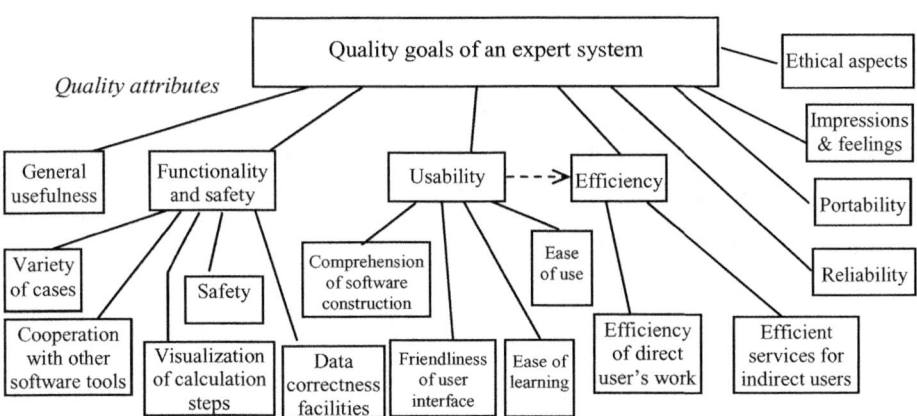

Fig. 1. The quality tree of an intelligent software system

Product *Usability* is a key quality attribute from the user's point of view. It refers to the comprehensible software construction enabling easy navigation and access to required data and tracing facilities. It conditions the proper use of the considered product. Facilities of user interface enable ease of learning and ease of use of an intelligent system. Thus the *Usability* has been decomposed into four sub-criteria specified on the presented quality tree. Conformity with domain terminology and applied notation (including graphics) is expected. The high level of software usability translates also into the efficiency of user's work (the dash line on Figure 1 symbolizes that fact) and, in consequence, in high productivity in users' organization. *Usability* is then decomposed into a rich set of detailed features and their related measures.

Efficiency in the presented approach has been decomposed into two subsets: *Efficiency of direct user's work* with the developed software tool and *Efficient services* provided *for indirect users* (if any) – the efficiency related to designed services should be assessed separately by the direct and indirect users. Specified measures of the second sub-criterion are related to an inquirer's or an applicant's service in a public organization, for example. The examples given below are the author's proposals:

- Average time of performance of each service specified for indirect users
- Time required by data acquisition procedures (if they are time-consuming)
- Total time required to find a solution (to fix a business matter, for example)
- Number of required documents/data that should be presented by an applicant
- Percentage of real life cases met in practice and considered by the system
- Number of failures in data including their incompleteness met in one day of work
- Number of words/records/documents required to correct the particular data
- Frequency of net problems monthly (which cause delays in service)
- Paper savings monthly (number of pages generated earlier and nowadays, if any).

Reliability of software applied in civil engineering refers to the required ability to operate, stability, and savings of resources.

From the user's point of view, *Portability* of an intelligent software system is equivalent to its easy installation on various applied computer platforms. Then a transfer to new platforms requires minimum of rework.

The last two criteria in the presented approach are referred to so-called soft features. The criterion of *User's impressions and feelings* has been introduced to consider various attitudes, behaviours, and emotions of software users who are different people than software developers. Some examples of measures of users' impressions are: satisfaction with a software tool, general assessment of its work, comfort of work with the considered tool (its usage is not stressful), product impact on an atmosphere at workplace, work with the tool is rather interesting than boring, product is in accordance with user's likings, screen views are aesthetic, etc. These a bit subjective measures help to understand if people will keep applying the software tool instead of looking for another one.

Ethical aspects include social expectations referred to the considered tool with respect to social interests, especially when applied in a public organization (but not limited to that kind of cases). Developers of an expert system may be unaware of various threats the usage of the developed software product may cause, dealing with: privacy, honesty, respect to particular persons, risk of crime when working with the specified tool, etc. The ETHICOMP conference series provides an international forum for discussions concerning ethical and social aspects of the technological progress.

Each quality criterion is then decomposed into particular quality measures. Further details related to the reported case are presented in the next section.

4 Questionnaire Survey to Assess Software Quality – The Case Study

The reported software quality assessments were performed six times – the first one in 2002 and the last one in 2009. The first four editions have been reported in [1]. They were a kind of pilot tests.

The presented guidelines refer to problems to be solved:

- design of the quality tree of the considered expert system; selection of quality measures to be assessed by software users as described in the previous section;
- design of a questionnaire (related to the developed quality tree) and acceptable forms of answers which should be processable,
- required sample of respondents needed in the survey,
- processing the obtained results.

The guidelines presented below to software quality assessment are described as the case study on a base of the author's experience. The intended aim is to improve those software features which are poor from the users' point of view.

4.1 Design of a Questionnaire

The devised quality tree reflects the aim formulated above. There are the following quality key attributes introduced on the quality tree developed for the considered expert system [2]: *Functionality* (including *Safety*), *Usability* decomposed into 4 sub-criteria as shown in the Figure 1 and combined with efficiency of use, *Reliability*, and *Portability*. They have been decomposed into specified measures. *Usability* has been decomposed into altogether 26 measures. The *General assessment* has been added separately to help expressing user's general opinion about the product. It represents the user's satisfaction with the product – it is the main quality measure of the assessed software tool. The devised set of 41 quality measures concerns the user's point of view. No social expectations are associated with the considered expert system since it is intended to support designers of constructions in civil engineering and no indirect users of a product are considered.

Techniques developed and used in marketing, sociology, and recommended also in education, are applied to design a questionnaire, to specify its recipients, to perform pilot tests, and to improve the questionnaire itself. The designed questionnaire has an initial part to learn users' skills in computing.

The questionnaire structure reflects the devised quality tree of the assessed software product – the questionnaire items of the main part have been divided into 8 groups related to criteria and sub-criteria of the assessment. Each group of items has a name corresponding to the quality criterion (attribute) and focusing the user's attention on a given subject. Each questionnaire item is related to the particular quality measure.

After first two editions of a survey it was necessary to improve the questionnaire itself because some items were interpreted in different ways by respondents. In next two editions the set of values and their explanations were attached to each measure as possible answers to avoid misunderstandings, for example:

M24. The initially required help of an experienced program user

[1 – necessary, 2 – desired, 3 – partial, 4 – occasional, 5 – unnecessary]

In the last two editions of the questionnaire, the psychometric scale devised by Rensis Likert was applied. Each questionnaire item has a form of a statement, like this related to M24, for example:

M24.*The help of an experienced user is not required in the initial period of using the program.*

Then a respondent is asked to indicate his/her degree of agreement with this statement, using a five-point scale applied at schools (in Poland the highest mark is "5" equivalent to the American "A" and "1" is the worst one equivalent to the "E"):

5 – I fully agree,
4 – I rather agree,
3 – I have doubts,
2 – I rather disagree,
1 – I completely disagree.

Some space is left at the end of a questionnaire for user's suggestions and opinions.

4.2   User Profile and Sample of Respondents

In general, the author's recommends learning the user's profile. In particular it is recommended during the first edition of the questionnaire survey. Software authors may be wrong in their opinions concerning users' characteristics. The recommended and confirmed several times by the author in practice way to learn who users are is to place an initial part at the beginning of the questionnaire. It contains the following items, for example:

- Age: under 30, over 30 and below 50, over 50
- Gender: *male, female*
- Level of education: secondary, higher (bachelor or master degree)
- Self-assessment of skills in computing
- Self-assessment of experience in using the analyzed software tool.

All items mentioned above were applied in the questionnaire conducted in several public organizations. They were intended to help learning potential problems that system users may face with when using the analyzed tool. The results show that the age does not play any essential role any more. The gender of the respondent is perceptible only in items concerning the required need of an experienced user of the analyzed software system and the comfort of work with the delivered software system. It seems that female workers prefer to communicate directly with other people and not only via computer system.

In the performed by the author questionnaire surveys concerning other software tools the respondents have been inquired also about their several other features, like: educational profile (technical, non-technical), professional position (manager, team leader, or ordinary worker), skills in English (in the case when software users are not native English speakers and software tool is not translated into its users' family language), and experience in using other specified software tools. In one case respondents were asked if they use computers only at work or also in other places: at home or in an internet café. This research performed in 2002 showed that more than 60% of clerks use computers at work only. One more question has been referred to the frequency of using the analyzed expert system: daily, once a week, or rarely. Author's experience has showed that there is no need to inquire respondents about their home location or country region – there is no influence of these features on software quality assessment. And even some respondents have ignored these items to demonstrate that they do not want to be identified this way in the survey which is intended to be anonymous.

There were 5 items in the initial part in the reported questionnaire surveys concerning the expert system used by civil engineers. The respondents were asked about:

- General skills in computing
- Number of software tools of general purpose being used by the respondent
- Number of software product developed for civil engineers being used by the respondent
- Proficiency in using AUTOCAD system
- Frequency of using computer (every day, once a week, for example).

The first and the fourth of the above items were to be self-assessed by respondents. Results obtained in the initial part of questionnaire have shown each time that civil engineers are well skilled in computing – all of them use computers on a daily basis, all are experienced users of popular general purpose tools like MS Excel. And all of them know and use the AutoCAD system.

There are essential questions on how many users or software quality evaluators are needed to achieve a targeted performance of software quality assessment? The research in this area has recently confirmed that a general rule for optimal sample size would be the 10±2 rule [11]. Thus the sufficient number of respondents may vary from 8 to 12, depending of a kind of the software tool being assessed, because their educational level, skills, and liking are often similar.

The considered expert system applied in civil engineering has been assessed by its direct users (from 38 up to 81 respondents). The time of an assessment is set a priori with its users in one month. There is no need to gather all respondents at the same place and time. It took ca 15 minutes for each respondent to fulfil the questionnaire.

4.3 Processing Obtained Results

All answers given by respondents are recorded in a report sheet. Every row of the sheet concerns one quality measure and contains its number, name, and ratings given by individual respondents. The following values are calculated:

- number of answers given by respondents to the considered item,
- sum of values of the given answers,
- obtained minimum value,
- obtained maximum value,
- mean value,
- number of the obtained "1",

- number of the obtained "2",
- number of the obtained "3",
- number of the obtained "4",
- number of the obtained "5".

These data make possible to learn:

- What is the progress in quality in the sense how many measures and which in particular have obtained the higher mean value than before?
- What is the mean value of the general assessment representing user's satisfaction with the product and what is its comparison with ratings in previous surveys?
- What measures have obtained the highest values (more than 4.0)?
- Which measures have obtained a substantial dispersion of values? Diagrams and charts are recommended to illustrate it.
- How many and what measures have obtained worse mean values than before?
- What measures have obtained the lowest values in the present survey?
- What measures have obtained poor ratings (it means values of "1" or "2")?
- What are ratios of particular ratings to the ratings obtained in the previous two surveys?

There is recommended here to present the selected results obtained in the last 3 editions of the survey in a tabular form and, in subsequent columns, the ratios of mean values related to individual measures obtained in the compared editions. These data constitute the basis of conclusions and further actions. The values of selected measures, mentioned in the further text and including the product general assessment (M41), are presented in Table 1.

Table 1. List of 14 selected measures, their values, and their ratios related to the last three surveys

Measure ID	Mean value in 2009	Mean value in 2007	Mean value in 2005	2009/2007 ratio	2009/2005 ratio
M3	4.29	4.12	4.00	1.04	1.07
M4	4.27	4.12	4.14	1.04	1.03
M5	3.75	3.93	3.71	0.96	1.01
M6	3.85	4.00	3.71	0.96	1.04
M7	4.62	4.53	4.47	1.02	1.03
M22	3.85	3.76	3.50	1.02	1.10
M23	4.85	4.82	4.93	1.01	0.98
M24	4.36	3.75	3.07	1.16	1.42
M25	4.44	3.87	4.47	1.15	0.99
M26	4.73	4.59	4.14	1.03	1.14
M30	4.44	3.88	3.80	1.14	1.17
M33	3.50	2.88	3.07	1.22	1.14
M35	3.58	3.18	3.43	1.13	1.04
M41	4.64	4.55	4.08	1.02	1.14

The analysis of results of the last three iterations of the assessment shows that the users are satisfied with the considered product and assess it highly. In the last edition the mean value of as many as 35 out of 40 particular measures was not less than 4.0 (32 in 2007 and 30 in 2005, respectively). The mean value of M41 expressing the *general satisfaction with the considered product* has obtained 4.64 in 2009.

Mean values of 29 measures were higher in 2009 than in 2007, in particular: M3.*Mode of cooperation with the AutoCAD system, providing an effective way to check the correctness of the input data*, M4.*Possibility of presenting subsequent steps of calculations*, M7.*Comprehensibility of all provided software options and their use*, M24.*Initially required help of an experienced program user*, M26.*Number of mistakes made currently by the user in a time unit, compared with that at the beginning*, and M35.*Protection against running the program for incorrectly given load values*. The M23.*The time required to learn how to use the program* gained the highest mean value, namely 4.85.

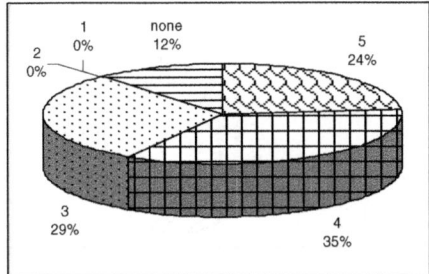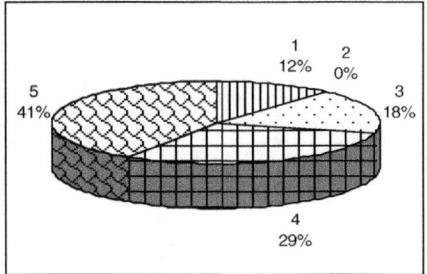

Fig. 2. The dispersion of ratings related to the measure M5.*Possibility of on-line correction of data describing the given construction* in 2007 (on the left) and 2009 (on the right)

The mean values of three measures were the same, and nine values were worse including the M5.*Possibility of on-line correction of data describing the given construction*. The M33.*Protection against an unauthorized access* was accessed as the worst one although the system is not available via net and a great progress has been noticed in this case. It is interesting that the obtained results do not always illustrate an effort made to improve the particulate feature.

The dispersion of the obtained measures is less and less after each edition of software assessment − users' ratings related to particular measures are going to become similar. The set of available ratings, including the highest and the lowest possible mark, has been used only in five cases related to: M5.*Possibility of on-line correction of data describing the given construction* (illustrated in Figure 2), M6.*Possibility of on-line correction and modification of data concerning loads of the construction*, M22.*Ability to customize views of screen objects to the user's likings*, M33.*Protection against unauthorized access*, and M35.*Protection against running the program for incorrectly given load values*. Examples of value dispersion related to other two selected measures are illustrated in Figures 3 and 4.

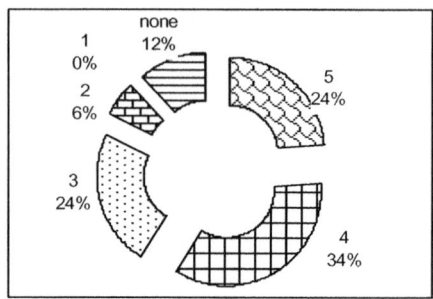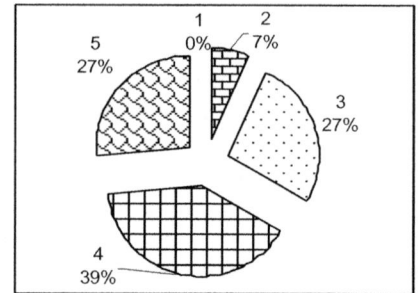

Fig. 3. Dispersion of values of the ratings obtained for the measure M25.*Estimated number of mistakes made by a user in one hour of the software use after the initial period of use* obtained in 2007 (on the left) and in 2009 (on the right).

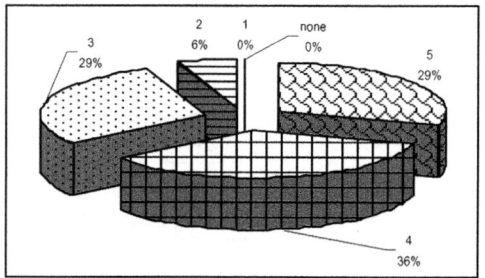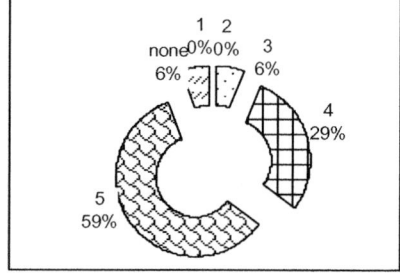

Fig. 4. Dispersion of values of the ratings in 2007 (on the left) for the measure M30.*Sufficient number of the provided messages and alarms; clear content of the messages and alarms,* and the obtained in 2009 (on the right).

5   Specifications of Software Quality Improvement Based on Ratings and Remarks Given by Users

All ratings, remarks, and suggestions given by users were carefully analyzed after each questionnaire survey. Fortunately, many of the polled users showed their willingness to influence the software product. But the number of all expressed suggestions was decreasing in subsequent editions of the survey – one in two respondents in 2005, one in three in 2007, and one in four in 2009 gave his/her particular suggestions concerning the software improvement. The remarks and suggestions varied a lot, from proposal of applying larger size of letters indicating particular points of construction on a specified chart, to the demand to copy automatically individual views of a design to allow a user to analyze and discuss them later. Also the danger of losing previous data has been identified when the number of analyzed points describing a given construction is changed. Users required to specify and to explain precisely the meaning of particular data used on the screen. In particular it refers to the notion of the level of a concrete slab floor or a ceiling at the end of design activities.

Specifications of improvements were formulated on the base of poor ratings given by users to some items and users' suggestions given in an assessment of a subsequent version of the product. They were grouped into three subsets concerning, respectively:

1. Improvement of the specified software feature, including presentation details of specified screen views,
2. Close cooperation with the AutoCAD system and data transfer in both directions,
3. Extended number of types of analyzed constructions.

Three enumerated lists of suggested changes were worked out each time, separately for each group. Each item on the list has its initially specified attributes: identifier, name of the suggested change, date of registration, description of the required change, justification of the change with reference to the goals of the product and its quality measures.

Then the weight was assigned to each change (improvement) on a base of the team leader's experience. The weight is associated with the need of the change and the number of users who demand it. It involves also possible influence on the product. As a result, three subsequent attributes of the change were added to each item on the list of selected changes: weight marked by a distinctive colour, estimated cost expressed in days or weeks of work, and the name of a programmer responsible for introducing the change. The red colour indicates changes accepted by the team leader to be introduced in the next version.

The developed lists were transferred to programmers who were obliged to value several other attributes and then to document what real modifications of the system have been made. The maintained history of all changes and their justifications indicates favourite areas of programmers' work although these efforts have not always been reflected in assessment by users. What programmers do first is to improve the interface with the AutoCAD system. Several pre- and postprocessors cooperating with the Auto-CAD system have been subsequently developed and modified after each assessment.

The authors of the considered expert system have eliminated some flaws and shortcomings pointed out in the conducted questionnaire surveys. Some examples of improvements are concerned with:

- Ability of the improved external pre-processor to transfer from the AutoCAD system not only data concerning geometry of a building but also its loads,
- Provided precise and detailed messages concerning errors detected in input data,
- Available analysis of shear wall construction with alternate stiffness along the height of the building,
- Added printout of geometrical characteristics for the shear wall structure,
- Extended printout of the allocation of the mass of the considered construction,
- Automated visualization of default images.

So the improvements of the considered expert system have been made exactly to users' expectations expressed during the software product assessment by the questionnaire survey.

6   Conclusions

The evaluation of software quality from its users' point of view and related product improvements are topical problems in software engineering. In the author's opinion, only a regular and systematic feedback from users may help to solve the problem of software quality. It decidedly refers to expert systems to meet its users' various expectations. The user's point of view usually differs from the developer's one. In turn, the satisfied users make all business successful.

In the presented approach, the core of the continuous feedback from users is the assessment of each developed version of the expert system. The questionnaire survey is the recommended instrument of this feedback. It enables software designers to learn the users' point of view on a software quality. Today's users are skilled enough to play an active role in a software process and become conscious of their rights to assess quality of delivered software products, especially those developed for public organizations. Users, by their ratings, remarks and suggestions, influence the further software product development.

In the presented paper the quality aspects of an expert system are referred, as the case study, to the software system supporting calculations in civil engineering. The quality criteria decomposed into quality measures extend the set recommended in the ISO 9126. The quality tree is specified for the analyzed expert system. Not only stricte technical but also some soft features like user's feelings and impressions are considered – it is the author's contribution. Software developers have to accept that some quality measures may be assessed subjectively by users. The guidelines on how to conduct the survey and make use of the obtained answers are described.

The author has experienced that many users are eager to present their suggestions on how to improve a product and to cooperate with software authors. The evidence shows that feedback from users is easy to elicit, has been readily accepted by programmers, and resulted in successful software improvements. Ratings and suggestions given by users' constitute the basis for specification of the required changes. Thus the directions of software product improvement exactly reflect the users' ratings, opinions and suggestions. After six iterations of software development and product quality assessment performed by its users, the mean value of users' satisfaction with the considered system is evidently high (4.64). And the obtained ratings of particular quality measures are also higher than in previous surveys.

The questionnaire itself also needs to be periodically improved. The wording in the final version of the questionnaire is clear – questionnaire items are unambiguously specified. All possible expected answers are expressed using the Likert scale.

The described solution is not limited to engineering tools but also might include expert systems used by public administration, judiciary, hospitals, etc. There are so far no specific legal mechanisms enforcing software producers to improve their products. Despite all differences the periodical assessment of a software product may be also incorporated in the evolutional development of various business expert systems.

The range of user expectations increases – users formulate new requirements after their basic needs are satisfied. The Maslow's statement is applicable also to intelligent software systems, applied and assessed in a changing environment, including changes in business, legal rules, technology and the growing computing skills of software users. So the results of subsequent assessment may be even worse than the previous ones, although many improvements have been done in the meantime.

The described idea of software improvement based on quality assessment of an expert system by its users is nowadays in line with the concept of reality mining required, for example, to develop context-based services in interactive social networks – users become the subject of software development and an adaptation of software services to the given community of users is needed. Sophisticated solutions concerning e-institutions may be rejected if they do not meet user expectations. Quality improvements must respond to and also anticipate users' needs – only close cooperation with users may help here.

References

1. Begier, B., Wdowicki, J.: Feedback from Users on a Software Product to Improve Its Quality in Engineering Applications. In: Sacha, K. (ed.) IFIP. Software Engineering Techniques: Design for Quality, vol. 227, pp. 167–178. Springer, New York (2006)
2. Begier, B.: Software quality improvement by users' involvement in the software process. Publishing House of Poznan University of Technology, Poznan (2007)
3. Boehm, B., Basili, V.: Software Defect Reduction Top-10 List. Computer, 135–137 (2001)
4. Capability Maturity Model Integration (CMMI^{SM}), http://www.sei.cmu.edu/cmmi/general
5. Chen, L., Soliman, K., Mao, E., Frolick, M.N.: Measuring user satisfaction with data warehouses: an exploratory study. Information & Management 37, 103–110 (2000)
6. Conrath, D.W., Sharma, R.S.: Toward a Diagnostic Instrument for Assessing the Quality of Expert Systems. ACM SIGMIS Database 23, 37–43 (Winter 1992)
7. Cooke, J.: Constructing Correct Software. The Basics. Springer, London (1998)
8. Damodaran, L.: User involvement in the systems design process – a practical guide for users. Behaviour & Information Technology 15, 363–377 (1996)
9. Doll, W.J., Torkzadeh, G.: The measurement of end-user computing satisfaction. MIS Quarterly 12(2), 259–274 (1988)
10. Highsmith, J.: Agile Project Management. Addison-Wesley, Boston (2004)
11. Hwang, W., Salvendy, G.: Number of People Required for Usability Evaluation: The 10±2 Rule. Communications of the ACM 53(5), 130–133 (2010)
12. ISO 13407 Human-centred design processes for interactive systems, International Organization for Standardization, Genève (1999)
13. Iivari, J., Iivari, N.: Varieties of User-Centeredness. In: Proceedings of the 39th Hawaii Conference on System Sciences. IEEE, Los Alamitos (2006) (received reprint contains no page numbers)
14. Ives, B., Olson, M.H., Baroudi, J.J.: The measurement of user information satisfaction. Comm. of the ACM 26, 785–793 (1983)
15. Kujala, S.: User involvement: a review of the benefits and challenges. Behaviour & Information Technology 22, 1–16 (2003)
16. Kujala, S.: Effective user involvement in product development by improving the analysis of user needs. Behaviour & Information Technology 27(6), 457–473 (2008)
17. Link, S., Hoyer, P., Kopp, T., Abeck, S.: A Model-Driven Development Approach Focusing Human Interaction. Software Process: Improvement and Practice 14, 90–139 (2009)
18. Manifesto for Agile Software Development, Agile Alliance (2001), http://agilemanifesto.org/
19. Martin, R.C., Martin, M.: Agile Principles, Patterns, and Practices in C#. Pearson Education and Prentice Hall, Indianapolis (2007)
20. Mattsson, J.: Exploring user-involvement in technology-based service innovation. ICE-Project, Roskilde Univ. and Aalborg Univ. (2009), http://www.ice-project.dk
21. McHaney, R., Hightower, R., Pearson, J.: A Validation of The End-User Computing Satisfaction Instrument In Taiwan. Information & Management 39, 503–511 (2002)

22. Quality Criteria for Website Excellence,
    `http://www.worldbestwebsites.com/criteria.htm`
23. Petter, S.: Managing user expectations on software project: Lessons from the trenches. International Journal of Project Management 26, 700–712 (2008)
24. Saturn Quality Aspects, Web Development Company, India (2008),
    `http://www.saturn.in/advantages/quality-aspects.shtml`
    (accessible in November 2008)
25. Subramanyam, R., Weisstein, F.L., Krishnan, M.S.: User Participation in Software Development Projects. Communications of the ACM 53, 137–141 (2010)
26. Vilpola, I.H.: A method for improving ERP implementation success by the principles and process of user-centred design. Enterprise Information Systems 2, 47–76 (2008)

Author Index

GPSR Compliance

The European Union's (EU) General Product Safety Regulation (GPSR) is a set of rules that requires consumer products to be safe and our obligations to ensure this.

If you have any concerns about our products, you can contact us on ProductSafety@springernature.com

In case Publisher is established outside the EU, the EU authorized representative is:

Springer Nature Customer Service Center GmbH
Europaplatz 3
69115 Heidelberg, Germany

Batch number: 09490872

Printed by Printforce, the Netherlands